Justice in Islam

Justice in Islam

*The Quest for the Righteous Community from
Abu Dharr to Muhammad Ali*

RAYMOND WILLIAM BAKER

OXFORD
UNIVERSITY PRESS

Oxford University Press is a department of the University of Oxford. It furthers
the University's objective of excellence in research, scholarship, and education
by publishing worldwide. Oxford is a registered trade mark of Oxford University
Press in the UK and certain other countries.

Published in the United States of America by Oxford University Press
198 Madison Avenue, New York, NY 10016, United States of America.

© Oxford University Press 2022

All rights reserved. No part of this publication may be reproduced, stored in
a retrieval system, or transmitted, in any form or by any means, without the
prior permission in writing of Oxford University Press, or as expressly permitted
by law, by license, or under terms agreed with the appropriate reproduction
rights organization. Inquiries concerning reproduction outside the scope of the
above should be sent to the Rights Department, Oxford University Press, at the
address above.

You must not circulate this work in any other form
and you must impose this same condition on any acquirer.

Library of Congress Cataloging-in-Publication Data
Names: Baker, Raymond William, 1942– author.
Title: Justice in Islam : the quest for the righteous community
from Abu Dharr to Muhammad Ali / by, Raymond William Baker.
Description: New York : Oxford University Press, 2022. |
Includes bibliographical references and index.
Identifiers: LCCN 2021056069 (print) | LCCN 2021056070 (ebook) |
ISBN 9780197624975 (hardcover) | ISBN 9780197624999 (epub)
Subjects: LCSH: Justice—Religious aspects—Islam. |
Justice, Administration of—Islamic Empire—History. |
Justice, Administration of—Arab countries—History.
Classification: LCC BP188.16.J88 B35 2022 (print) | LCC BP188.16.J88 (ebook) |
DDC 297.5/622—dc23/eng/20211203
LC record available at https://lccn.loc.gov/2021056069
LC ebook record available at https://lccn.loc.gov/2021056070

DOI: 10.1093/oso/9780197624975.001.0001

1 3 5 7 9 8 6 4 2

Printed by Lakeside Book Company, United States of America

In remembrance of Elaine and her inspirational gifts of compassion, wisdom, and spirituality.

Be just: that is closer to true righteousness.

Qur'an 5:8

Contents

Acknowledgments	ix
1. Introduction: Anchored in Justice	1
2. Abu Dharr al Ghifari: Symbol of Justice, Lawyer of the Poor	16
3. Hassan al Banna and Sayyid Qutb: Founders, the *School* of the Muslim Brothers	38
4. Shaikh Muhammad al Ghazalli: The People's Shaikh	70
5. Sa'id Nursi: *Jihadist* of the Word	87
6. Grand Ayatollah Muhammad Hussein Fadlallah: Poet to Strategic Visionary	114
7. Grand Ayatollah Baqir al Sadr: Martyred Theorist of the Islamic Alternative	152
8. Ali Shariati: The Believing Revolutionary	176
9. Muhammad Ali: Global *Caller* to Islam	200
10. Conclusion: The Companion, the Prophets, and the Unseen	231
Notes	241
Bibliography	255
Glossary of Non-English Terms	259
Index	263

Acknowledgments

A word of thanks: With great appreciation, I wish to thank Mostafa Mohamed, my senior researcher for this project. Mostafa's phenomenal memory and sharp analytical skills have been indispensable. Omar Mahmoud, a former student and lifelong friend, somehow found time, despite extensive travel and heavy professional commitments, to critique a substantial part of this manuscript. His insightful commentary stimulated major improvements. Muhammad Ismael al Hakim, my personal assistant for almost two decades, provided indispensable support and a calming presence for which I am most grateful. My brother Don has yet again provided unfailing support. I would like to close these acknowledgements with a special thanks to Cynthia Read, executive editor at Oxford University Press, for her tactful guidance through the publishing process. There is something quite magical about the lightness of her touch and the insight and wisdom it consistently conveys. I personally claim full credit for the shortcomings and misapprehensions that are still to be found.

1

Introduction

Anchored in Justice

A Muslim friend frequently stays with me in Alexandria, Egypt, where I now live most of the year. We have a Friday ritual. I go to write every morning in one of the classic Greek coffee houses arrayed along the Mediterranean shore of Alexandria. At the Brazilian coffee house, I have known two of the baristas, now in their seventies, since the late 1960s. I have recently moved "my office" to the very classic and newly renovated Delice coffee shop just down the street, with its view of the central Alexandria square and the sea beyond. The landmark Cecil Hotel looks out on the square. My wife Elaine and I stayed there on our first trip to Egypt in 1968, just after the devastating June War.

My friend Muhammad Ismail works in the apartment. He then goes to the Friday communal prayer, often in the imposing al Qa'id Ibrahim Mosque which is a stone's throw from my building on the Corniche of the Mediterranean. When the prayers end, we both head back to the apartment. Since all the communal Friday prayers end roughly at the same time, there is no problem coordinating our return.

Muhammad is always eager to discuss the Friday sermon over coffee. This morning of Friday, February 3, 2017, just as I was beginning serious research for this book, the centerpiece of the sermon was an Abu Dharr legend! Such a fortuitous coincidence is too unlikely to dare make up. I am simply reporting what happened. Inevitably, the theme of the sermon was justice, the core value that anchors Islam. The sermon narrative, Muhammad related, centered on the fate of a man who had killed a neighbor in a dispute. By custom, his life was forfeited to the family of the deceased. The man pleaded with the family of his victim for time to return home and put his affairs in order for the sake of his children. He pledged that he would honor his oath to return to face his death for the murder he had committed. The family agreed. They did so, however, only on condition that someone stand in his stead in case he failed to return. That substitute figure, by prevailing communal notions

Justice in Islam. Raymond William Baker, Oxford University Press. © Oxford University Press 2022.
DOI: 10.1093/oso/9780197624975.003.0001

2 JUSTICE IN ISLAM

of justice, would forfeit his own life should the man not return to honor the agreement.

The man who committed the crime pleaded for someone to play that role. No one did, fearing that he might not return. Then, legend has it, Abu Dharr al Ghifari, beloved companion of the Prophet Muhammad, stepped forward. He agreed to provide that assurance to the family. Caliph Omar Ibn al Khattab sanctioned the arrangement. The man left to rejoin his family. He did return, only very slightly delayed. Abu Dharr stood unflinchingly in his place. The family of the murdered man was so moved by the honorable behavior of the man and by Abu Dharr's brave homage to justice that they requested that the caliph pardon the murderer. He did so. The caliph later asked Abu Dharr why he had taken that monumental risk. Abu Dharr explained that the arrangement reflected a communal conception of a solution that matched his own sense of justice. He told the caliph that he had stepped forward simply as a Muslim and therefore a lover of justice. The Abu Dharr al Ghifari of that sermon and the contemporary struggles for justice he inspires are the subjects of this study.

Abu Dharr and Justice

'Adl, the Arabic word for justice, occurs more frequently in the Qur'an than any of the names of the Muslim prophets. In Islamic tradition, the Prophet's companion Abu Dharr al Ghifari (d. 652 AD) stands as a venerable symbol for justice. As history and legend, Abu Dharr represents both the worldly and spiritual dimensions of this core Islamic value. The Prophet Muhammad himself saw in the character of his companion a connection to the abstract value of justice. The Prophet memorialized this linkage with an unambiguous *hadith* (saying of the Prophet) that connects his companion to the Islamic prophet Jesus. In Islam, Jesus is revered for his asceticism, kindness, and love for the poor, qualities that will be familiar to Christians. The Iranian Islamic intellectual Ali Shariati summarizes an extraordinary portrait of Abu Dharr elaborated by the Prophet: "A person who was so learned in knowledge that his breast was overflowing with it." Shariati tells us that the Prophet's description continues that "the blue sky never cast a shadow upon—and the dark earth never saw, a more truthful man than Abu Dharr." The depiction records that "Abu Dharr is more famous in the heavens, than the earth." Most importantly, the prophetic description concludes that "the modesty and piety of

INTRODUCTION 3

Abu Dharr resembles that of Jesus, son of Mary."[1] This authoritative linkage of the companion as symbol of justice with the Muslim prophet Jesus has served through the centuries to reinforce the understanding that Islamic justice anchors the faith in both its worldly and spiritual dimensions.

Missing in the general Christian understanding of Islam is an appreciation for the importance and distinctive character of the Muslim prophet Jesus. In truth, Christian culture makes seeing Jesus as an Islamic figure all but impossible. Islamophobia is at times discussed today as though it were a new phenomenon. It is not. It pervades all historic formations grounded in Christianity. Unseemly animus toward Islam has been a part of Christian culture for centuries. Like all deeply embedded hostilities, it distorts reason, limits the imagination, and blunts awareness of inconvenient realities. The centrality of the Muslim Jesus to Islamic tradition is one such obscured reality.

Christians have made the figure of Jesus of Nazareth the center of their faith. They have been reluctant to take note that Muslims have a revered Jesus of their own. Things would be easier if the Muslim Jesus remained confined to Islam's story as history and unfolding as theology. Such is not the case. This book explores the profound influence of the spirituality of the Muslim Jesus on the *contemporary* Islamic Awakening. This study is an explicitly interpretive one rather than a traditional work of social science. While the inquiry draws on the oceanic scholarship on Islam from both the Islamic and Western world, scholarly references are kept to a necessary minimum. Energy and space are given instead to distillations of what I have learned from some fifty years of direct experience of living, working, and traveling in Islamic lands.

The book is written from a point of view that brings into view the Islamic roots of the call for transformation that animates the Awakening of our own time. Particular attention is given in this study to developments in the Islamic strategic triangle of Egypt, Turkey, and Iran. As an extended essay, the book makes the argument that the Awakening in its multifaceted dimensions cannot be understood unless the influence of the animating spirit of Islam's Jesus is recognized and brought into conscious view. The strategy deployed to accomplish this core objective is the straightforward one of the textual analysis of the writings of the major Arab, Turkish, and Iranian Islamic intellectuals who have guided the Awakening. An unanticipated research discovery, reported here, is the way that evocations of the spirit of the Muslim Jesus is pervasive but often coded in the writings of the most important

4 JUSTICE IN ISLAM

intellectuals of the Awakening. At times, references are made directly in the name of the prophet Jesus. More frequently, the spirit of Jesus is evoked by references to Abu Dharr al Ghifari, the beloved companion of the Prophet Muhammad. In these writings Abu Dharr is treated as a figure who shared core qualities with the Muslim Jesus. The centrality of Jesus in Islam is poorly understood in the West. Therefore, for the most part, Western publics lack the minimal background on Islam to understand that coding. Rare are those Christians who know that Jesus, the son of the Mary, is a revered prophet in Islam. Even more unusual are those who appreciate that for many Muslims, Jesus holds a privileged place in the company of the Prophet Muhammad.

Images of Jesus and Muhammad walking hand in hand have enlivened the Islamic spiritual imagination for centuries. Non-Muslims rarely see them. Cultural blinders block those realities that define Islamic spirituality. Jesus is seen by Muslims as a figure of exemplary kindness, humility, and asceticism who is greatly loved by their Prophet Muhammad. All too often, young Christians in the West are imbued with a fearful distrust of all things Islamic. Hostility to Islam may not always be conscious. It is, however, always there.

The very notion of "Islam's Jesus" will be beyond the pale for many who come to this book with a Christian cultural background. That limitation has unfortunate consequences. Muslim readers, in contrast, will find the notion of the spiritual centrality of Islam's Jesus unexceptional. Islamic culture offers multiple templates for envisioning Jesus. Muslim youth come to know Christianity, as well as Judaism, in a very different way than their Christian or Jewish counterparts learn of Islam. As children, Muslims are taught that Islam came into a world where both Judaic and Christian monotheisms were already a positive presence. The Qur'an teaches in clear and direct language that Jews and Christians both received the divine message of the one God, as did Muslims. In all three faiths, the *same* one God is the creator of the universe and all the life that pulses through it. The tensions and even hatreds that have marred the relationship of the three great monotheisms have far less to do with Judaism, Christianity, and Islam than with the actions of Jews, Christians, and Muslims.

Actions do matter. Unjust actions, like imperial expansion, occupation, and exploitation, register with great force. Acts of violence and terror against the innocent always damage the perpetrators as well as their victims. It is critical to understand that hostile behavior toward one another by Jews, Christians, and Muslims most often comes in contradiction to the moral and ethical teachings of their respective faiths.

INTRODUCTION 5

In the Islamic tradition, Jesus looms large. He stands in the line of prophets that extends from Adam to Muhammad (570–632). A Qur'anic verse pronounces that all of Islam's prophets have equal status.[2] Yet, Muslim children also learn about a special relationship between their Prophet Muhammad and the prophet Jesus. The closeness between these two prophets in Islam is celebrated.

Jesus's stature in Islam makes him a figure to be emulated. Jesus has a secure place in the midstream Islam of the Qur'an. He is a revered figure, like all the prophets in Islam. Jesus, the son of Mary, is evoked by name several dozen times in Islam's holy book. He is given a variety of reverential titles. As we will see, the Muslim Jesus is represented differently in some important ways than the savior of Christianity. However, in Islam, the figure of Jesus always commands the utmost respect. For Muslims, few accolades can match comparison to Jesus. Abu Dharr al Ghifari was set apart by the Jesus-like attributes attributed to him. The Prophet Muhammad saw in Abu Dharr the same qualities of selflessness, love for the poor, and passion for justice that defined the person of Jesus.[3]

Sufism, Islamic mysticism, has its own equally spiritual understanding of Jesus. The son of Mary looms large in the mystical tradition. Mysticism boasts more than one Jesus-like figure. The mystical tradition is characteristically comfortable with that plurality. Love, light, and breath are all Sufi symbols. They all open to the mysteries of spirituality. All are associated regularly in Sufi literature with the figure of Jesus. A number of Islamic mystics are known through direct references to Jesus. Most prominent is Mansur Hallaj (858–922), one of the greatest such figures in Islam. Hallaj was charged with blasphemy and crucified in ways reminiscent of the martyrdom of the Christ.

The starting point for assessment of these varied Islamic references to Jesus must be the extraordinary reverence that Muslims accord their prophet Jesus. To be sure, that reverence does not translate into agreement with all Christian ideas about Jesus. Most importantly, Islam finds no place for the core Christian belief that Jesus has a divine character as the son of God. Muslims consider Jesus as one among the prophets in Islam. He has the stature accorded all prophets from Adam to Muhammad. In Islam, the prophet Jesus is known simply as the son of Mary. Like the Prophet Muhammad himself, Jesus is regarded in the Islamic tradition as fully human. He is taken, however, as an exceptional human being who came into the world by immaculate conception. Muslims share with Christians this

6 JUSTICE IN ISLAM

understanding of Jesus's birth. Muslims, like Christians, take Jesus as an exemplar for all humanity. He is characterized as extraordinary in ways that Christians will find familiar. Muslims celebrate Jesus' humility, asceticism, and love of the poor. Muslims, however, do not regard these characteristics as unique to Jesus. They are viewed as shared with the Prophet Muhammad and other prophets in Islam, such as Adam, Moses, Job, and Abraham. The miracles of Jesus, such as healing the sick and resurrecting the dead, are all viewed as coming *with God's permission*. No similar miracles, it should be noted, are attributed to the Prophet Muhammad.

Disrespect of Jesus by Muslims is quite simply unthinkable. The epithets hurled from Christian lands at the Prophet Muhammad through the centuries have no parallel in Muslim characterizations of Jesus and his mother Mary. Mary is revered in Islam as the *virgin* Mother of Jesus. Travel anywhere in the Islamic world and you will find girls and women who have been given some version of her name. Mary is mentioned more frequently in the Qur'an than in the Bible. She is the only woman mentioned by her own first name in the Qur'an, rather than being identified with a family or tribe. An entire chapter, or *surah*, of the Qur'an carries the name Mary. Few non-Muslims have any idea of this reverence accorded to Mary and her son in Islam. Muslims feel genuine shock and incomprehension that so many who follow Jesus and share their own love for Mary and her son often do not reciprocate with even minimal respect for the Prophet Muhammad.

When the Prophet's companion, Abu Dharr al Ghifari, is compared to Jesus, the comparisons could not be more positive. Abu Dharr is judged to share many qualities with Jesus of Nazareth, as represented in Christianity. His modesty and self-denial are legendary. He worked tirelessly for the less fortunate. Of all the values Abu Dharr shared with Jesus, his passion for justice stands out most insistently. A central truth emerges from both the sparse history and luxuriant legends of the Prophet's companion. All that we know of Abu Dharr teaches that his deep love for the Prophet was paired with a love just as intense for social justice.

The Muslim Jesus who is most relevant in our contemporary Age of Islamic Awakening is very much this ardent lover of justice. The Islamic Awakening swept through Islamic lands in the late 1960s and early 1970s. It expressed itself in those early decades as a renewed embrace of Islam as faith and civilization. Those powerful sentiments of a turn to Islam took varied forms. There were midstream, conservative, as well as radical claims to the Islamic legacy. Most importantly, the midstream trend, the *Wasittia*,

INTRODUCTION   7

insistently spoke of the great reverence and love Muslims felt for the Jesus of the Qur'an.

Implicit in the general turn to Islam has been a critique of Western secular civilization and the legions of "Westernizers" it has attracted in Islamic lands. Midstream Islam should be seen as an alternative preferred by millions of Muslims to challenge Western secular culture. The military power and technological prowess of states with materialist secular ideologies are judged undeniable. Recognized, too, are the often elevated standards of human rights, and the even more impressive work of committed social movements to extend their reach. So too is the general level of prosperity brought to Western societies.

By the late 1960s, however, flaws of Western secular culture, such as excessively materialistic values, ruthless competition, and a propensity to violence, had also become apparent to even those Muslims most attracted to the achievements of the West. Despite these critiques, commitments of the political elites to secularism in Islamic lands for the most part held. However, the always tenuous hold of that secular vision on mass populations weakened. The Islamic Awakening drew its following from the hearts and minds of ordinary, disaffected Muslims.

For many in the Islamic world, the value of competition as a core driver in the market societies of the West was a deeply flawed substitute for the values of justice and compassion emphasized in Islam. Important conclusions flowed from that core judgment. The secular worship of competition in all its forms inevitably produces hurtful disparities in wealth and opportunities. Projected internationally, it leads to exacerbated worldwide contests for power and influence. The United States, for many the exemplar of Western secularism, came to be seen as a nation responsible domestically for shocking inequalities and disturbing social violence, alongside endless wars abroad.

Islamic intellectuals took note of these discouraging developments. Across Islamic lands, they began the serious intellectual work of elaborating the Islamic alternative as a better pathway than Western secularism to address the injustices of the modern world. They were, in one sense, theologians. They were also strategic thinkers who sought to elaborate an alternative global vision that could challenge the hegemony of the Western secular vision.

I have followed these efforts of Islamic intellectuals from close at hand. I have found these brave efforts impressive and worthy of the respect that comes with serious critical engagement with their work. The Islamic figures featured in this book have all made what I judge to be positive contributions

8 JUSTICE IN ISLAM

to a massive Islamic intellectual, moral, and political challenge to the West. They are included precisely because of their successes, inevitably limited but no less important for that. My goal is to provide as truthful and honest account of their actions and beliefs as possible. It would make no sense to apologize for the positive tilt in their direction that defines the overall thrust of this book. It does seem appropriate, however, to make that affirmative angle of vision clear to readers from the outset. The work of these Islamic intellectuals has been serious and productive. It undergirds the Islamic Awakening of our time. The Islamic Awakening has impressive intellectual moorings that deserve respectful attention.

Objective vision is an illusion in the social sciences. However, a balanced view is possible. Those seeking a balancing negative view of the project of the Islamic Awakening will find an extensive bibliography. Major Western scholars, including Bernard Lewis, Fouad Ajami, and Daniel Pipes, have all made notable contributions to that bourgeoning critical literature.[4] My own mentor at Harvard, Samuel Huntington, sums up this hostile orientation with what remains the most impressive rhetorical flourish in his *Clash of Civilizations and the Remaking of World Order*. Islam, he famously argued, has "bloody borders." In subsequent clarifications, he added that Islam's "innards" were bloody as well. For the most part, the international corporate media follows this same general orientation. American political leadership has for the most part fully embraced this notion of a clash with a violent Islam that "hates us."[5]

Inevitably, the successes of the Awakening elicited a powerful counter-reaction. It came with a vengeance in Egypt, my second home now for almost fifty years. It found expression across Islamic lands. A great deal has changed since the early years of the Awakening. By the second decade of the twenty-first century, the period of this writing, the Islamic intellectuals and movements of the Awakening are everywhere under attack. Today, the strength and importance of the Awakening must be measured not only by its gains, but also by the sweep and power of the opposition it has stimulated.

Centrist Islamic intellectuals project a sober and realistic understanding of the forces of reaction that midstream Islam, the *Wasittia*, now faces. They warn that a grand reactionary coalition has emerged to counter the enlightened dimensions of the Awakening. Their strategic vision offers no surprises in the characterization of the main features of the reactionary alignment. The Saudi royals are understood to lead the regional charge against Islamic centrism, though the United States provides major support. Shi'i Iran is demonized. Vicious sectarianism is actively cultivated. Egypt's military dictator falls in line behind the Saudi leadership. The Saudis are untroubled that the Egyptian tyrant's hands and military uniform are stained by a dismal record of oppression that includes "the worst mass murder in Egypt's history."[6] How could they be, given the Saudi regime's own record of vile human rights abuses? The right-wing Israeli government smiles and reaps the bountiful contributions of regional reaction to the project of a Greater Israel. The United States averts its eyes, while mumbling incoherently about human rights and a fantasy "peace process" and even a "deal of the century." Intermittently, more sober and ominous demurrals are registered about a rush to war with Iran. In the end, however, America is seen by unsentimental centrist intellectuals to stand resolutely with reaction and a militarized foreign policy.

The trials of the Awakening in the second decade of the twenty-first century do cast a pall on the Islamic alternative. It cannot, however, obliterate decades of gains for the Islamic center. The Islam of the Qur'an justifies neither oppression nor the corruption of exorbitant wealth. Islam of the center stands with resistance in the name of justice. Resistance in the Islamic tradition is always and everywhere defined as the struggle for a freer, more just, and more compassionate social order. Abu Dharr has persisted through fourteen centuries as a symbol of that unending struggle in Islam for a better world defined in these value terms. Those centuries have witnessed more than their share of tyranny, cruelty, and corruption. That depressing political record more than matches current conditions. Yet, it is also true that the centrist Islam of the Qur'an has made itself available for periodic waves of renewal and reform.

The contemporary Islamic Awakening can be counted as the fourth such historical wave of Islamic renewal. It is not over. The Christian Jesus returned to his father in heaven. The Qur'an remained on the earth to provide support for the work of the Muslim Jesus. This difference has had momentous consequences. The Qur'an provides indispensable spiritual and practical guidance for worldly reform and renewal. Today, its message of justice shores up the besieged forces of Islamic renewal.

The record of resistance struggles inspired by the core Islamic value of justice cannot be undone by neglect or distortion. That record demonstrates that whatever the outcome of contemporary struggles in particular contexts, the resilient message of social justice will remain as inspiration. This fourth wave of renewal in the modern era will not be the last. Justice will be the lodestone of the struggles to come. Abu Dharr as a symbol of justice will stand in the wings, ready to step forward. The Prophet's companion will make himself available for unexpected appearances yet again.

I first encountered Abu Dharr and the legends surrounding his name in my graduate studies in classic Arabic and Islamic Studies at Harvard in the 1960s. Even in writings with the patina of centuries, Abu Dharr came to life for me as a vivid, irascible character with an unshakable commitment to justice. He is remembered as bold and unconventional in all respects. He is represented as one of those rare and always disconcerting individuals who speak the truth simply and directly. Possible negative consequences did not intimidate him. Abu Dharr never hesitated to call even the most exalted to task for unjust behavior.

As a graduate student in the 1960s, I found a great deal to admire in Abu Dharr. I found it surprising that so little attention is given in studies of Islam by Westerners to this unconventional companion of the Prophet with so much to recommend himself. My own admiration for this contrary figure so beloved by the Prophet Muhammad has shaped the way I approach Islamic studies to this day. Islamic communities are inevitably communities of interpretation. No characterization of Islam is complete unless it takes account of the progressive interpretation of the faith that the Prophet's companion has represented through the ages. As my understanding of Islam has deepened with decades of reading, traveling, and living in Islamic lands, the Islam of my experience and imagination always reserves a special place for Abu Dharr, his rebellious spirit, his passion for justice, and his constructive contrariness. These qualities have made Abu Dharr a vivid presence for me among the Prophet's many companions.

When considering cultures and faith traditions other than one's own, it makes no sense to ignore the things to which people aspire. Aspirations, though often unrealized, do tell us a great deal about them. Dreams define the places communities seek to go, whether or not they succeed in actually making the journey. Yet, more often than not, such knowledge of loftier aims and images of better selves is used in the Western literature on Islam simply to highlight the gap between hopes and realities. That exercise has value as a reality check on inflated self-evaluations. However, the effort to understand a lived religious tradition also demands understanding the highest aspirations the tradition sets for its adherents. The shortfalls of others, given our own impressive failings, should occasion no great surprise and exaggerated emphases. Heroic figures, dreams, hopes, and especially values should not be left out of Islamic studies.

INTRODUCTION 11

There is a rich Western library that documents the shortcomings and failings of Islamic civilization. This study of Abu Dharr and his rarely noted contemporary influence makes few contributions to that well-stocked library of Islam's negatives. Abu Dharr's story is therefore for the most part left out. This book offers a corrective interpretive essay that leans purposefully to the positives in Islam as faith and civilization. The tilt to the positive in Islam inevitably brings Abu Dharr into clear view. The reasons for such an approach are simple. Islam has persisted for some fourteen centuries. The usual litany of Islam's failings and shortcomings cannot explain that simple historical fact. Today, Islam is generally regarded as the fastest-growing faith in the world. Some percentage of those converts are quite clearly opportunistic, with Saudi oil money undoubtedly playing its role. Nevertheless, it is unreasonable to think that the steady stream of converts from the major religions and regions of the world are all misreading the faith they have freely chosen to enter. There must be more to Islam.

As many Islamic scholars announce, conditions today in the Islamic world are among the worst in Islam's long history. Like all the great monotheisms, Islam has been subject to narrow, literalist interpretations. Such narrow and dispiriting views have a history, too. They are the dark shadows that obscure the centrist Islam that is the protagonist in this book. The Islam of the shadows is today experiencing its own resurgence. Its adherents thrive in the environment of death and chaos that endless wars in the Middle East have created since the time of the disastrous American assault on Iraq in 2003. "Ending the Iraqi state," the aim of the US invasion, proved to be a gift to the most violent extremist movements.

The Islam of dark shadows gives license to violent extremist intellectuals. They misread the legacy in the most destructive ways. The sacred texts are systematically distorted. The Qur'an is pushed to the side in favor of weak and invented *hadith*s or traditions of what the Prophet said and did. A foundation of lies and distortions is built for the launch of violent extremist movements. They are as "Islamic" as the Inquisition, the burning of women judged to be witches, or the sanctification of slavery are "Christian."

Even dark and distorted ideas, however, are still ideas. Interpretations of Islam do take shape that celebrate nihilistic violence with black flags and unspeakably cruel actions. Attempts are made to wrap these unmitigated horrors in Islamic garb. For a minority of benighted souls, charismatic "caliphs" and "amirs" concoct an intoxicating brew of cruel deceits. Qur'anic passages are wrenched out of context. They are made part of the mix. Weak

12 JUSTICE IN ISLAM

or invented prophetic *hadiths* are most often the main ingredients. They are intended to strengthen the bogus claim of extremists to Islamic legitimacy. Those without hope and a future find the illusion of both under the black flags. They are encouraged to believe they are soldiers for the faith. In reality, they are doing the bloody work of building the foundation for a new *jahilliya* (age of ignorance).

Ignorance is not confined to those who wave black flags. Through the centuries, the Islam of the Qur'an has proven itself the most effective antidote to extremisms of all varieties. The antidote weakens, however, when extremists find powerful outside support. At times, the support has been deliberate. Saudi financing has flowed in a regular stream to purveyors of extremist Wahhabi Islam and analogous distortions of the faith. Reaganites supported Islamic radicals as "freedom fighters" in Afghanistan. At other times, that support has been less focused and purposeful. Windfalls from corruption and sheer incompetence have simply gifted extremists in Iraq with suitcases of dollars and huge stockpiles of abandoned weapons.

Ignorance of the centrist Islam of the Qur'an is the most dangerous shortcoming of the West. Islamophobia is but one of its consequences. It is not the most consequential. Extremist Islam relies on a complex of ideas. *Not even the most powerful military the world has ever known can kill ideas.* In the end, dark and distorted ideas must be understood and countered by better ideas. Islam of the Qur'an has proven itself through the centuries as the best source of such ideas. Blinding ignorance of Islam and of the Islamic landscape into which Western militaries have blundered is dangerous. Knowing little of midstream Islam, the secular West too often conflates centrism with extremism. The West, with its debilitating lack of knowledge of Islam, consistently pursues policies that damage moderation and fuel extremism. There is, for example, a profound ambivalence about the midstream Muslim Brothers. The Brotherhood undoubtedly suffers from serious failings in both actions and theory. However, through their decades-long history, the Brothers have on balance been a bulwark against the most dangerous and destructive forms of Islamic extremism. The Wahhabi Islam of the Saudis, in contrast, has inspired and rationalized the vilest of extremisms. At times, the Brothers are supported as moderates; more often they are considered no better than the terrorists. In sharp contrast, Saudi Arabia and its extremist Wahhabi Islam are consistently and uncritically embraced. It is effectively shielded by American power from rational criticism.

INTRODUCTION   13

Virtually unnoticed in the West, Islam of the center enjoyed an unmatched global renewal as an Islamic Awakening.[7] The reservoir of centrist ideas deepened. These ideas of centrist Islam are the most effective corrective for the distortions of extremism. It is noteworthy that the Islamic Awakening has given the Jesus-like figure of Abu Dharr al Ghifari a significantly expanded space of appearance in Islamic lands, though the scope of that presence has varied. In the West, the quiet manifestations of the Awakening are routinely crowded out of international airways by the attention-grabbing stories of the spectacular violence of the extremists. Individual acts of brutal murder eclipse the hopeful signs of the resurgence of midstream Islamic values.

Attention to Abu Dharr al Ghifari provides a gateway to that neglected story. Abu Dharr, as history and legend, is one of those admirable figures of centrist Islam who are so little known in the West and too often neglected in Islamic lands. He is the standard bearer of the value of justice that defines midstream Islam. To bring him forward is in no way to deny the reality and importance of the rogues and tyrants who have stained Islamic history. Al Qaeda, the Islamic State, and all their evil progeny are important to track. They have, however, received more than their due from scholars and journalists. Moreover, they thrive on publicity. The work of tracking them is best turned over to international security forces. The task of countering their violence is best left to police, security forces, and the military as last resort.

Scholars should have a broader mandate. They should not act as publicists who magnify the importance of a terrorist minority. They should in no way reinforce the ludicrous claim that the extremists have successfully hijacked Islam. They have not. There is no good reason to treat extremist aspirations as though they have been realized. It is irrational to treat a violent minority as though it represents the world's 1.8 billion Muslims. As a first order of business, the ideas and values of midstream Islam should be rescued from neglect. Westerners need to know that alongside the divine Jesus of their own traditions there stands an admirable Prophetic Jesus who, like his divine counterpart, comes as a "mercy" for all humanity.[8] Abu Dharr and other exemplars of the midstream tradition deserve greater attention. Such an approach goes against the current wave of animus to all things Islamic in the secular West. The rise in such inhibiting hostility represents a gain for the violence of terrorists who have plagued so many of world's great cities. Yet, it is also true that many ordinary citizens in the West have embraced their Muslim neighbors. They have also, in large numbers, refused to follow Western political leaders who foster irrational hatred and fear of Islam. Muslims in

14 JUSTICE IN ISLAM

substantial numbers have vigorously condemned the violent criminality of those who claim to act in the name of their faith. No matter how often the lie is repeated, it is simply not true that moderate Islamic intellectuals have failed to condemn criminal extremism.

There is no reason to consolidate the gains of murderers by excessive attention to their crimes and denigrations of those Muslims who stand bravely against them. On the contrary, in such a climate it makes more sense to direct attention to the Islam of the Qur'an and the strong *hadith* in line with its message. For just this reason, now is an opportune time to direct attention to Abu Dharr al Ghifari, beloved companion of the Prophet Muhammad. His story is the story of the Qur'anic Islam centered on justice that shaped him. It is also the story of the Muslim Jesus for whom he has often acted through the centuries as a representative. Whenever and wherever Abu Dharr is invoked, the spirit of Islam's Muslim Jesus makes itself felt. Non-Muslims who have not had the chance to know one of the world's major faiths can look to the legends and history of Abu Dharr as a guide to midstream Islam. Muslims whose memories of Abu Dharr may have faded can renew their acquaintance with the Prophet Muhammad's beloved companion and symbol of Islamic justice.

Attention to admired figures and the values they exemplify has a rightful place in studies of Islam. Abu Dharr, as such a figure in Islam, does not have a static presence. At times, his memory fades, only to be renewed in often unexpected ways. In my own personal experience, he very quickly escaped from an initial graduate studies framing in Islamic studies as a companion of the Prophet Muhammad. Abu Dharr, I came to realize, respects neither the borders of time nor place. In research for my last book on the spiritual springs that fed the Islamic Awakening, much to my surprise, Abu Dharr seemed to be everywhere.[9] The more politically consequential the subject, the more likely was an appearance by this most venerable symbol of Islamic justice. The learned Islamic scholars whose work I most admired and followed regularly would invariably and often quite unexpectedly introduce him into our conversations. They evoked Abu Dharr by name, whether they were Sunni or Shi'i, Arab, Turkish, or Iranian. Somehow, Abu Dharr made it a habit to show up in a meaningful way, no matter where my research took me in the Islamic world, though more insistently in Iran than elsewhere. Those uninvited appearances made this book centered on the Prophet's companion as the symbol of Islamic justice and representative of the prophet Jesus inevitable.

INTRODUCTION   15

The aim of this interpretive study is to bring the Islam of the centrist Islamic Awakening into view. It is the Islam that centers on the core Qur'anic values of justice. In this book, the value of justice is given the human face of Abu Dharr, the Prophet Muhammad's beloved companion. Justice is treated here, as it is by the intellectuals of the Awakening, in the spirit of the Muslim prophet Jesus. Abu Dharr's habit of making himself an unannounced presence has not been restricted to my research life, as the personal story with which this preface opens illustrates. Across the Islamic world, shaikhs, imams, and ordinary believers make sure that Abu Dharr as a symbol of justice is not forgotten. The brief anecdote with which this Introduction opens makes that much clear. Abou Dharr's presence here in Alexandria, as this book opens, is reassuring.

2

Abu Dharr al Ghifari

Symbol of Justice, Lawyer of the Poor

Justice in Islam has a spiritual as well as a worldly dimension. It is the brightest jewel in the Islamic moral universe. "To render justice," as the eleventh-century jurist Muhammad Abu Bakr al Sarakhsi explained, "ranks as the most noble of acts of devotion, next to expression of belief in God. It is the greatest of all the duties entrusted to the prophets . . . and it is the strongest justification for man's stewardship of the earth."[1] Muslims learn from a greatly loved and endlessly cited verse of the Qur'an that actions for justice, rather than the performance of religious rituals, is the highest form of righteousness. Since first reading this verse decades ago, I have always found it among the most moving in the Qur'an:

> It is not righteousness that ye turn your faces to the East and West [as performance of prayer requires] but it is righteousness to believe in God and the Last Day, and the Angels, and the Book, and the Messengers; to spend of your substance, out of love for Him, for your kin, for orphans, for the needy, for travelers, for those who ask, and for the ransom of slaves; to be steadfast in prayer, and give *Zakat* [donation to support those in need], to fulfill the contracts you have made; and to be firm and patient, in pain [and suffering] and throughout all periods of panic. Such are the people of truth, the God-fearing.[2]

Humanity is charged by God not only to believe, but to *act* to build just and compassionate communities. *Istikhlaf* is the Qur'anic term for this responsibility.[3] It defines a mission for humanity at once sacred and historical. To build a community is a practical achievement of the highest order. In building a *just* community, men and women are given intimations of the Divine. The experience of actually living in a just and caring community draws them still closer to God. Muslims in such a social world are more able to live in the way God and their Prophet Muhammad intended for them.[4]

Justice in Islam. Raymond William Baker, Oxford University Press. © Oxford University Press 2022.
DOI: 10.1093/oso/9780197624975.003.0002

To guide this work of building, the Qur'an provides a profile of the just community. In the community envisioned, differences in levels of prosperity and station may rightly reflect the variety of human capabilities and commitments. However, the Qur'anic vision strictly warns against great disparities of wealth between the rich and the poor. More pointedly, the Qur'an instructs that wealth should circulate throughout society. It should not be confined to the upper social strata only.[5] A foundation of practical compassion must also assure that the needs of the most vulnerable are addressed. Obligations to the poor must be fulfilled as religious duties and not as charity. Needs must be met in ways that respect the dignity of the poor. The Prophet's attitude toward assistance to the poor is captured in a *hadith* that explains that "one who looks after a widow or a poor person is like a *mujahid* [warrior] who fights for Allah's Cause, or like he who performs prayers all the night and fasts all the day."[6]

For his tireless efforts on behalf of the least privileged, Abu Dharr al Ghifari was known to his contemporaries as the "lawyer of the poor." The Prophet's companion escapes all attempts to reduce him to an ideological or sectarian prop. Rather, Abu Dharr al Ghifari, like the prophets of Islam, belongs to all Muslims. To study Islam as a worldly force is to encounter Abu Dharr. It also means to feel through him the spirit of the Muslim Jesus with whom he is so closely bound. The encounter with the companion often has a jarring quality. The Prophet's companion speaks the truth simply and directly, unafraid of consequences.

On the very first meeting, Abu Dharr shakes off the dust of history to call one and all to join struggles against injustice. The companion's expectations of those who take the Qur'an as lodestar are high. Not even the richest or most powerful escape accountability. In Islam, steep demands are normalized. The Qur'an repeatedly insists, however, that Islam does not break new ground. Rather, Islam brings *dhikr* (remembrance) of great truths humankind "already knows."[7] That pregnant phrase reminds humanity of the steady stream of messengers God has sent to humanity. The earlier revelations notably included Judaism and Christianity. However, they were by no means limited to them. Islamic tradition at times assigns 124,000 as the number of previous divine messages.[8] The number should be understood as a symbolic one, meant to indicate that God's messengers to humanity have been countless. Islam, understood by Muslims as the last of these divine messages, neither discounts nor denigrates any of the earlier revelations. Islam in this way comes as a reaffirmation to humanity of the essence of all the earlier divine messages.

18 JUSTICE IN ISLAM

God created *fitra* (human nature). The Message of Islam and the responsibilities it imposes come to humanity in a form that is consonant with that essential character. As the final form of God's revelation, Islam strikes a balance.[9] Its message is neither too worldly, like Judaism, nor too other-worldly, like Christianity. Islam responds to human capabilities in a measured way. It calls men and women to their better selves in ways that do not overwhelm them or underestimate their capabilities. Islam does not make demands that humanity cannot fulfill. The Qur'an states clearly that "God does not on any soul place a burden greater than it can bear."[10]

Islam did not come to a passive Abu Dharr. The companion actively pursued the faith. Doing so, Abu Dharr consolidated his radical break from the polytheistic tribal society into which he was born. The legends of his embrace of Islam establish him as a strong and self-directed figure. Even before his first meeting with the Prophet Muhammad, he had made his own journey to monotheism. The essentials of the faith were a natural part of his being. In embracing Islam, Abu Dharr found confirmation of truths intimated by his own experience. Abu Dharr worked throughout his life to strengthen his faith on foundations secure from within.

Abu Dharr heard stories of the appearance of a unique man among the Kureish tribe. Some considered the stranger a prophet. He asked his brother to go and learn what he could of the man. Encouraged by his brother's report that the stranger called for the worship of the one God, Abu Dharr traveled to Mecca to take the measure of the man.

When the prophet of the one God explained to him more fully the essentials of the Message, Abu Dharr immediately embraced Islam. He is regarded as the fourth or fifth person to enter the faith. Pronouncing himself a Muslim, Abu Dharr immediately readied himself to call others to Islam. The Prophet Muhammad cautioned his early convert that the people of Mecca were not yet ready to receive the Message. It would be best, the Prophet counseled, to sound the call cautiously at first with close circles of family and trusted friends. The Prophet himself had done precisely that. However, the impetuous Abu Dharr was so deeply moved by the Message that he could not contain himself. He rushed immediately to the public square in Mecca. There, he loudly pronounced the *shahada* (the Muslim profession of faith). Abu Dharr bore public witness that there was but one God and Muhammad was His Prophet. He called all who could hear his voice to embrace the faith built on those essentials.

The Meccans responded angrily to this bold stranger. They took offense at his disruptive proclamation of a new prophecy. They were attached to their numerous gods. They devotedly worshipped the stone idols that represented them. Abu Dharr's declaration that there was but one God represented a challenge to the most fundamental beliefs and religious practices of Meccans. He also seriously threatened the economic foundations of their way of life. Pilgrims traveled from all over Arabia to visit the numerous shrines in Mecca. These pilgrimages provided an important stream of revenue.

The angered Meccans set on the hapless Abu Dharr. They beat him severely. According to the most trusted accounts of the incident, Abu Dharr was saved only by the intervention of the Prophet's paternal uncle, 'Abbas ibn 'Abd al Muttalib (568–653). Legends tell us that 'Abbas threw himself over Abu Dharr to protect him. Unchastened, the very next day the impetuous Abu Dharr returned to the same public space. This man, known to be modest, indeed humble, nevertheless could erupt with reckless boldness. Abu Dharr once again loudly pronounced the *shahada* in Mecca's central square. He bore proud witness to his new faith that there was but one God and that Muhammad was His Prophet.

Yet again, 'Abbas barely managed to rescue him from the angry crowd. 'Abbas calmed the situation by cautioning the Meccans against killing a member of the Ghifari tribe. The territory of the tribe lay on a major trade route that connected Yemen to Syria. Abu Dharr's tribesmen had a reputation as fierce fighters. They exacted tribute from all who passed through their tribal land. They raided those who refused their demands. The Prophet's uncle reminded the Meccans that their caravans had to pass through al Ghifari territory. Their goods and their very lives would never be safe if the blood of a Ghifari stained their hands.

'Abbas worried that Abu Dharr might not survive a third assault. He feared that efforts to contain the anger of the Meccans might fail if put to the test a third time. He alerted the Prophet to the danger. The Prophet once again urged his passionate convert to return to his family and his own al Ghifari tribe to sound the call to Islam. This time Abu Dharr accepted the Prophet's cautionary counsel to avoid unnecessary provocation. He did so with the salutation to the Prophet of *salamu 'aleikum* (peace be upon you). The claim is at times made that Abu Dharr was the first to use this phrase. In any event, it became the preferred greeting for Muslims. It is heard today when Muslims conclude each of their regular prayers and whenever they greet each other.

20 JUSTICE IN ISLAM

Strict asceticism reinforced the aura of humility that surrounded Abu Dharr. The contrast to the bold actions of which he was capable imbued his renunciation of worldly goods with a diffuse spiritual character. When visitors came to his home, they could not but notice the extreme sparseness of its furnishings. Abu Dharr always told them simply that his needs did not exceed minimal belongings. He explained that he kept at hand only the essentials. He did, however, put aside a small reserve to allow for a modest measure of generosity. Abu Dharr would also tell visitors that he sent his most prized possessions ahead to the world to come. The most important things in his life were his faith and his fervent commitment to social justice. Neither was available as a material object to be displayed.

Abu Dharr sought to travel unencumbered to the world to come. The Prophet's companion reasoned that the worship of God alone frees humanity from all other forms of enslavement, whether to persons, passions, or possessions. Abu Dharr explained that obsession with material acquisitions and other forms of wealth stands as perhaps the most common form of self-imposed bondage. Abu Dharr held close only those things absolutely necessary for a life that could fulfill the genuine needs of self and family. He believed that no Muslim should ever succumb to the worship of *more*.

The Prophet's companion went further still. He gave his asceticism a progressive political meaning. He explained that the Islam of the Qur'an announces that no king, leader, or military figure should ever be venerated like a god. With its grounding in the principle of *tawhid* (the Islamic belief in the oneness of God), the strict monotheism of Abu Dharr modeled non-violent Islamic resistance to all manner of tyrannies. It is no accident that the plethora of authoritarian rulers in Islamic lands often face important opposition from Islamic intellectuals and movements of Islamic inspiration. It matters little whether dictators cast themselves as shahs, monarchs, "presidents for life," or clerics with a mandate to rule. Abu Dharr explained that the servile worship that all absolute rulers demand violates the principle of *tawhid*. Islam thus imbues the heart and mind of ordinary Muslims with a latent spirit of resistance to all forms of tyranny as a core religious obligation. That spirit may elicit no response. It may lay dormant. Muslims may not be able to act on it. Still, it is always there. Islamic lands may be littered with corrupt kings, cruel dictators, or tyrants in religious dress, as they are today. Foreign invaders may impose by force or seduction their way of life, languages, and forms of governance, as they have attempted to do over the last two centuries. However, just below the passive surface, Islam preserves

ABU DHARR AL GHIFARI   21

a spirit of resistance in the hearts and minds of its legions of ordinary followers. To be sure, religion is not the only source of the will to resist. Leftist and broadly humanistic trends often feed the same impulse. Cooperation in the name of justice among all such trends is clearly sanctioned in Islam.

Islam may at times lose force with co-opted elites. Yet, as Shaikh Muhammad al Ghazalli, one of the most important Sunni clerics of the twentieth century, frequently observed, the Islam of the Qur'an and *Sunnah* remains alive and robust in the hearts and minds of the common people. No other political or ideological movement has quite the same mass reserves of deep commitment. Islamic activism only appears to come out of nowhere. Its most important resources are within. Shaikh Ghazalli consistently identified Abu Dharr as an important inspiration for tapping these interior reservoirs of resistance. Explicit references to Abu Dharr are threaded through Ghazalli's most influential works.

The death of the Prophet Muhammad in 632 A.D. was a terrible blow to the nascent Islamic community. Succession struggles proved devastating. It is shocking that three of the first four caliphs were assassinated. In Abu Dharr's eyes, the problems of succession became particularly grave with the ascendency of the third caliph, Osman ibn Affan (577–656). Abu Dharr came to see in the behavior of Osman signs that power and wealth were corrupting righteous caliphal rule. A pattern of amassing wealth under the personal control of the caliph emerged. More troublesome still to Abu Dharr was Osman's practice of filling key positions of the expanding administrative and military structures of the caliphate with members of his own family and tribe.

Osman's appointments notably included his nephew Mu'awiyya (602–680) as governor of Syria. Mu'awiyya proved a competent administrator. His strong rule brought a measure of prosperity to the territories he controlled. However, legend records that aspects of his rule alarmed Abu Dharr. Abu Dharr objected, in particular, to Mu'awiyya's misuse of community funds. He judged most egregious the building of a caliphal palace. The very idea of a palace represented to Abu Dharr a radical departure from the modest and integrated way that the Prophet Muhammad had led the community as Islam's first caliph. The Prophet had lived simply among his followers. Abu Dharr judged that a palace would set the ruler apart. It would encourage an unwarranted feeling of subservience to the ruler on the part of ordinary Muslims. Abu Dharr directly questioned the caliph's departure from the Prophet's example. He judged that if the funds for the palace were private, they bore witness to an unwarranted display of flagrant wealth. If they were public, their

22 JUSTICE IN ISLAM

appropriation for a palace constituted theft from the resources of the community of Muslims.

Righteous Rule and the Islamic Awakening

Abu Dharr held Caliph Osman accountable for such departures from the Qur'anic vision of the just ruler. He warned that a privileged caste of power and wealth was taking shape. His response was bold and creative. It should not be overlooked that it was also non-violent. Abu Dharr organized no armed faction or conspiracy against the caliph, despite his intense opposition to the way the caliph was leading the community. To register his protest, Abu Dharr simply went alone to the mosque. There, he recited over and over the Qur'anic verses that condemned abuses of political power and wealth.[11] His message was clear and effective. It had Qur'anic sanction. Violence was not needed.

Mu'awiyya nevertheless complained to his uncle that Abu Dharr was undermining his rule in Syria. The caliph summoned Abu Dharr. The Prophet's companion recounted to the caliph in simple and direct terms the basis for his objections to the way his nephew was governing. He also made it clear that he held the caliph accountable for his nephew's departures from the Qur'anic vision of just rule. The caliph was taken aback by the boldness of Abu Dharr's admonitions. Yet, the angered caliph could not easily restrict a companion of the Prophet from reciting verses of the Qur'an in the community mosque. Silencing Abu Dharr would be no easy task. The caliph understood that the life of a companion so close to the Prophet could not be taken, without threat of open rebellion. Abu Dharr had succeeded in modeling a peaceful yet successful mode of protest. Nonviolent resistance represents an important, though frequently overlooked, dimension of the legacy of Abu Dharr. Modern-day Western mythology of "Islam of the sword" obscures the clear moral preference for nonviolence that threads its way through Islamic tradition from the time of Abu Dharr forward.

The protections Abu Dharr enjoyed from the wrath of the caliph extended only so far. In the end, the exasperated caliph exiled the troublesome companion to distant Rabadha, an isolated desert settlement some 125 miles northeast of Mecca. Sometime later, the caliph sent gold coins to Abu Dharr. He knew conditions in this bleak exile would be difficult. Abu Dharr would be in need. The caliph hoped this gesture to a disciplined companion might open a pathway to Abu Dharr's accommodation to his style of rule. Instead, Abu Dharr immediately returned the coins. The indentured servant from the caliph who brought them pleaded with Abu Dharr to accept the gold pieces. The servant explained that he had been promised his freedom if he was successful in delivering the coins. Abu Dharr responded simply that he would lose his own freedom if he accepted them. Despite his need, Abu Dharr sent the coins back. With the coins, he delivered a message. He suggested to the caliph that it would be far preferable to distribute them to the growing numbers of the community in need under his rule.

Such evocative legends of Abu Dharr represent a treasure of the classic Islamic heritage. Their truth resides in their elaboration of the centrality of justice to the Islamic vision of righteous rule, rather than any measure of their historical accuracy. They illuminate the meaning of the core value of justice in Islam. They should be understood as interpretive commentary on the justice-centered ideal of righteous action at the heart of midstream Islam. These endlessly recited stories have preserved and elaborated Abu Dharr's memory in the Islamic imagination through the centuries. They have kept alive the vision of just rule and moral governance at the heart of efforts of successive waves of Islamic reform. As we shall see, this compelling and unifying vision draws together the diverse voices of the contemporary Islamic Awakening.

To be sure, the memories of Abu Dharr are not without controversy. Not everyone is enamored of a lover of justice. At times, there have been discrediting charges lodged against Abu Dharr. I recall, in particular, the reports that circulated in Egypt in the early 1970s that traditionalist circles in al Azhar were going so far as to question whether Abu Dharr was a legitimate companion of the Prophet at all. The evidence-free accusations were subsequently abandoned. They are now mercifully forgotten. More durable have been persistent and more focused charges that Abu Dharr was a materialist who had deviated from Islam. In the modern era, these charges crystallized in accusations of "communism." Such charges have been misdirected. They find no justification in the centrist Islam for which Abu Dharr spoke. The Islam of the Qur'an does not question the right of private property. It finds nothing inherently evil in the workings of the market. There is only a Qur'anic aversion to the amassing of extravagant wealth and its monopoly by a narrow stratum of the population. A formal investigation into the charges of communism by al Azhar, under the direction of Abdul Meguid Salim, exonerated Abu Dharr. The committee found that Abu Dharr's admonitions

24   JUSTICE IN ISLAM

had gone no further than the Qur'anic prohibitions against amassing excessive wealth and limiting how widely it is shared. In the end, the accusations against a controversial figure of the classical age only served to revitalize his memory and clarify its relevance to contemporary concerns.

More serious have been the periodic attempts to diminish the stature of the Prophet's companion by embroiling him, retroactively, in the damaging Sunni-Shi'i split. Abu Dharr's time of closeness to the Prophet and most prolific reporting on Prophetic words and actions in fact predated Islam's first great *fitna* (civil strife), notably the Sunni-Shi'i schism. The *hadith*s Abu Dharr recorded are an integral part of the Islam of all Muslims. Nevertheless, there are differences in how Abu Dharr himself has been remembered by the two major communities of Muslims, the Sunni majority and Shi'i minority. They reflect the way Abu Dharr's role in the succession struggles after the Prophet's death is understood. Two contrasting viewpoints on leadership of the community emerged. The first approach sought to select as successor the man from the circle around the Prophet judged most capable to rule. This approach ultimately prevailed as the majority Sunni position. The second reflected the views of the most fervid partisans of Ali ibn Abi Taleb (ca. 600–661), the Prophet's cousin and son-in-law. This minority view argued that the caliphate should be kept in the family of the Prophet. This idea has survived in what was to become the minority Shi'i sect of Muslims. Today the Shi'i are variously estimated to represent up to 15 percent of the world's Muslims. They remain steadfast in the view that succession should be reserved to the Prophet's family.

Shi'i scholars emphasize Abu Dharr's close relationship to Ali and his early support for Ali's candidacy as caliph. They also accord Abu Dharr heightened status as one of the four foundational figures of Shi'i Islam. In Shi'i sources, it should also be noted, Abu Dharr is consistently presented in bolder and more vibrant colors than the typical representations of Sunni scholars. At the same time, Shi'i have been inclined to view the other *sahaba* (companions of the Prophet Muhammad) much less favorably than the Sunni majority community. Shi'i scholarship blames the *sahaba* for the delay in awarding the caliphate to Ali. Eventually, Ali did become the fourth caliph and led the community from 656 to 661. However, in the Shi'i view, the delay in his appointment as caliph ultimately served to alienate the institution of the caliphate from the Prophet's lineage.

Controversies notwithstanding, Abu Dharr has consistently embodied an enlightened interpretation of Islam for *all* Muslims. Abu Dharr's resilience through the centuries owes a great deal to a dimension of his story that receives sparse attention. Abu Dharr has weight as a reliable recorder of the words and deeds of the Prophet. As a companion, Abu Dharr enjoyed close access to the Prophet. In general, the companions were followers of Muhammad who were in personal contact with him. Abu Dharr made more than most of that proximity. From his intimate vantage point, Abu Dharr recorded actions of the Prophet that he witnessed and words that he himself heard. In all, Abu Dharr authored some 281 *hadiths* of the Prophet.

Some of the traditions recorded on Abu Dharr's authority carry exceptional weight. With his substantial body of *hadiths*, Abu Dharr built his scholarship into the very foundations of Islam. One such *hadith* could serve as the epigraph for this chapter: "O, my servants, I have forbidden oppression to Myself, And I have made it forbidden amongst you, So, do not oppress one another."[12] This tradition is a valuable resource for Muslims everywhere who resist tyranny and love freedom.

For fourteen centuries, Abu Dharr has moved by right with this core message through all the Islamic world. Everywhere, he brings a galvanizing conception of Islamic justice with him. The texts of the Qur'an and important traditions like those recorded by Abu Dharr himself have been woven into the life routines of Muslims. References to Qur'anic verses and the *Sunnah* (the record of all the deeds and words of the Prophet) enrich everyday speech.

Words matter greatly in Islam. Calligraphy is an art form expressed in all manner of ways, from high art to mundane decoration. The entire façade of a large bank building across from my first apartment in Cairo is decorated with Qur'anic verses in elaborate script. For special occasions, few speakers can resist turning to Qur'anic verses and *hadith* of the Prophet Muhammad for the *gravitas* that formal occasions are felt to demand.

Affirmation of the foundational principle of *tawhid*, the oneness of God, is always first among the messages of the sacred texts. Elaboration of the meaning of justice begins with *tawhid*. On the theoretical plane, the greatest injustice in Islam is *al shirk* (the association of any partner with God). The Qur'an could not be more explicit. A verse proclaims: "Say, He is God, The One and Only, God the Eternal, Absolute; He begetteth not, Nor is He begotten; And there is none Like unto him."[13]

As theology, these understandings set Islam apart from Christianity, with its central notion of the trinity. On the worldly plane, the Qur'an and *Sunnah* inspire battles against abuses of power and wealth.[14] Neither the powerful nor the rich are ever to be worshipped.[15] These struggles, too, have a spiritual

26 JUSTICE IN ISLAM

dimension. They, too, find their anchor in *tawhid*. Islam's radical monotheism refuses veneration of anything or anyone other than God.

At times, Abu Dharr has been ignored. At other times, his presence has faded. Yet, as the Prophet's beloved companion and important *hadith* scholar, Abu Dharr simply cannot be erased from Islamic tradition. Throughout their long history, Muslims have regularly turned to this classic figure for inspiration in their struggles for justice. The contemporary turn to Islam across Islamic lands represents precisely such a moment in the global history of Muslims.

Abu Dharr and the Islamic Awakening

The Awakening began to work its effects in the late 1960s and early 1970s. Remarkably, during those years Abu Dharr made regular appearances. Scholars from across Islamic lands explicitly invoked his name and example. The most prominent intellectuals of the Awakening drew inspiration from Abu Dharr. Whether Arabs, Turks, or Iranians, they identified the Prophet's companion as a force inspiring their work for the reform and renewal of Islam. Abu Dharr lives in the scholarly literature of the Islamic Awakening.

Today, Abu Dharr's is a voice that should be heard, not just in the Islamic world, and now more than ever. Familiarity with his legends enriches our understanding of an influential progressive interpretation of Islam that continues to have relevance. The Islamic Awakening has renewed Abu Dharr's importance. The Prophet's companion is now better known in Islamic lands as a fighter for justice. Yet, it remains rare to find any ordinary non-Muslim in the West who has even heard of him. What is stranger still is the relative neglect of Abu Darr by Western scholars of Islamic studies. Among the countless "introductions" to Islam in the major Western languages, one almost never finds an entry for Abu Dharr al Ghifari.

This lapse is symptomatic of a larger problem. In the West, a dark shadow is routinely cast on coverage of Islam and the Islamic world. Emphasis is regularly placed on retrograde Islam, particularly as exemplified by the most violent extremist groups. The spectacular destruction of Western wars waged in Islamic lands is mirrored in the terrible crimes of Islamic extremists. These horrific acts contribute to the calculated exacerbations of violent sectarian conflict by local and international actors. Ordinary citizens are caught in the crossfire. Islam itself comes under attack. For many in the West, the world of Islam comes into view only as a site of irrational violence.

Humanity cannot afford to be so ignorantly dismissive of one of the world's great religious and cultural traditions. Too many analysts and commentators see the alternatives available to Muslims as criminal extremism, on the one hand, or some version of Western secularism, on the other. The moral and political message of centrist Islam is lost to view. It is as though Islam and Islamic civilization have nothing to offer for a common human future other than violent wrongdoing or the ultimately demeaning imitation of others.

At a time when Islam for many has been reduced to little more than criminality and terror, the history and legends of Abu Dharr as exemplar of the Islamic value of social justice have greater importance than ever. The story of Abu Dharr is more than the narrative of an important figure from the classical Islamic era. His legends illuminate the venerable centrist understanding of Islam with an activist commitment to justice at its core. *Tawhid* is often mistaken as the primary Islamic value. It is not. *Tawhid* is actually something more. Monotheism is the *premise* of all Islamic thought, including thought about values. With *tawhid* taken for granted, the Qur'an discusses the values that Muslims should make their own. Justice ranks first. The sheer number of Qur'anic references to justice makes that priority perfectly clear. Only God is referred to more frequently than justice in the Qur'an. This emphatic Qur'anic emphasis on justice means that, however oppressive the particular circumstances of Muslims, the call for justice can always be heard. The Qur'an cannot be silenced. Muslims strive to act on its injunctions, if they are able. If they cannot, their faith instructs them to hold its message in their hearts and minds for the day when action will be possible. The call for justice is an intrinsic part of the call to Islam itself. It can be muted. It can be ignored. It cannot be abrogated.

Abu Dharr's identification with struggles for justice through the centuries has kept him at the moral center of the "venture of Islam."[16] The centrist Islam of the Qur'an is the Islam of justice. The Qur'an as the word of God is everywhere in the Islamic world, as I am reminded by the Qur'anic recitation playing in my Alexandria coffee shop where I write every morning. Almost as ubiquitous are expressions of the wisdom of the Prophet Muhammad. The *hadiths* of the Prophet record his words and deeds. *Hadith* collections, alongside biographies of the Prophet, should be thought of as repositories of prophetic wisdom. The collections represent the efforts of Islamic scholars to preserve the most accurate record possible of the guidance the Prophet brought to humanity. Individual *hadith* must be assessed for their reliability. Scholars judge the likely accuracy of the *matn* (substance of what is reported) by the reliability of the *isnad* (chain of sources for its reporting). As a result, the confidence in the soundness of *hadith* is understood to be variable. Nevertheless, the cumulative wisdom of the Prophet Muhammad, attested in important part by sound *hadith*, defines the normative way, or *Sunnah*, of the Prophet. The Qur'an and the *Sunnah* combine to provide the foundations of a faith for all Muslims that has justice at its core. For many, the Qur'an is the Law and the *Sunnah* a body of explanatory notes.

Islamic communities, secure in their monotheism, are always communities of interpretation. Determination of what justice demands in particular times and places is the first priority of the Islamic interpretive project. Abu Dharr identified himself completely with this quest for the realization of justice. Through the centuries, Abu Dharr al Ghifari has been an inspiration for parallel local struggles. The countless legends of Abu Dharr have their primary importance as communal annotations on the rich meaning of justice, rather than as historical records. The legends must be read for their symbolic and metaphorical meaning. Often the same legend is recounted in a variety of ways. Shi'i sources differ from Sunni sources. The Turks have a way of recounting the legends of Abu Dharr that center on questions of moral choice. This Turkish style of remembrance differs from that of the Arab focus on the abstract meaning of core concepts. The Iranians, too, have distinctive emphases shaped by their own historical experience and by their rich literary traditions. More often than not, among Iranian scholars, traditions find articulation in poetic style. In all these ways and more, details of the legends and the styles of their presentation vary from one version to another. The core meanings, however, remain remarkably consistent.

For all the complications, the legends of Abu Dharr make it perfectly clear that strivings for justice in Islam are inherently social and political. They cannot be simply spiritual. With justice as its critical value, Islam could not possibly separate politics and religion. Islamic justice is a social and political rather than individual value. It has historical as well as metaphysical or spiritual implications.

Justice finds its worldly grounding in the just communities Muslims are called to build. This characteristic is sometimes taken too literally to mean that clerics must rule. It does not. At times, particular religious figures may make that claim, as the Ayatollah Khomeini did in Iran. However, this position has no Qur'anic sanction. It can and has been challenged on solid Islamic grounds, including by Iranian Islamic scholars.

The Mystical Domain of the "One and Many"

Istikhlaf, the Islamic call to build a just community, requires not only justice but also its critical corollaries of freedom and compassion. The value of justice must be realized in grounded circumstances of time and place. Justice serves as the lodestar of efforts to fulfill the obligation of *istikhlaf.* At the same time, a measure of freedom is required to enable struggles for justice. The major intellectuals of centrist Islam have also consistently argued that in the modern world a just community will be one that protects fundamental freedoms. They have also made it clear that compassion and love are critical components of the imagined Islamic community.[17]

Abu Dharr understood justice as a value that is always also a call to action. The Prophet's companion models a spiritual commitment to justice as pleasing to God. He also displays, at every turn, a practical readiness to act on justice's behalf.[18] Far more than Christianity, Islam has a decidedly pragmatic and activist character. In the Qur'an, the realm of values and beliefs is always linked to action. The notion of salvation by faith alone, for example, is alien to Islam. The Qur'an articulates both *'aqida* (beliefs) and *mu'amallat* (behavior). They mark two interwoven pathways that God provides for 'the betterment of humanity.

Building the just community, in particular, requires the freedom to act for its realization. Unfreedom may prevail in Islamic lands, as it does today. However infertile the soil for freedom may be at particular times, the Qur'an assures that the idea of freedom is kept alive. An *aya* states clearly that even on the most sensitive issue of belief itself, God grants *al nas* the freedom to choose: "Let him who will Believe, let him who will reject [it]."[19] Believers are held responsible for the choices they make. Alongside justice and freedom, Islam gives the value of compassion great emphasis. Enlistment in the collective effort to build the just community is understood to find its deepest motivation in fellow-feeling for those wounded by injustice. Compassion always has a role, alongside justice and freedom, in the Islamic vision of community.

Interpretation is intrinsic to all efforts of *istikhlaf.* The core intellectual challenge requires that unchanging sacred texts, articulating core Islamic values, be related to the changing contexts where justice and its correlative values are to be realized. Abu Dharr, as a symbol of justice, assists in humanizing this interpretive challenge. The compelling simplicity of justice as a value has been one face of Abu Dharr. The complexity of the diverse pathways to its realization has sketched another. In this way, Abu Dharr has

30 JUSTICE IN ISLAM

represented the articulation of the value of justice as simultaneously singular and multiple. To accept Abu Dharr as a guide for understanding important dimensions of Islam is to enter the mystical domain of "the one and the many." This territory is not alien to me. It is the domain of the Islamic mystics that I first encountered in my graduate work in Islamic studies some forty years ago. Mystical figures from that cosmopolitan world of Arabs, Turks, Iranians, and countless other ethnicities have remained lifelong friends and spiritual interlocutors since then. It is in the spiritual world of the mystics where admiration of Abu Dharr and reverence for the Muslim Jesus have flowered.[20]

The indispensable mystical companion for this book has been Ibn al Arabi (1165–1240). When I travel between the United States and Egypt, as I do frequently, I now rarely bring books with me. In our time of VPNs, online access, e-books, and astonishingly rapid downloads, I decided several years ago that it was time to part company with many old friends in the interest of a lighter backpack. The exception in packing for my trip to Egypt for this past year of writing was Ibn al Arabi's *Bezels of Wisdom*. A book that pays serious attention to Abu Dharr as symbol of Islamic justice became inevitable when I constantly encountered references to him by the major intellectuals of the Islamic Awakening. Abu Dharr appeared most often against a backdrop of explorations of Islamic mystical learning in the writings of the major intellectuals of the Awakening. I convinced myself that I should have a mystic as companion for this particular book journey. Ibn al Arabi came insistently to mind. With Ibn al Arabi's masterpiece *Bezels of Wisdom* in my carry-on, I felt better prepared to puzzle through the unexpected and the unknowable, as I pursued the peripatetic Abu Dharr as he moved, hand in hand with the mystics, through the centuries and across Islamic lands.[21]

Translation of the abstract value of justice into social realities inevitably introduces complications. The singular yields to the manifold. Those who respond to Islam's call to build a better world all turn to justice as a unifying symbol to give unifying purpose to their disparate collective efforts. With no contradiction, they also look to justice as a multifaceted value to guide their specific efforts to resist injustice in their own particular circumstance. Inevitably, the galvanizing power of simplicity makes room for the nuances of complexity. Tailored relevance to particular circumstances becomes possible.

One of the unexpected discoveries of my most recent research on contemporary *Islam haraki* (movement Islam) has been a deeper appreciation of the way Islamic mysticism seeps deeply into the politics of the major centrist movements of Islamic resistance.[22] The effects are not peripheral. They have made themselves felt in powerful ways. They are to be found at the heart of the most important movements. Hassan al Banna, the Egyptian founder of the Sunni Muslim Brothers, belonged to a Sufi order from his early teens. The Muslim Brotherhood, founded in 1928, has been and remains today the most important of centrist Islamic political movements. Even after leaving his Sufi order, Banna continued his lifelong effort to deepen his mystical knowledge. Sayyid Qutb, the most important and most original intellectual the Brothers' movement produced, had his own deep roots in Islamic mysticism.

The paradox of "the one and the many" lies at the heart of mystical learning. I first encountered this notion in the work of Ibn al Arabi. Dr. Ilse Lichtenstadter, my classical Arabic and Islamic philosophy professor in graduate studies at Harvard, insisted that in order to develop a proper sense of the power and subtlety of the Arabic language, her students had to read a wide variety of very different texts.[23] Suddenly, I found myself face to face with excerpts from Ibn al Arabi's *Bezels of Wisdom*. The excerpts seemed embarrassingly brief. Nevertheless, they still represented an immersion experience with few parallels in all the decades since. I clutched Dr. Lichtenstadter's hand and somehow managed to convince myself that I had stayed afloat. The language was beyond challenging, the creative and chaotic ideas even more so. In the decades since, I have been amazed at how many times the most tough-minded and practical Islamic political activists confess to the lasting and always daunting influence of their own encounters with Ibn al Arabi.

The *Bezels of Wisdom* was written late in Ibn al Arabi's life. He describes the work as the summation of a lifetime of reflection. *Bezels* centers on the idea of prophecy, so critical not only to Islam but to all the great monotheisms. In one sense, all of the prophets are unified by the notion of prophecy itself. Yet, they are also diverse in their experiences and gifts. Ibn al Arabi teaches that as prophets, they were one. In the variations and elaborations of their prophetic wisdom, they were many.

This fundamental insight structures the *Bezels of Wisdom*. Bezels are the settings for precious stones. Al Arabi's study of wisdom treats each of multiple facets of prophecy as a jewel with its own distinctive setting. The beauty of the jewel emanates in part from interactions of the stone with its setting. The stone remains essentially the same, while different settings introduce variability. Each chapter of *Bezels* explores a distinct facet of wisdom through settings shaped by a different prophet. The wisdom of love, for example, is

32 JUSTICE IN ISLAM

explored with Abraham, of light with Joseph, of intimacy with Elias, of the unseen with Job. Taken together, the chapters open to endlessly suggestive reflections on the multiplicity of the spiritual dimensions of wisdom.

Such a brief, linear summary inevitably mutes the deliberate incitements of the actual writing of the master. Downplayed are the challenges of the free associations, the confusions of the sharp and unexpected turns of nonlinear thinking, the trials of the shockingly creative and at times bewildering leaps of imagination. Still, the summation does give a helpful glimpse of a simple "skeletal frame" on which all of Ibn al Arabi's provocative jewels of wisdom could be arrayed.[24] Ibn al Arabia taught that the settings of the jewels could be discontinuous, without diminishing the unifying beauty of their collective impact. The intervals between them could be expansive, yet still contribute to a holistic aesthetic experience.

In these subtle ways, Al Arabi modeled a simple yet effective structure that demands presentation of a core unitary concept. It then invites elaboration of the diverse settings in which the singular concept finds variable expressions. The "one" in the present study stakes shape as a unified concept of the value of justice, distilled from the Qur'an and *Sunnah* and symbolized by Abu Dharr. The "many" emerge from the detailed accounts of very distinct local struggles for justice.

Abu Dharr everywhere stands in a singular way for justice. At the same time, multiplicity finds expression in the quite different meanings of justice as expressed in particular settings where Abu Dharr plays an inspirational role in battles for justice. Through the centuries Abu Dharr has persisted as a singular symbol of justice. His message of the centrality of justice in Islam is always the same. However, the abstract value of Islamic justice that he represents assumes a wide variety of distinctive forms as it is takes hold in diverse circumstances across Islamic lands. It may be impossible to assess the historical accuracy of particular legends of Abu Dharr. However, we can document how the stories, whether history or legend, have shaped the Islamic conception of justice.

To read the works of the leading intellectuals of the Awakening is to learn immediately that Abu Dharr is integral to the interpretive project that underlies the Awakening. No effort at all is required to place the Prophet Muhammad's beloved companion at the heart of the Awakening. *He is already there.* Major Islamic activists have consistently called on him as their inspiration. They have invoked him explicitly for support. Their extensive writings testify forthrightly to his importance to their cause. Whether

Sunni or Shi'i, whether Arab, Turk, or Iranian, major Islamic intellectuals find occasions to invoke Abu Dharr as a reference for their particular fights for justice.[25]

The abundant scholarship that has fueled the Awakening opens a rich vein to update the portrait of Abu Dharr al Ghifari. From the storehouse of legends of the Prophet's companion, the intellectuals of the Awakening make instructive choices. The emphasis here is not on whether particular legends are factual or not in their historical details.[26] What matters instead is what the legends reveal about the situated understandings of Islamic justice brought into play by its most enduring symbol. Abu Dharr emerges refreshed in these writings as the confident author of his own identity. He is not defined by the social and political circumstances that pressed on him from the tribal society of seventh-century Arabia. He refuses the inherited dictates of his tribal society. He embraces Islam's fluid restatements of the known *old truths* of radical monotheism. Those truths are insistently political. Those truths, forgotten and ignored, have had a revolutionary impact in the clarity of their Qur'anic restatement. To be a Muslim means hearing the Qur'anic call for justice. Abu Dharr, as an early convert, responded. Rebellion against injustice is at the heart of the contemporary Awakening. It expresses itself in circumstances as different as resistance against foreign occupation in tiny Lebanon to a radical mass revolution against an externally imposed tyranny in weighty Iran.

Du'a: Callers to Islam

Abu Dharr acquiesced to the Prophet's urging that he return to the al Ghifari territories. With time, he succeeded in bringing his entire tribe into Islam. The Islamic intellectuals who feature in subsequent chapters, from the Egyptian Shaikh Muhammad al Ghazalli to the American convert Muhammad Ali, follow in his footsteps as *du'a* (callers to Islam). They are each, for their own time and circumstances, a brave and accomplished *da'i* (caller to Islam.) They are all very much in the mold of Abu Dharr.

Shaikh Muhammad al Ghazalli frequently identified the two essential qualities of a successful *da'i*.[27] A deep and conscious faith, grounded in the teaching of Qur'an and *Sunnah*, had greatest importance. God sent his final message in a clear and accessible form in the Arabic of the Qur'an. The Prophet's example as founder of the first community of Muslims

34 JUSTICE IN ISLAM

complements the Qur'anic Message. God bestowed on humanity the great gift of reason. The *da'i* is called to use that reason to study the Qur'anic revelation and the Prophet's example in efforts to discern the meaning of the Message for their own circumstances. It is a grave mistake to juxtapose revelation to reason as though the two were somehow antithetical. The example of the most important callers to Islam teaches that God gave humanity reason. He did so to enable human beings to reach an understanding of His revelation, adequate to their lives. God made reason and revelation complimentary. The Caller to Islam, Shaikh Ghazalli explained, is always an intellectual who necessarily relies on *revelation as understood by reason*. Both revelation and reason are received as God's gifts to humanity. They work in tandem. They supplement each other. They are to be embraced simultaneously.

Shaikh Ghazalli emphasized that the successful *da'i* would have not only knowledge of Islam, but also the ability to communicate it effectively to others.[28] However, the *da'i* persuades by more than skillful rhetoric. He must have not only a sound grasp of the core texts, but also an awareness of the real world conditions in which they will work their effects. The power of action also matters greatly. Each *da'i* will have not only a distinctive persona but also a tutelary public role. The Call is always the same. However, it is sounded and acted on in myriad ways in varied circumstances.

The great diversity that results represents a signal strength of Islam. Abu Dharr, lover of justice, had proven himself an early and effective *da'i*. Through the centuries he has been a model to be emulated. The beloved companion ended his life in exile. The conditions of his final years were harsh. Only his wife remained at his side. Abu Dharr's physical strength eventually failed him. He told his wife he was dying. She wept that the Prophet's companion would die so far from his community. She mourned that he would die without even a proper shroud for burial.

Legend records that Abu Dharr faced his death calmly. He told his wife that he knew from a prophetic *hadith* that, although he would die in exile far from his community, fellow Muslims passing by his place of exile would assist in his burial. When the foretold Muslim travelers did arrive, Abu Dharr made only one request. For the customary Islamic burial cloth, he did not want the shroud of an *amir* or aristocrat. He wanted to be buried in a shroud of the kind worn by the common people. When the travelers arrived, one of them reported that his own mother had sewn clothes for him that could serve as a modest shroud. The body of the Prophet's companion was washed, shrouded, and buried by the unknown Muslim travelers. Abu Dharr died, as he lived, humble and uncompromised.

* * *

The chapters that follow explore multiple facets of justice, all symbolized by the indomitable Abu Dharr. The major figures who feature in Chapters 3 through 9 are all *du'a* in the mold of Abu Dharr al Ghifari. They are all Islamic intellectuals in that distinctive way. A study of the Islamic Awakening from the vantage point of the major Islamic intellectuals who spearheaded this justice-centered wave of reform inevitably opens with the controversial and conflicted story of the Muslim Brothers. In Chapter 3, that story is told from the perspective of the two intellectuals and activists who shaped the Brotherhood and its legacy. They are the founder, Hassan al Banna, and the most influential Brotherhood intellectual, Sayyid Qutb. The chapter addresses the controversies the Brotherhood has generated. It acknowledges that the movement was in many ways flawed. The chapter insists, however, on the signal historic importance of the Brotherhood.

In Chapter 4, the Egyptian Muhammad al Ghazalli, a figure regarded by many as the most important Sunni scholar of the twentieth century, explores the wisdom of resistance in justice's name. Ghazalli characterized himself as a graduate of the *school* of the Muslim Brothers.[29] He eventually left the movement, but never disavowed its influence on his thinking and his activism.[30] Ghazalli was gifted with depth of thought and feeling that he succeeded in conveying with seductive simplicity of expression in both his writings and speeches. To accomplish both goals, Ghazalli took explicit guidance from Abu Dharr. Ghazali understood that Islam belonged to ordinary Muslims. Its articulations, he believed, must be available to them. He was very much the *People's Shaikh*.

In Chapter 5, the life work of the Turkish Islamic scholar and mystic Sa'id Nursi illuminates the way intense spirituality can act as handmaiden to justice in even the harshest circumstances. He drew on great personal reserves of love for Islam and confidence in the reign of justice it promised among the mass of ordinary Turks. Nursi and his followers created entirely new organizational instruments of resistance. They established networks based on the copying and studying of Nursi's Qur'anic commentaries. In those innovative social spaces, Abu Dharr appeared as the spirit of Islamic justice. Nursi's followers succeeded in sheltering Islam from the virulent onslaught

36   JUSTICE IN ISLAM

of Turkish secularists. The master's writings inspired networks of followers, known as the *Nurcu*. In his commitment to peaceful resistance, Nursi's role is as inspiring as the work of the Mahatma Ghandi or Martin Luther King, Jr. Turkish nonviolent Islamic resistance is rarely recognized as such.

Chapter 6 treats the Grand Ayatollah Fadlallah, poet, scholar, and social reformer. From his base in Lebanon, Fadlallah inspired Hizbullah, the most successful Islamic movement of national resistance in the modern history of the Arab world. At the same time and just as importantly, he established an empire of righteous social works that spanned the Islamic world from Lebanon to Pakistan. Those projects, too, were works of resistance. Fadlallah's theoretical explorations of the roots of both violent and nonviolent resistance have had a lasting importance. He was at the same time a strategic thinker of the first order. Yet, the Ayatollah is remembered above all as the poetic oracle of a compassionate Islam of good works.

Chapter 7 engages the work of the Iraqi Ayatollah Baqir al Sadr. The Ayatollah's prolific studies of the philosophical foundations of the contemporary quest for Islamic justice provide the focus of the chapter. Baqir engages the materialist alternatives to an Islamic worldview, assessing both capitalism and socialism. He does so in the context of an intellectual rivalry for the commitment of young people. Baqir appraised the strengths and, as attentively, the shortcoming of Islamic discourse in competition with materialist alternatives. He devoted his life to the buttressing of the theoretical foundations of a progressive *Islam haraki* (movement Islam). Baqir registered these intellectual achievements in defiance of a murderous tyranny.

In Chapter 8, the Iranian intellectual Ali Shariati will be seen to repeatedly credit Abu Dharr as the major inspiration for his progressive thinking. Shariati's inspiration contributed in a major way to Iran's revolution of 1979. He was second in importance only to Ayatollah Khomeini in galvanizing the Iranian people in support of the overthrow of the American-backed Shah and his brutal dictatorship. Shariati's role was critical in preparing Iranian youth for participation in the Iranian revolution under an Islamic banner. Shariati explicitly clarifies the ways in which the example of Abu Dharr drew Iranian youth to the Revolution.

Chapter 9 broadens the lens for this study of the progressive Islam that has inspired the most important contemporary battles for justice that define the Islamic Awakening. The subject is Muhammad Ali, the world-class American athlete and Muslim convert. Admired by Westerners and non-Westerners, young and old alike around the world, Ali stands as a symbol of a progressive

Islam for a global age. A man of very limited formal education, Ali nevertheless made his way by right into this circle of distinguished modern-day Islamic intellectuals. Islam has a respected place for Ali as a *da'i*. The *caller* to the faith need not be a shaikh, theologian, theorist, or philosopher. He can be an American athlete of international fame and limited formal education. Ali expressed love for an Islam of lightly worn but deep spirituality and a passion for worldly justice. He did so in a distinctive voice that sounded around the world.[31] An Islamic framing of Muhammad Ali's life makes clear how a lifelong spiritual quest, rather than simply dazzling athleticism, define the real essentials of his legend. The very public record of Ali's quest for justice against racism and other forms of social injustice reveals unexpected parallels to that of Abu Dharr centuries before. Ali projected a very personal spiritualism, unconventional intelligence, and a barbed tongue that Abu Dharr would admire. Ali's worldwide fame gave his status as a proud convert to Islam global significance. In his mature years, he combined his advocacy for his faith with a universalist activism for justice that crossed barriers of nation, ideology, and race. Muhammad Ali died in 2016, admired by millions from that rainbow human family that Islam embraces in its totality. Born and raised a Christian, Muhammad Ali died a global icon for the centrist Islam of the Qur'an and the *Sunnah*.

In the book's concluding Chapter 10, the Prophet Muhammad and the Muslim Prophet Jesus join hands. Together, these two prophets of Islam are seen to inspire the struggles for justice that have given life to the Islamic Awakening. The Islamic scholars who have made major contributions to the Awakening regularly introduce Abu Dharr al Ghifari, companion of the Prophet and venerable symbol of justice, into their narratives. Guided by the prophets and the companion, the major Islamic intellectuals provide leadership for battles to check the tyrannies of wealth and power across Islamic lands. The commonalities of their struggles give coherence to the Islamic Awakening of our time. Walking with the major Islamic intellectuals in the Islamic strategic triangle of Egypt, Turkey, and Iran provides an opportunity to see the Islamic world as they do. That distinctive perspective brings into view dimensions of the Islamic world for the most part unseen in the West.

3

Hassan al Banna and Sayyid Qutb

Founders, the *School* of the Muslim Brothers

Our time is a time of Islamic Awakening. The public *turn to Islam* is experienced across Islamic lands. I have witnessed the phenomenon firsthand in Egypt, where I have lived and worked for more than four decades. The markers are multiple. It is impossible to miss them. They are now a part of everyday experience.

Over these many years, I have also traveled widely in the Middle East, particularly in the Islamic strategic triangle of Egypt, Turkey, and Iran. Egypt is far from alone in its experience of the larger space in public life that Islam has come to occupy. The effects of the *turn* are widespread. It is my sense that they are welcome, for the most part, on the mass level, although unrealistic expectations have shadowed that welcome. Elites from the first have been more conflicted in their responses.

Dinner with the Brothers

As an American scholar, I have also been acutely aware of the disquiet the expanded role of Islam has occasioned in the West. The apprehension is most pronounced when Islam is given political expression. Americans, in their journalism and much of their scholarship, have generated an Islam of their own. I think of that Islam as the *Islamist imaginary*. It is an Islam inherently violent and hostile to the West. That imagined Islam is very real and very influential. It also has little to do with the grounded Islam I directly experience in the Islamic lands where I live and work.

Dinner with the Brothers made this point in clear ways. In the early fall of 2008, an Egyptian friend from a major publishing house was having guests for dinner in his elegant suburban apartment. In his invitation, he mentioned that he was entertaining a small circle of prominent Muslim Brothers. I had been living and working in Egypt for decades and had on-the-ground

Justice in Islam. Raymond William Baker, Oxford University Press. © Oxford University Press 2022.
DOI: 10.1093/oso/9780197624975.003.0003

experience interacting with virtually all currents active in public life, including the Brothers. I had a fairly good idea of what to expect. There were still surprises.

The evening opened with the first five or six of us sitting on the balcony. The Arabic was more sophisticated than usual. Otherwise, there was no mistaking the company of Egyptians. Within ten minutes of initial appreciation for the lush gardens in the large park across the street, the jokes that are so much a part of Egyptian culture began to flow fast and furious. Now, for a language not your own, humor of the spontaneous Egyptian kind represents a great challenge. In my travels, however, I had learned a trick: the more control you can exert over the direction of conversation, the stronger will be your comprehension.

At a certain moment, Saudi Arabia came up. I jumped on the topic with a puzzle. Which is older, I asked my fellow guests, the Saudi Kingdom or the Muslim Brotherhood? I placed my "bet" with a flourish on the Brotherhood. Now, the Brothers strongly disapprove of gambling, so the idea of a bet, even an innocent one, caught their attention. With a smile, I suggested that an American academic might well be better at betting than Egyptian Brothers. They immediately understood the playfulness in my comment. An animated discussion followed that I had much less trouble following.

To my great pleasure, the majority of the Brothers were convinced that the kingdom was older. We called on our host to check his history book. Most of my fellow guests had spent time in the kingdom. They had all been subject to unceasing Saudi effort to wrap their kingdom and their Islam in a vaporous aura of agelessness. The efforts have been surprisingly effective, and not just in the West. But the image conjured is largely a mirage. The Saudi kingdom was stitched together by the conquests of four provinces in Arabia in 1932. The Muslim Brotherhood was founded by Hassan al Banna in the Egyptian provincial city of Ismailia in 1928. With good nature, the Brothers accepted that the American *khawaga* (foreigner) had won the bet and, or so it seemed, a more welcoming place at the table.

By this time, the remaining guests had arrived. Our host signaled that we would be moving to the dining room. The venerable Brotherhood is often taken, with considerable justification, as the fountainhead of contemporary political Islam. The Muslim Brothers have also for decades, with far less justification, occupied an outsized place in Western hostile imaginings of what political Islam means. Westerners are inclined to see *the turn to Islam* as a political threat, or worse. They regularly and most often casually invoke the

40   JUSTICE IN ISLAM

example of the Brothers in their hostile imaginings. The vague indictment goes further. Islam itself is seen as a faith given to violent expression that eludes reason and moral restraint.

For all my strong reservations about such thinking, these settled conclusions did come to mind as we took our places. A recent event set the agenda for the dinner conversation. Earlier that week a massive mud and rockslide had done terrible damage to a poor section in the Mokkatam Hills, a range of hills in southeastern Cairo. My fellow guests were all middle class and highly educated. Table talk immediately organized around two themes: How could those whose lives had been disrupted be helped? What caused the slides to begin with? I could not have been better positioned. To my right was a medical doctor. To my left, a geology professor. The doctor had played a role in organizing volunteers for the injured, and painfully cataloged the injuries. The geologist lost himself in explanations of the causes and dynamics of mudslides. The details of a highly specialized geologist, to be honest, would be excruciating for me in any language. The seemingly endless, expert exposition of the dynamics of mudslide did, however, periodically return to the practical question of how such disasters could be averted. The evening paralleled countless others over the years. It passed without a glimmer of the *imagined* Brothers.

Setting the Course of the Brotherhood

The Brothers have a long and very well-documented real history. A useful entry point is an introduction of the two thinkers and activists who were most influential in setting the course of the Society of Muslim Brothers. They are Hassan al Banna (1906–1949), the actual founder, and Sayyid Qutb (1906–1966), the most significant theorist to emerge from the movement. Each exerted a molding impact on the Brotherhood. They are both "founders" in that sense. Their story, as organizational and intellectual pioneers of the society, merits attention.

Critics of political Islam in the West often accept an underlying image of Islam and the movements it inspires. Islam is very often seen as having *a bloody body and no heart or mind*. Banna and Qutb, each in their own way, confound that dismissive trope. Both loved Islam, felt the faith was under attack, and were prepared to defend it. Each also made serious contributions of ideas that aimed at making Islam a lived political and social force. Banna was the gifted organizer. His intellectual contributions came in a distinctive way. Banna expressed his innovative thinking in creative institutional forms. Qutb emerged as the deep thinker in more traditional ways. His most important writings centered on the core Islamic issue of social justice. He provided theoretical grounding for the practical social work of the Brothers. Both Banna and Qutb, in their very different intellectual styles, allowed their love for Islam to suffuse their work and give it a powerful emotional impact. From the outset, Banna and Qutb assured that the Muslim Brothers would have a legacy of both mind and heart that could be developed and refined.

There were, of course, inevitable shortcomings of mind. There were also misapprehensions of the heart. However, the Muslim Brothers from the outset were always far more than simply an aggressive body. The Brotherhood took shape as a *school*, to borrow the designation that Shaikh Muhammad al Ghazalli (1917–1966) popularized. The Brotherhood aimed to serve in cultivating Islamic activists who would provide a model for thinking and acting for Islam in Egypt and across Islamic lands. Many beyond Egypt's borders came to consider the Brotherhood experience instructive. They looked to the example of the Brotherhood for guidance in their own efforts to give the turn to Islam political and social depth. They always sought to do so in ways responsive to their own particular circumstances.

The example of the Brotherhood provided inspiration, rather than a blueprint. The chapters that follow document the effects of that inspiration. All of the intellectuals featured as important contributors to the Islamic Awakening were influenced directly or indirectly by the work of the Muslims Brothers. Many said so explicitly. The Brothers from the first faced severe challenges and damaging denigrations. Critics of political Islam charged that, in the end, all Islamic intellectuals and activists were alike. They all represented an undifferentiated extremist threat to civilized society.[1] A template emerged that to this day is systematically deployed by secularists to weaken and undermine their centrist Islamic adversaries. Essentially, it rests on denial of the very possibility of an Islamic center.

The formula has been applied with a vengeance to the Muslim Brotherhood. It has also had wide application further afield. When stripped to essentials, secular critics judge that Islamic movements all have an agenda of violence and little more. This view means that Hizbullah should not be understood as a Lebanese movement of legitimate resistance to a foreign occupation. Hamas is not to be understood as one variety of Palestinian national resistance to an aggressive settler colonialism. Both are simply organizations

42 JUSTICE IN ISLAM

of Islamic terrorists, *tout court*. Neither complex historical realities nor universal values, such as the right of resistance or self-determination, were ever to be made part of the assessment. Recognized rights under international law, such as self-defense or self-determination, are systematically denied any relevance to Islamic movements. In short, apparent moderation in Islam is always simply a cloak for extremism. By these lights, Islam itself and the movements it inspires have no constructive center.

The systematic mischaracterization of the Muslim Brothers has provided the most egregious application of this ahistorical formula for distortion. The effects are magical. Both historical facts and theological distinctions that do not fit the mold are conjured away. Reasoned criticism of the flawed record of the Brotherhood is certainly warranted. Yet, to equate the Brothers with extremist groups like al Qaeda or ISIS (the Islamic State) requires breathtaking theological and historical blinders. The Brothers have a well-documented history. As we have seen, it is older than that of the state of Saudi Arabia. The current wave of mindless repression directed against the Brothers is not new to their long experience. Nor are the varied means of their resistance.

Through the decades since the late 1920s, the influence of the Brothers has registered across Islamic lands, despite recurrent efforts to suppress them. It has been felt on both sides of the contemporary manifestations of the historic Sunni-Shiʻi sectarian divide. All of the major intellectuals of the Islamic Awakening, whether Shiʻi or Sunni, Arab, Turkish, or Iranian, experienced to varying degrees the influence of the Egyptian Brothers. In the West, the Brothers are routinely denigrated. An organization that, in my view, has functioned for decades as a centrist firewall against violent extremism is itself denigrated and undermined as terrorist. The Muslim Brothers have become not only extremists wearing a mask of moderation. They are transformed into outright terrorists. By these lights, they are indistinguishable in essentials from groups like al Qaeda and ISIS.

To be sure, the Muslim Brotherhood was born to resistance. However, resistance should not be conflated with mindless violence. Resistance is a historical force that reacts to injustice. Occupation is injustice on a gargantuan scale. The British occupied Egypt from 1882 to 1956 when the last military forces were finally withdrawn. The occupation was understood to be part of a larger historical pattern that made it all the more oppressive. In the long historical view, the Brotherhood has been shaped by its conflictual coevolution with the global revolution of Westernization. That anodyne expression is a euphemism for the Western drive for worldwide domination. The process was well on its way long before the Brothers came on the scene. The West's expansion dated from the sixteenth century, gathered momentum in the late nineteenth and early twentieth centuries, and continues to this day.

The Western notion of "progress" calls for development along a pathway charted by the West. In doing so, it rationalizes the forceful appropriation of resources from around the world. Those resources have helped generate power on an unprecedented global scale. The end goal is breathtaking and unforgiving. Whatever its rhetoric, the West aims to remake the entire world in the Western image. The costs in lives lost, political disruption, and cultural destruction are not given much attention. This underlying Western project is inescapably and profoundly violent.

The British brought the Westernizing wave to Egypt. Founded in British-occupied Egypt in the late 1920s, the Brothers first made their mark in militant demonstrations against this British presence on Egyptian soil. To resist, the Egyptian Muslim Brothers have consistently advanced an Islamic alternative to the Westernized future the occupiers planned. For eight decades, the venerable Brotherhood has battled with the Westernization project to preserve and elaborate its own distinctive vision of an Islamic future for Egypt. Consistent with their anti-colonial stance, the Brothers have also acted as fighters for besieged Palestinians against Zionist settler colonialism. European Jewish settlers displaced Arab Palestinians, absorbed their lands into an expanding Zionist state, and systematically undermined the Arab and Islamic character of Jerusalem. The Brother's role in Palestine was more modest than the claims often made for it by Brotherhood apologists. But they did have a role. Even that limited contribution did burnish their reputation with all those who felt deep sympathy for the historic injustice suffered by the Palestinian people. The Brothers have also consistently opposed the post-colonial, Westernizing military regimes that the colonizers left behind in Egypt and elsewhere. They have stood defiantly against the secularism these military "modernizers" advanced. They often suffered grievously for those efforts.

Brotherhood Resilience and Resistance

Virtually all academic and journalistic observers of the Muslim Brotherhood emphasize the at times astonishing resilience the Brothers have shown in the face of unrelenting Westernizing pressures by both national and

44 JUSTICE IN ISLAM

international forces. That standard narrative has surfaced once again with the current wave of repression the Brothers face under the military junta that has ruled Egypt since 2013. Lessons in resilience, however, are only part of the story of the Muslim Brothers. The Brotherhood is about a great deal more than an impressive ability to survive often violent oppression. Of greater importance is the model of an Islamic alternative that the movement advances. In the decades that have witnessed the Islamic Awakening, the Brothers have also played a role in the broader regional movement of Islamic Renewal (*al Tagdid al Islami*). They have never been the only Islamic force in the field. Nor have their contributions always been the most constructive. However, they have always been an important presence in the ranks of Islamic resistance.

As a vital social force in Egypt since the 1920s, the Brotherhood has gained impressive practical experience of work among the masses. No other political trend can match that record, particularly in its social and humanitarian dimensions. Consequently, the Brothers were exceptionally well positioned to make significant contributions to the Islamic Awakening that first took hold in the late 1960s. In academic and journalistic commentaries, the Muslim Brotherhood is generally viewed through a political lens as an oppositional force. The characterization has force. Yet, it is also true that the Brothers have contributed as much or more in intellectual and psychological terms to the practical advancement of an Islamic alternative to Westernization.

The Islamic Awakening has been fueled by deep thinking, passionate feelings, and sustained social practices. The Awakening cannot be understood in a political register alone. The long experience of the Brotherhood does not exercise a monopoly over the generation of those intellectual and psychological resources. However, their contributions *are* impressive. They are not, however, without serious flaws. The rigidity of the Brotherhood's organizational and ideological structures at times has created obstacles to the creative thinking and innovative actions that successful resistance requires. Shaikh Muhammad al Ghazalli, for example, left the Brotherhood because he found it too restrictive in intellectual and organizational terms. Equally revealing, however, is the fact that Ghazalli, despite his reservations, never disavowed the centrality of the Brotherhood to his own formation as an Islamic intellectual of world-class stature.

Despite the limitations of the Brotherhood experience, the movement has enriched the pool of ideas, emotions, and practical models for action on which the forces for Islamic Awakening have drawn. Most importantly, the Brothers have demonstrated that an Islamic political character of a movement could be crafted in ways to give it relevance to contemporary conditions. All the struggles of the movement have been strengthened by the power of a distinctive and painstakingly developed Brotherhood identity. Identity as a Muslim Brother rests on a distinctive interpretation of the faith developed first by Hassan al Banna and elaborated further by Sayyid Qutb. That faith component has been decisively fueled by Islam's inherently assertive character. It is shaped as well by the drive to reform the Islamic legacy in both theoretical and practical terms. The religious and social elements are tightly interwoven. At the core of the comprehensive Brotherhood identity is the unbreakable commitment to an Islamic alternative to Westernization and the Western-inspired secularism it brings. The Brothers have carefully cultivated the psychological strength to act collectively on behalf of the Islamic alternative that originates with the society. That alternative is given a particular rather than universal character by the society. The Brotherhood has no monopoly in speaking for Islam.[2] At times, however, their practice has suggested that they believe the reverse. There is, in fact, ample room to critique the Brotherhood society on Islamic ground.

On the level of practical reality, the Brothers have strived to elaborate a lived Islamic alternative in defiance of the overwhelming and often harsh power of the Westernizers. They have done so in competition with competing Islamic groups. The society has also strived since its founding to make itself a seedbed of practical social experimentation. Efforts have aimed at pioneering ways to renew and reform Islam on the mass level and in practical terms.

Hassan al Banna and Sayyid Qutb both taught that the best strategy to refuse colonial and postcolonial realities was the nurturing of an embryonic alternative Islamic social order within the existing body politic. Such a "community-in-the-making" would grow organically and peacefully within the larger society. Followers would have the immediate opportunity to participate in this alternative Islamic social reality in their everyday lives. The aim was to provide Brothers and their families with clear, reassuring, and real-world contrasts to alien Western interventions. Those alien intrusions would be seen clearly to disrupt their culture and way of life. Most ominously, these Western penetrations would be clarified as threats that could undermine Islam. The Brothers aimed to show how they could be resisted. They demonstrated how the experience of the embryonic Islamic society could salve the wounds. It could also channel constructively the frustrations and, at times, fury caused

46   JUSTICE IN ISLAM

by "remaking" in the crucible of an alien vision. The lived realities of life as a Brother would translate abstract commitments to resistance and reform into realistic everyday actions. Even partial realizations of the projected Islamic alternative could be lived in the moment and with like-minded partners.

By struggling to make their version of an Islamic alternative real, the Brothers aimed to drain the Westernizing project of its appeal. It has mattered little to the Brothers whether the Westernizing project was advanced by the colonizers themselves or by *anti-Western Westernizers*, like the Nasserists. The work of the Brothers struck a responsive chord. In Egypt by the mid-twentieth century, they had many more than half a million followers, though the exact membership can only be roughly estimated. The Brothers built their influence into the social fabric of the nation. They exhibited impressive skills in adapting to rapidly changing conditions as Egypt shifted from monarchy to republic. The shifts in the political configuration were dramatic. As a republic, Egypt had first a socialist, pro-Soviet orientation and then a capitalist, pro-American direction. Through the 1980s and 1990s, the Egyptian Brothers carried lessons learned from these adaptations across the Islamic world. At the same time, they continued work to consolidate their own strong position at home. Both Turkish and Iranian Islamists paid attention to the work of the Egyptian Brothers and acknowledged lessons learned from the pioneering experience of the Brotherhood. The influence of the Muslim Brothers was transnational.

In Egypt, the Brothers represented one of the best organized opposition forces to the long years of the Mubarak dictatorship. They did not, however, spearhead the revolution of 2011 that ended Mubarak's rule. The revolution came on the wings of spontaneity and essentially without disciplined organization. My Cairo apartment is a stone's throw from iconic Tahrir Square, the epicenter of the revolution. My frequent interactions with activists in the months before the eruption indicated that diffuse leftist and nationalist sentiments prevailed among the youth cadres that flooded the streets and provided what leadership the uprising developed. Islamists were a presence but, in my observation, they were in no way dominant. A generational split divided the collective reaction of the Brothers to the increasingly assertive expressions of uncoordinated mass dissatisfaction. The aging Brotherhood leadership held itself aloof, while younger Brothers joined the youth of other trends in their loose call for radical change. In the end, an essentially spontaneous mass revolution erupted on January 25, 2011. The almost thirty-year dictatorship of Husni Mubarak was over.

The mass uprising gave Egyptians a genuine revolutionary moment. The effect was magical, though short-lived. It also created unearned opportunities for the Brotherhood. With the fall of Mubarak, Egypt did experience a brief period of democracy. Taking advantage of the openings the democratic moment created, the Brothers threw themselves into electoral politics. They demonstrated a prowess in democratic contests that few anticipated and fewer still have remembered. A presidential election was held in two rounds in May and June 2012. In an unforeseen triumph, Muhammad Mursi (1951–2019), the Brotherhood candidate, won the Egyptian presidency by a slender majority in the country's first-ever democratic presidential election. The Carter Center, with a delegation headed by the former president himself, was the most prominent of international monitors. President Carter later reported to the world press that the Center "confirms the integrity of Egypt's latest parliamentary elections and its compliance with international standards of fairness."[3]

The moment of triumph of the Brotherhood did not last. An unforeseen twist came a little less than a year later, on July 3, 2013. Well-founded dissatisfactions with flawed Brotherhood governance brought Egyptians back into the streets. Their numbers appeared to exceed those who took to the streets in the revolution itself. Secular trends threw their full support behind these second-round mass actions. They overshadowed the Brothers.

A military junta seized power on July 3, 2013. It was a military coup with a difference. The military return to power came with substantial mass support. The liberals and the left joined the demonstrations with enthusiasm. They threw themselves into the arms of the military. Egypt's new rulers jailed the elected Brotherhood president. The new regime then launched a massive and violent repression of the Brothers. In developments that should have been anticipated, the military rulers acted with the same repression against not only Islamic actors but all others who challenged the dictatorship-in-the making.

There was no mystery to the widespread dissatisfaction that brought people into the streets to end the brief democratic interlude that the Muslim Brothers dominated. The record of practical governance by Egypt's Brotherhood president leading up to the coup was deeply flawed. To be sure, the forces arrayed against the embattled president were formidable. Still, the inexperienced Mursi compiled a depressing record of missed opportunities and inept actions. That record was all the more disappointing because the

48   JUSTICE IN ISLAM

Muslim Brothers had initially performed so well in the electoral space the Egyptian revolution briefly opened. In the two years immediately following Mubarak's ouster, they continued to do so. Egyptians voted for the Islamic political alternative in reasonably free elections and monitored referenda at least six times. Not once did the secular and liberal parties mount a serious electoral challenge to the Islamic parties. The decades of serious social work and spiritual guidance among ordinary Egyptians paid electoral dividends. The parties of politicized Islam, with the Brotherhood in the lead, triumphed in an impressive number of these democratic contests.

The electoral successes of the Brothers and the easing of repression during the year when Egypt had a Muslim Brother as president makes the story of the subsequent military coup and all-out assault on the Brotherhood all the more unsettling, During the summer of 2013 the Brotherhood suffered hundreds of arrests. Many in the leadership fled abroad. Persecution in the wake of the July coup surpassed in viciousness even that endured during the Nasser years. On August 14, 2013, the government assault culminated in the mass killing of more than a thousand members and sympathizers in attacks on two squares in Cairo. The squares had been occupied by demonstrators in support of the deposed Muslim Brother president. Human Rights Watch, the highly respected Nobel Prize–designated international human rights organization, pronounced the killings "the worst mass killings in the country's modern history."[4]

In the wake of the slaughter in two of Cairo's public squares, Egypt had a military dictatorship with a serious claim as the most brutal in the country's long history of tyranny. In September 2013, the battered Muslim Brotherhood was officially banned by Egyptian authorities. The campaign to eliminate the Brothers from public life crested with a cabinet announcement in December 2013, declaring the Brotherhood a terrorist organization. No persuasive evidence to substantiate the charge was offered. That omission hardly mattered. The Brotherhood appeared finished.

Not so: true to their history, the Brotherhood responded to the campaign of repression with characteristic defiance. The group's London-based spokesman, Abdullah al-Haddad, elaborated:

> The Muslim Brothers are part and parcel of Egyptian society. Corrupt illegitimate judicial decisions cannot change that. . . . [The Muslim Brotherhood] will continue to be present on the ground: they cannot kill an idea, they tried before and failed—they are trying again, and they will fail again.[5]

In the face of brutal oppression, it is unclear if the Brothers will in fact survive. Their tenacious history suggests they will, although once again the Muslim Brothers will have to adapt and to do so this time in more profound ways.

Extant organizational structures can be smashed by a determined military dictatorship. Political access can be blocked. With so much of their leadership in exile and so many of the cadres under arrest in the horrific circumstances of Egyptian prisons, a purely power calculus would suggest that the Brotherhood may well be reaching its end point. A closer look at the long history of the Brothers and closer study of the movement's founder and most important ideologue would suggest that the Muslim Brotherhood inherits institutional, intellectual, and psychological resources that may well allow them to write a different future.

The Founder and the Most Important Ideologue

Appreciation for that possibility of survival begins with close attention to the role of Hassan al Banna, the movement's charismatic founder, and Sayyid Qutb, its most impressive ideological thinker. Both figures played a crucial role in shaping the Brotherhood. Together, they define the organizational and intellectual legacy of the Muslim Brotherhood. Both men were murdered. Both, in the short time given to them, succeeded in generating lasting theoretical resources and sustaining emotional energy to give the Brotherhood an improbable future. Martyrdom only enhanced their intellectual and psychological weight in the unfolding of the Brotherhood trajectory.

Shaikh Muhammad al Ghazalli, a revered Sunni scholar, has characterized al Banna's role in a way that best captures the power of his indispensable role. Ghazalli saw the founder as a synthesizing vehicle for varied reformist and oppositional influences from Muhammad Abduh (1845–1906), Jamal Eddine al Afghani (1838/9–1897), and Rashid Rida (1865–1935). From Afghani, Ghazalli judged that al Banna took a sense of the dangers coming from the West, from Abduh the idea that the *ummah* should reform itself, and from Rida guidance to deeper understanding of the Qur'an as the foundation for that reform.

Ghazalli believed that Hassan al Banna sowed knowledge the way a farmer sows seeds. The revered and learned shaikh identified himself as

50 JUSTICE IN ISLAM

a lifelong student of al Banna. He believed that al Banna had a rare skill that allowed him to explain complex theological concepts in simple terms. Ghazalli believed that the Islamic world had not seen an Islamic figure with ability on this level since the great classical scholar Abu Hamed al Ghazalli (1058–1111).[6]

The adaptation of traditional conceptions to the modern world seemed to come naturally to Banna. He was born in 1906 into a pious, lower middle-class family in the village of Mahmudiyya to the northwest of Cairo. Banna attended village schools. But he did so with a difference. Banna's father was a religious teacher who often led the communal prayers in the village. He closely supervised his son's religious instruction. By the age of fourteen, Banna had memorized the Qur'an. While still in his early teens, he began regularly attending the mystic circles of the Hasafiyya Sufi Order. Banna totally immersed himself in the activities of the order. He attained the status of an initiate. It is quite remarkable, though rarely noted, that Banna remained an active member of the Order for some twenty years. For a brief time, he even wore the tasseled turban and white outer garment of the Hasafiyya Order. In setting the roots of the Brotherhood, Banna did not neglect Islam's mystical dimension that was so much a part of his own formative religious experience. In time, however, Banna, and the Brotherhood with him, developed a highly critical view of Sufism. That negative view remains characteristic of the Brotherhood today. Brothers came to consider Sufi practices as a corruption of the faith. The Sufi pattern of support for existing governments, whatever their character, also heightened hostility.

Hassan al Banna's conception of the society he founded was an innovative one. Outside observers have done their best to force the Brotherhood into recognizable Western molds as a covert political party, social movement, or fellowship of faith. Yet, the Brotherhood, as Banna conceived it, could not be contained by any of these boxes. Banna himself explained simply and directly the spiritual dimensions of his followership:

> My Brothers: you are not a benevolent society, nor a political party, nor a local organization having limited purposes. Rather, you are a new soul in the heart of this nation to give it life by means of the Qur'an.[7]

The Brothers from the outset saw themselves, quite literally, as a nascent society with a distinctively Islamic character.

The Worldly Islam of the Muslim Brothers

Hassan al Banna possessed the imaginative power to envision organized actions in a wide variety of spheres. He cast them all in a way that brought them within the reach of ordinary Muslims. The simplest of movement activities were somehow able to encapsulate the founder's expansive Islamic vision of reform and resistance. Through the engaging activities he fostered, Banna created new institutional arrangements on all levels. He imbued them with a defining Islamic character.

The depth of Bamma's insights can be read from the success of the very hands-on practices he initiated for his followers. The Brothers tutored in basic literacy. They taught "proper" forms of worship. In group settings, they discussed issues of Islamic morality. However, the real burst of their transformative energy took the form of social activism among the common people. The Brothers established schools and clinics. They built factories, making sure that wages and benefits were higher than in state-owned enterprises. They launched a modern scout movement. They organized night schools for workers, as well as tutorial programs to support advancement of civil service employees. The greatest strength of the Brothers emerged from such direct social activism that Banna made the very heart of the movement. They infused practical social programs with their distinguishing conceptions of Islamic teachings.

Banna's animating idea for all these activities was simple and powerful. In these creative and accessible confines, he taught that the Brothers could live what they judged to be an alternative, more meaningful, and more moral life. In contrast, the Marxists, with whom the Brothers often competed for the loyalties of the youth, focused on study groups to explore ideas. However, the ideas themselves were often only loosely connected to everyday Egyptian life.

Banna understood the community works he fostered as essential planks of his strategy of resistance as building an alternative. To resist colonial encroachments, he aimed to create a practical platform for reform of the heritage. Politically, the mainstream Brothers stressed moderation and gradualism in the service of a very long-term vision of Islamic renewal and social transformation. They strongly opposed the use of violent means to achieve their aims. Banna himself explicitly opposed any headlong rush to power.

For all the successes registered, Banna's achievements were not without disturbing contradictions. There was an inherent tension between the cohesive yet adaptable social networks he built and the rigidly disciplined

52 JUSTICE IN ISLAM

leadership structures that he put in place to manage them. Governance by the Brotherhood leadership was secretive and authoritarian. The absence of an explicit overall theoretical understanding of the political and economic dimensions of the mission of the Brothers also created its own dangers. Banna emphasized the call to Islam, rather than a drive for political power. However, he was aware that power would in fact be necessary to accomplish some of the goals he set for the movement.[8] Banna never resolved these persistent ambiguities in his thinking about power. Nor, for that matter, did the Brothers under Banna's leadership develop a coherent economic philosophy. In practice, these shortcomings meant that the Brothers attempted to work for reform through existing structures. Despite their support for some progressive measures, especially in modest land reform, health, and education, the Brothers left the structures of economic privilege largely in place.

Perhaps most fateful of all shortcomings was Banna's ambivalence and contradictory responses on the question of violence. Like all the major trends in the field in the tumultuous 1940s, the Brothers developed an armed apparatus to which they assigned a defensive role. The *tanzim sirri* (secret apparatus) proved difficult to control. It threatened to turn the society in a more overtly political direction, laced with violence. Banna's gradual and moderate vision of change through Qur'anic wisdom and the sound counsel he had provided had difficulty holding its own in the face of calls to take more forceful political paths to hasten the strengthening of Egypt's Islamic character. Banna famously spoke against the violent actions of militants with a political agenda. In the strongest language, he charged that they "are not Brothers, they are not Muslims."[9]

Despite such strong pronouncements, there were nevertheless damaging inconsistencies in his statements. At times, he spoke loosely of *jihad* (struggle for the faith in both spiritual and physical senses). Banna's lack of precision left the way open to a militant interpretation of his words. Moreover, Banna never incorporated his warnings against power abuses into an effective institutional mechanism to contain the more politically assertive elements within the Brotherhood. They naturally gravitated to the secret apparatus. Their intermittent violence, including the assassination of political figures, eventually turned back on the Brotherhood.

In February 1949, at the age of forty-three, Hassan al Banna was assassinated by an Egyptian government agent near his office in Cairo. He reportedly was shot seven times. He was then denied medical care. Banna died from the neglect of his wounds. His murder in 1949, most likely by the palace, left the Society more vulnerable to its extremist elements. The political vision that the extremists championed, with the scent of violence surrounding it, haunts the Brotherhood to this day.

The Utopian Political Vision of Sayyid Qutb

The practical social experimentation spearheaded by Banna found its complement in the soaring theological and literary commentaries of Sayyid Qutb. Qutb's prodigious writings on Islam include insightful essays on the literary dimensions of the sacred texts. Most importantly, he authored *In the Shade of the Qur'an*, a sophisticated, multivolume interpretive commentary on the Qur'an that is widely read to this day. That work established Qutb as an Islamic intellectual of stature. However, it is his more analytical study of *Social Justice in Islam* that brings him into sharpest focus for this book. Qutb referred to Abu Dharr al Ghifari so frequently and with such admiration in *Social Justice* and related works on social questions that he can be appropriately considered a protégé of the Prophet's seventh-century companion. However, it is Sayyid Qutb's political writings that have left the most lasting, if not the most balanced, view of his legacy as an Islamic thinker.

In his *Milestones* in particular, Qutb authored a sweeping political alternative to Banna's social Islam in its most cogent and controversial expression.[10] Qutb's political writings contain very forceful and incisive condemnations of the predatory violence of colonial powers in the Islamic world. He also attacks the scourge of corruption and brutality of the successor secular, military regimes. In his view, these failings had their roots in the colonial situation rather than the legacy. His arguments on both counts are well reasoned and well founded. Few intellectuals of the broader Islamic Renewal would disagree with either of these fundamental assessments.

Qutb, however, went further. He called for resistance not only to the depredations of colonial powers, but also to the tyrannies of Westernizing, postcolonial regimes. These oppositional positions, too, enjoyed widespread support among centrist Islamic trends. However, for midstream intellectuals like Shaikh Muhammad al Ghazalli, Qutb crossed a red line in his thinking when he pronounced existing regimes "un-Islamic," rather than simply deeply flawed.[11] Qutb argued that these systems shared the character of regimes that took shape before Islam brought its light to humanity. They, in

54 JUSTICE IN ISLAM

effect, were *jahilliyya* (bearing the irremediable flaws of the pre-Islamic age of ignorance). By these lights, these systems of rule and the societies they governed were only nominally Islamic. The formulation implied that they were open to the charge of *takfir* (declaring Muslims to be unbelievers, i.e., apostates). Qutb's stance was read as a declaration of war against existing regimes across *Dar al Islam* (the Islamic world) and against the global order of which they were a part.

Sayyid Qutb was taken to argue against accommodation with both the postcolonial regimes and the Western-dominated world system of which they were a part. His charge of *jahilliyya* forcefully smashed a centuries-old Sunni accommodation with ruling power. The power of his radical rejectionism can be felt only with a strong sense of the historical record that he contemptuously rejected. In the wake of the assassination in 661 of Ali ibn Abi Taleb (ca. 600–661), the fourth caliph, the Sunni community acquiesced in the capture of the caliphate by the ruler in Damascus. The Umayyad Dynasty followed, with its essentially secular character and reliance on hereditary rule. Both characteristics, in Qutb's view, contravened the Prophet's example of righteous rule. Henceforth, the majority Sunni community would accept dynastic rule that had little to do with Islam. It did so on condition that internal order and the territorial integrity of the *ummah* (Islamic community) were maintained. The accommodation compartmentalized the religious and the political into separate spheres. Religious matters would be left largely to the *'ulama* (Islamic scholars). Political governance of the *ummah* would be the domain of rulers.

Qutb created the intellectual platform from which a reasoned call could be made for a decisive break with this centuries-old compromise. In opening that door, Sayyid Qutb turned explicitly to the legacy of Abu Dharr. Qutb saw in the legends of the rebellious Abu Dharr venerable precedents for his own radical thinking. Abu Dharr, in Qutb's eyes, appeared as a kindred spirit who had played a remarkable role as a radical intellectual close to the Prophet. He legitimated the idea of righteous rebellion in Islam. Sayyid Qutb seized on and amplified that legacy. It is not always remembered, however, that the target of Abu Dharr's rebellion was limited to the pattern of governance set by the Caliph Osman and, more particularly, by his nephew Mu'awiyya whom the caliph had made governor of Syria. Abu Dharr did not model a challenge to all authority. The companion challenged corrupt governance. He did so in the name of just rule. He did so nonviolently.

With startling boldness, Sayyid Qutb generalized the precedent Abu Dharr had established. He exceeded its restraint. Qutb boldly pronounced the Sunni historic compromise with ruling power to be the greatest mistake in the history of *Dar al Islam*. In Qutb's view, this compromise had a certain logic in the Western Christian cultural context. In the West, there was historically a recurring conflict between secular and religious realms. Science and faith were understood to be at damaging odds. The separation of the two realms in the interest of science-based progress had a cultural logic. That logic, he argued with considerable force, did not hold in the Islamic world.

Islam, in sharp contrast to Christianity, posed no such threat to science, nor did reason-based science impinge on the faith. Islam presented itself as a religion compatible with, indeed dependent on, reason. Reason was understood as a handmaiden that allowed Muslims to more fully understand their sacred texts. With that understanding, the Sunni compromise that left the political sphere to secular rulers and the religious sphere to Islamic intellectuals was both unnecessary and damaging. Qutb concluded that this misconceived compromise of the majority Sunni community explained, more than any other single factor, how the Islamic world lost its place of world cultural and intellectual leadership.[12]

Sayyid Qutb applied this historical assessment to the contemporary challenges facing the *ummah*. He judged acceptance of the Western imperial order and of the regimes supported by it unacceptable. *Milestones* called for the formation of a vanguard that would galvanize true Muslims by persuasion, "physical power," and *jihad*, to implement Qutb's radical challenge to Sunni tradition.[13]

In the standard Western dismissal of Sayyid Qutb, it is rarely noted that as an analysis, the most important centrist intellectuals have for the most part agreed with much of Qutb's critique of foreign interference and dictatorship. They did not, however, accept the implications in his work that the road to reform and constructive accommodation was effectively closed. Moreover, they feared that such a position opened the door to an even more violent repression of the Islamic trend in Egypt and elsewhere. In the view of the mainstream, the "dark ideas" of Qutb's later writings, notably *Milestones*, reflected an interpretation of Islam that had more to do with the terrible provocations of the Nasserist state and the criminal depredations of dominant secular powers than with the message of Islam.

56 JUSTICE IN ISLAM

Western critics are given to charging that Islamic moderates have failed to challenge such extreme positions. The charges are without merit, no matter how endlessly they are repeated. In fact, centrist Islamic intellectuals produced volume after volume of refutations of the more extreme Qutbist positions.[14] Virtually none of this important work, most of it untranslated from the Arabic, is read or discussed in the West. That literature does receive attention in Egypt and the Arab and Islamic world, however. For the overwhelming majority of Muslims, Islamic centrists have in fact been remarkably successful in countering the influence of extremist readings of Qutb's ideas.

It is important to note that, while Qutb did reach very radical conclusions on the theoretical plane, there is no persuasive evidence that he himself ever participated in direct actions that relied on the "physical power" to which he referred in *Milestones*. In this regard, Sayyid Qutb followed the pattern set by Abu Dharr. The Prophet's companion never organized a faction against the Caliph Osman. He did not hesitate to criticize his nepotism and misuse of community funds. He did so directly to the face of the caliph. He did not, however, foster a conspiracy or violent revolt against his rule. Abu Dharr clearly had the resources and support to do precisely that. His demurral defines the rightful limits of his legacy of radicalism. Abu Dharr was a radical in thought and impulse. However, he was not an activist who took direct action, nor did he model direct action for others.

It is a serious misjudgment to see Sayyid Qutb as an engaged advocate of armed struggle. Rather, Qutb's vision was utopian on a grand scale. He looked to the "vanguard" of which he wrote not as a violent underground movement. It was rather to be the seedbed of a utopian Islamic society that would grow organically as an essentially peaceful movement until it formed a truly Islamic community "in some Islamic country." He reasoned that "only such a revivalist movement would eventually attain the status of worldwide leadership, whether the distance is near or far."[15]

The frequent comparisons made between Qutb and Lenin are thus without merit. Qutb was no Lenin. Sayyid Qutb did not act to create and lead a revolutionary party of militant Islamic revolutionaries, committed to employing violence to impose their will. There is more mystical utopianism in *Milestones* than the ruthless realism of *What's to Be Done*, Lenin's most influential revolutionary tract. Both men spoke of a "vanguard." However, they did so with vastly different meaning. On the political plane, Qutb advocated utopian ideas. He did so in a highly speculative way. Qutb's writings could at most be charged with unknowingly inspiring others to actions that went beyond the cautious boundaries of his own politics. Lenin, in contrast, himself led the first workers' revolutionary vanguard in history. Qutb's political philosophy was closer to anarchism than the militant Marxism and highly disciplined party dictatorship that Lenin advocated and succeeded in installing in revolutionary Russia.

At the same time, Sayyid Qutb was no democrat. His radicalism as an Islamic thinker, however, also does not make him an advocate for theocracy, as his critics often charge. Qutb was decidedly unimpressed with Western-style democracy. He experienced it directly in the United States during a lengthy period of study there. He judged American democracy harshly as riven with racial and class discrimination. Qutb also detested the flagrant sexuality of American social mores. He had total disdain for the inequalities of the consumerist and materialistic American society that he believed democracy enabled.

Yet, it is a mistake to read those critical views of the most influential versions of democracy as advocacy of theocracy. In Qutb's view, Muslims should stand against both "rule by a pious few, or democratic representation." Sayyid Qutb, in full anarchist mode, actively opposed *any* system where men are in "servitude to other human beings" and to the worship of material things. He deplored "human lordship and man-made laws" that he judged as "un-Islamic and a violation of *hakemeyya* (God's sovereignty) over all his creations." [16] At the same time, Sayyid Qutb never advocated Islamic theocracy. He advanced no brief for Islamic scholars as preferred rulers. In sharp contrast, he quite explicitly opposed theocracy as strongly as he did Western-style democracy.

For his opposition to dictatorship and for his utopian speculations, Sayyid Qutb was imprisoned for ten years, periodically tortured, and eventually hanged. One incident from his decade-long imprisonment left an indelible mark. It can stand for all the brutalities that scarred his body and assaulted his spirit. In 1957 Qutb witnessed the slaughter of twenty-one imprisoned and defenseless Brothers by armed and unthreatened prison guards. The prisoners had simply balked at reporting for backbreaking manual labor. A regime capable of such crimes, in Qutb's view, was not redeemable. The conclusion carried force.

In a final show trial in 1966, with none of the most elemental requirements of a legitimate court procedure, Qutb and five other Brothers were charged and convicted of plotting to kill the president and other state leaders. The

58   JUSTICE IN ISLAM

trial came in the wake of an alleged Muslim Brother attempt against the life of Gamal Abdul Nasser. It has never been firmly established that such an attempt was real, rather than a staged rationalization for a campaign of repression against the Brothers. It is instructive that the "evidence" used against Qutb in the trial consisted essentially of passages from his most radical writings, primarily *Milestones*. If hard evidence of a plot that implicated Qutb existed, it made no appearance at the trial.

Qutb himself vigorously denied the charges of criminal and treasonous actions. He did so with great eloquence and memorable impact. At the same time, Sayyid Qutb adamantly refused to disavow his ideas. He understood fully what the price would be. Stories are told about the smile that passed over his face as he confronted death. Nasser reportedly had offered Qutb a reprieve on condition that he renounce his ideas. Qutb rejected the offer. This refusal was unsurprising. Years earlier, he had declined a high-level position in the new military regime. A legend has grown up around Qutb "kissing the gallows."[17] Qutb's principled martyrdom utterly captivated a great many youths in the Islamic world in the late 1960s.

This same Sayyid Qutb is now a man routinely described as "the grandfather" of modern terrorism. The epithet usually comes in a few declarative sentences that brook no rebuttal. The indictment typically jumps from a sketch of Qutb's undeniably radical ideas, to his show trial and hanging, and then to the heinous crimes of later terrorists. There is no discussion of how these contemporary extremists have distorted Qutb's thinking in the most reckless ways. Instead, the suggestion takes shape that violence erupted from Qutb's pen. He is seen as inspiring and justifying murderous actors from al Qaeda to ISIS.

It makes little sense to drag Sayyid Qutb in this way into the company of later terrorist figures like al Qaeda's Osama bin Ladin and Ayman Zuwaihri or, more recently, ISIS's Abu Bakr al Baghdadi. It also makes any reasonable understanding of his actual role in the critical history of the Muslim Brothers virtually impossible. Qutb was never linked directly to any violent or criminal act. Sayyid Qutb was executed by the Nasserist state for his critical thinking and evocative adversarial rhetoric. Whenever accounts of Qutb's life and thought implicitly justify that judicial murder by reference to crimes committed by others, years or even decades later, Sayyid Qutb is murdered once again.

Sayyid Qutb never argued for the cleansing power of violence as a way to ameliorate the damage to the psyche, caused by violent authoritarian rule and racist foreign interventions. Qutb, however, did denounce terrible injustices and exploitation. He modeled the right to resist such depredations in an Islamic vocabulary. Anticipating the outlandish charges that would be made against his thinking, Qutb explained:

> It is not that Islam loves to draw its sword and chop off people's heads with it. The hard facts of life compel Islam to have its sword drawn and to be always ready and careful.[18]

Throughout his writing, as exemplified in this important passage, the general stance is defensive in anticipation of violence from the foreign occupiers or repressive successor regimes. Qutb himself did not choose violence. Violence chose him. It left its marks.

The pervasive caricature of Sayyid Qutb blocks from view the real human being. Qutb may have been given to a measure of extravagant rhetoric. Yet, he was also a principled man and intellectual of depth and refined sensibility. In any serious attempt to understand the sources of the exceptional strength and endurance of the Muslim Brothers, the intellectual Sayyid Qutb must stand second only to the activist founder Hassan al Banna in stature and enduring importance. These two men, with their strikingly different talents and temperaments, built the resilient foundations of the Society of Muslim Brothers. For reasoned understanding of the Muslim Brothers, a fully rounded historical picture of Sayyid Qutb is imperative. His influence has been multifaceted and far-flung. It has flowed abundantly across *Dar al Islam*. He left the footprints of a giant across Islamic lands, from Bosnia to Turkey and on to Iran and Central Asia. He has been a large and continuing presence in all these places, though his writings were often banned and his name pronounced only in whispers. There is weight and there is substance to Qutb.

The productive passions of both Hassan al Banna and Sayyid Qutb guaranteed that the Muslim Brothers would have an inheritance of mind and heart. Both men were, like the figures who loom large in each of the chapters that follow, intellectuals in the Islamic sense of influential *du'a* or Callers to Islam.

The Rise and Fall of Brotherhood Rule

After long decades of struggle that saw the murder of both Banna and Qutb, the Brotherhood appeared to come into its own in the wake of the

60 JUSTICE IN ISLAM

revolutionary uprising of 2011. On June 30, 2012, the Brotherhood candidate Muhammad Mursi was elected Egyptian president in the only democratic elections in Egypt's long history. Mursi's unexpected victory came as a stunning surprise across the political spectrum.

The momentous elections that brought the Brotherhood to power were the democratic fruit of Egypt's revolution of 2011. However, those benefits for the Brothers were undeserved. While there was some Brotherhood support for the uprising, the Muslim Brotherhood did not play anything like a leadership role in the mass upheaval that toppled the thirty-year dictatorship of Husni Mubarak.

My apartment in Cairo is a stone's throw from iconic Tahrir Square, the epicenter of the revolution. Conversations with activists on the streets in the weeks that led up to the eruption impressed me with the stronger presence of a youthful left and progressive nationalist, rather than Islamist, animating spirit.

In truth, however, revolutionary upheavals are notoriously unpredictable in their outcomes, which rarely have much to do with the aims of the actual revolutionaries. Egypt's revolution was no exception to this pattern. When the revolutionary wave subsided and elections were possible, it was the Brothers, rather than leftists or nationalists, who emerged victorious. When elections were held, it was the Brothers who triumphed. Egypt's mass revolution produced a democratically elected Muslim Brother president.

That anomalous outcome did not go uncontested. An eclectic amalgam of diverse social forces almost immediately coalesced to challenge the Muslim Brotherhood victory in the sole democratic elections in Egypt's long history. Muhammad Mursi came to the presidency with liabilities. Mursi did not come from the first rank of Brotherhood leadership. He was put forward only when more influential and experienced leaders were disqualified on technicalities. He was derisively known as a Brotherhood *spare tire*. As president, he only very rarely showed any gift for leadership. Often even his capacity for more mundane administration seemed questionable.

To be sure, conspiracies by a large cast of adversaries worked aggressively against the president. Mursi faced a year of mounting criticisms and sporadic protests. Finally, a mass upheaval, only partly manipulated, flooded the streets. Across the board, people had had enough of the chaos and disorder that marked Mursi's year in office. They took to the streets in numbers that many claimed to be the largest in Egypt's history. Egypt reverted to a comfortable pattern of military dictatorship. Elites and ordinary citizens came together to throw themselves into the arms of the military. The disheartening results should have been predictable.

Military Coup and Its Aftermath

What happened in Egypt in the wake of the coup that removed Mursi and brought Egypt's current military ruler to power has little to do with Islam. The military junta that seized power had a secular character. In very short order, the new rulers turned decisively against all manifestations of political Islam. To justify its authoritarian rule, the current regime has been eager to wrap itself instead in a nationalist mantle. They invoked the authoritarian nationalism of Gamal Abdul Nasser (1918–1970), who ruled Egypt from 1956 to 1970. An aura of a sham Nasserism was generated. That effort of ideological justification failed. As the idea of a return to Nasserism faded, a naked dictatorship came into clear view.

Islamic scholars recognized and acknowledged the new political realities early on. Tunisia's Islamic intellectual and political activist Rashid Ghannouchi has incisively explained why. No admirer of Nasserism, Ghannouchi did point first to Nasser's record of suppression of the Brothers. He went on to register the stifling of political freedoms more generally. Yet, Ghannouchi emphasized as well the bold and in many ways progressive agenda that Nasser set for Egypt. Ghannouchi explained:

> The security and political oppression of the Nasser years was obscured by an impressive number of expansive economic, political, and cultural projects. They included land reform, the spread of education, the expansion of al Azhar, engagement with the Palestinian cause, striving for the unification of the Arab nation, anti-imperialism, and leadership in the non-allied movement.

Against the background of this Nasserist record, Ghannouchi asks:

> What project does the new ruler carry for his people and nation, other than a pseudo-intellectual cover for brutal repression that has reached such low levels as to accuse the legitimate President [Muhammad Mursi] of the "crime" of collaborating with Hamas.[19]

Assessing Brotherhood Governance

Clear-eyed and balanced assessments of the brief period of Muslim Brotherhood governance are now becoming possible. They include incisive critiques by prominent Islamic intellectuals.[20] The Brothers did narrowly win an internationally monitored election for the Egyptian presidency. *They did not, however, win the right to speak in Islam's name.* Once in power, Brotherhood leaders too often acted as though they had. They did so at times with an insufferable arrogance. Some in the Brotherhood leadership also came to speak falsely of their movement as the driving force behind the success of the 2011 revolutionary uprising. It was not.

The Brothers in the presidential palace were not only arrogant. They were inept as well. They made too little progress in restoring security, giving substance to their calls for social justice, and sharing power in meaningful ways with other political trends. Brothers in power made little note of Abu Dharr's message to love and act for the poor. They knew how to run mosques, service projects, and entrepreneurial business enterprises. Administering state structures and engaging in the political give-and-take that successful governance requires were quite different matters. No transition from a thirty-year dictatorship to a democratic political system could realistically be dominated by one political trend. No constitution written without the effective participation of a representative range of the nation's political forces could hope to command legitimacy across the political spectrum. In Egypt, no majority party could display insensitivity to the legitimate concerns of women and Christians and still claim to speak for the nation. The Brothers committed all these sins. They caused self-inflicted, costly, and unnecessary wounds.

In the end, Muhammad Mursi was only given less than a year in power. It should be registered that, despite the brevity of his time as president, he did manage to launch important plans and projects. They ranged from an ambitious development proposal for the Suez Canal Zone to enhancements of the food subsidies program.

Unfortunately, time ran out. The painfully slow pace of reform was coupled with serious missteps. President Mursi made his most egregious political miscalculation when in November 2012 he issued an executive decree that placed his presidential power above that of all other government branches, most notably the judiciary. From a presidential perspective, there was good cause for that infamous decree that set off a firestorm of protest. From the outset, the judiciary, in place from the Mubarak era, had set about systematically undercutting the Muslim Brother president's ability to govern. Nevertheless, this action by executive decree looked very much like a power grab to place the president above the law. The outcry was deafening. It included sharply critical assessments by prominent Islamic intellectuals.

The president did rescind the provocative order under this intense and multi-sourced pressure. The reversal came too late. Mursi had handed his political enemies a smoking gun. The dam broke. In the eyes of too many Egyptians, the president had lost the legitimacy his slender electoral victory had conferred.

At this juncture, a wise and experienced political leader would have recognized the untenable political reality, resigned, and established procedures for early elections. Egyptians in more than sufficient numbers had given Mursi a ringing vote of no-confidence. For the sake of Egypt, democracy, and the Brotherhood itself, Mursi should have taken that decision. Fatefully, he failed to do so.

There was nothing inevitable about the course of action Mursi adopted in the face of the massive demonstrations of June 30. The Society of Muslim Brothers was never a monolithic bloc with a fixed authoritarian and theocratic trajectory dictated by its Islamic roots. Decisions emerged in the context of power struggles at the highest leadership levels. They reflected competing policy orientations within the Brotherhood. Different factions had quite distinctive policy preferences. Outcomes were in no way predetermined.

In particular, the Islamic formation of the Muslim Brotherhood did not preclude a more flexible and accommodating politics. Islamic critics of Mursi's decisions make this case by contrasting the rigidity of the Brothers in Egypt with the flexibility and political adroitness of the Islamic Ennahda party in Tunisia.

At the highest organizational levels of the Brotherhood, two factions were locked in dispute over grand strategy for the society. A useful simplification would be identification of a first group of forward-looking reformist Brothers and a second of more conservative faction. The first group proved itself more inclusive of younger followers and more open to the contemporary influences of a globalized world. At the same time, members claimed continuity with that aspect of al Banna's legacy that emphasized the proselytizing "call" among ordinary Muslims rather than politics. Their goal was to work at the societal level to strengthen Islamic values and create effective Islamic social institutions that would allow full normalization of the Brothers' role in Egyptian society.

64 JUSTICE IN ISLAM

The second, more conservative Brotherhood faction embraced these proselytizing goals as well. However, they subordinated them to an unacknowledged drive for political power that would facilitate their realization. The conservatives are sometimes referred to as Qutbists, although the label is misleading as it is often used. This group did accept the political thrust of Sayyid Qutb's later work. They also did lean to elitist political attitudes, like Qutb. However, the conservatives, like the reformers, accepted peaceful, democratic change. They did not embrace the frequent misreading of Qutb that saw him as an advocate of violent change. The conservatives, like the reformers, sought to come to power through the ballot box.

Muhammad Mursi came from the second tier of this conservative faction. In the end, Mursi became the face of the conservative triumph. Fears to the contrary, Mursi's year as president did not result in assertive efforts to use the presidency to Islamize Egyptian society in any systematic way. There was no concerted drive for the implementation of *Shari'ah*, though the issue did come up in discussions on the new constitution. There were numerous Brotherhood appointments to important governmental posts. Yet, such a practice is standard everywhere when a new and different administration assumes power. However, a government with only a very slim mandate should have exercised more restraint.

Despite reasonable concerns about the placement of Brotherhood figures in key media and educational organizations, the national press and higher education under the Brothers were freer than under Mubarak and infinitely more so than what the return of harsh dictatorial military rule would bring. Despite these important positives, critics of Brotherhood governance have a strong case. It would be stronger if they acknowledged the serious constraints within which President Mursi was forced to govern. The president was locked into both Camp David and the neoliberal economic order underwritten by the United States. American dominance of the Middle East region assured that these restrictive economic and political frameworks would remain in place, no matter who occupied the Egyptian presidency.

Even within these constraints, Mursi did find some room for maneuver. He was able to signal that a new orientation might just be possible in the long term. His earliest foreign policy initiatives suggested that he might try to bring Egypt closer to the Islamic world. He made the point by not traveling to a Western capital on his first trip abroad. Rather, he visited Teheran very early in his presidency. Mursi also actively courted the best possible relations with Turkey. The president also relaxed to the maximum degree the border pressures placed by Egypt on the Palestinians. None of these gestures represented a substantial reorientation of Egyptian foreign policy. However, they did signal that a limited but still meaningful change might well be possible over the longer term.

Domestically, Mursi was even more severely handicapped from the outset. The president never effectively controlled the army, the police, or even the security apparatus. As with the dominance of Americans and Israelis in the foreign policy arena, he had little choice but to bow to superior power. The president signaled that the privileges of all of Egypt's military and security institutions would remain intact. Abuses of power by these structures had long been an established part of Egyptian life. The abuses continued under Mursi. However, in my observation they did so at a lower level of intensity. Most egregious of the violations on Mursi's watch was the violence deployed against football fans in Port Said in 2012. During three days of protests more than seventy were killed and some 500 wounded, due to the disproportionate lethal force of the out-of-control security forces.[21]

Opportunities were missed. The pressures from a mystically conceived *deep state* were invoked to explain why real change proved so elusive. That abstract notion lent a vague legitimacy to an institutional pattern that in no way deserved it. The president could have exposed the mystifying diversion of an Egyptian *deep state*. Deconstruct the concept and you have a predatory and corrupt military with massive economic holdings, and a repressive police and security apparatus, supported by a bloated bureaucracy. An authoritarian ideology that the Egyptian people must be ruled by the rod justified this complex of debilitating structures.

Mursi could have appealed directly to the people and explained honestly and openly just how retrograde these institutions had become. At a minimum, the president could have made clear in frank language just how little room for substantial new initiatives he had. Above all, Mursi could have acted to do something forceful—*anything*—for the mass of poor Egyptians to show them that the president stood with them. There were some gestures to the lower middle class, notably some salary and minimum wage increases. There were also efforts to protect and even modestly enhance the subsidies for bread, flour, and cooking oil, critical to the masses on the edge. The poor required and deserved more.

On the macro level, the economy suffered under Mursi's leadership. Foreign currency reserves dropped precipitously. The government was unable to defend the Egyptian pound. It steadily lost value. Since Egypt depends

66 JUSTICE IN ISLAM

on imported food, including wheat for bread, the poor suffered dispropor-
tionately as prices of basic imports rose. Public-sector companies and the
workers they employed were hit hard as well.

The president lost his hold on the people. The always thin electoral legitimacy he enjoyed faded. Mursi was told all of these things by the wider array of
Islamic and nationalist figures around him who were more in touch with the
street than his narrow inner circle of top Brotherhood figures. Participants
report that Mursi always listened politely. He never acted in the meaningful
way demanded by deteriorating conditions. Even as power slipped away, the
president showed a complete failure of realism about just how tenuous his
grip on the presidency really was. Instead of facing this reality and reaching
out, the embattled president wrapped himself endlessly in the mantle of his
democratic election. At the same time, he seemed to address himself more
and more to Brotherhood cadres and less and less to *al nas*, the common
people.

These mistakes and missed possibilities took their toll. Yet, any fair ac-
counting of the Brotherhood experience must also acknowledge the dark
forces of counter-revolution and reaction arrayed against Egypt's first democratically elected president. The army, the police, and the security structures
did actively conspire against the Muslim Brother president. The business
elite that thrived under Mubarak and had gravitated to his son Gamal joined
their efforts. Elements of the old statist regime welcomed all opportunities
to obstruct and undermine the president. Oligarchs financially supported
the efforts of the mobilized young people of the *Tamarod* movement to organize protests. They have been only too glad to tell the world of their hand in
deposing the Brotherhood president.[22]

Mursi confronted a truly astounding range of conspirators, eager to bring
him and Brotherhood governance to an end. Throughout the year of his
rule, the attacks by the opposition media on the Muslim Brothers were unrelenting. They lacked minimal journalistic standards and were remarkably
innocent of any factual basis. The judiciary, led by the Mubarak-era Supreme
Constitutional Court, systematically undermined all the president's attempts
to build democratic institutions to fill the void created by the long years of
Mubarak's dictatorship.

Mursi also confronted enemies further afield. The very fact that Mursi
came to power via the ballot box alarmed regional states, notably including
the Emirates, Saudi Arabia, and Israel. They all feared a "democratic contagion." They masked that fear of democracy with useful but unfounded

talk of the Brothers as violent extremists. Garden variety conspiracies also made their contribution to the weakening of the president. With the military and the business elite in firm control of the economy, they were not hard to manipulate.

In the months of deterioration before Mursi's ouster in the military coup of 3 July 2013, I noticed in my morning walks in central Cairo that the lines at gas stations seemed to start earlier each day and grow longer and longer. Then something wondrous happened for those beleaguered drivers. Within just a few days of Mursi's removal, gasoline deliveries resumed and gas returned to the stations in Cairo, Alexandria, and other larger cities. The lines disappeared from the first days of the president's removal. In parallel fashion, the electricity that had shut down periodically and fluctuated disruptively during Mursi's months in power suddenly stabilized at a time when the military regime was cultivating popular support. Egypt's new military rulers brought with them the blessings of gasoline and electricity.

Mass Murder in August 2013

In the wake of the military coup on July 3, 2013, the Muslim Brothers and their supporters turned their demonstrations in public squares into peaceful occupations. They created collectives of nonviolent resistance by men, women, and children. The demonstrators numbered perhaps as many as 30,000. In those spaces, there were impressive displays of generosity and compassionate caring, as I learned daily from friends in the squares. These were assemblies of ordinary citizens who had welcomed the end of the Mubarak dictatorship. They endorsed the coming to power of an elected president. Food was prepared for hundreds, a respectful security system created, crude sanitation facilities set up, and makeshift medical clinics established. The occupation continued for some fifty-five days, extending through Ramadan. The Holy Month saw communal *iftars* (the "breakfasts" that break the Ramadan fast), prayers, and various celebratory programs. The programs highlighted the talents of the children who were in the squares in large numbers.

The military responded to the prolonged occupations on August 14, 2013, with nightmarish brutality. They slaughtered some 900 souls in Rabaa al 'Adawiyya square and another 87 in al Nahda Square. Whatever the final count of men, women, and children killed and maimed, the massacre is, as

68   JUSTICE IN ISLAM

Human Rights Watch proclaimed, the worst mass killing in Egypt's modern history. The Nobel Prize–credentialed, international NGO judged that the new regime had clearly committed a crime against humanity.[23] In their subsequent investigations, Human Rights Watch found less than 20 weapons among the approximately 30,000 demonstrators. When the merciless onslaught came, the demonstrators were unable to defend themselves. This essential defenselessness gives the lie to the official stories of large numbers of armed terrorists threatening the public order.

Subsequent charges against the Brothers and the trials of leading members were for the most part evidence-free and unmindful of the most fundamental legal procedures. In the face of the vicious repression, the Brotherhood and a growing number of diverse supporters on democracy and legitimacy grounds continued to demonstrate across Cairo and around the country. As the reality of the mass murder became better known, they called for the end of military rule and the restoration of the legitimately elected president.

At the center of all these disheartening events stood the battered, deeply flawed, yet resilient and nonviolent Muslim Brothers. All serious observers agree that the Brothers displayed a damaging unwillingness to work constructively with other trends. There is not, however, the slightest justification in the best academic studies for the persecution of the Brothers as terrorists.[24] There is, at the same time, no question that an inexperienced and poorly supported president and an at times arrogant and close-mind Brotherhood leadership also made their contribution to the tragic demise of Egypt's all too brief democratic experiment

* * *

The fate of the Muslim Brotherhood itself is another matter. The Brothers have historic weight and continued contemporary relevance not only as an organization, but also as an idea and an identity. The Brothers were pioneers of the Islamic Revival. Subsequent shortcomings do not obviate that important role. Military and security measures can damage and perhaps even destroy organizational structures. They can imprison and kill Brotherhood leaders and ordinary members. They can drive them from public life. They can force key figures into exile.

A galvanizing idea and a sustaining identity, however, are not so easily dispatched. A military dictatorship can crush a movement. But in the long run, it cannot erase decades of history. The Brotherhood legacy, in all likelihood, will endure for new generations of Islamic activists to make their own. The intellectual work of Banna and Qutb will likely survive to provide indispensable guidance. So, too, will the presence of Abu Dharr as a venerable symbol of the ageless Islamic value of social justice enshrined in the Qur'an.

To that end, it should be noted that venerable figures like Shaikh Muhammad al Ghazalli, who was so profoundly influenced by the Muslim Brothers, remain alive in the hearts and minds of legions of followers. Ghazalli's deepest roots are in the Brotherhood. However, as an Islamic intellectual he moved beyond the limitations of the Brothers. The lifework of the shaikh stands apart from the history and ultimate fate of the Muslim Brothers. Yet, Ghazalli always acknowledged just how much he owed to the Brotherhood. He consistently refused to participate in the maligning of the martyred founders, Hassan al Banna and Sayyid Qutb. Ghazalli testified to the contributions of both men to the Brotherhood. At the same time, Muhammad al Ghazalli criticized the restrictions imposed by the Brothers and he left his leadership role in the society. However, he never completely severed ties with the Brotherhood. The shaikh preserved the connection in important part because of his own intimate connection to both martyrs. Over his lifetime, he viewed Banna as his teacher and Qutb as his teacher's student, notably in the work for social justice that he set in motion. Ghazalli made himself an Islamic intellectual of world-class stature. He rose above movements, sects, and nationalities. As we shall see in the next chapter, Ghazalli's scholarship and his engagement in public life, driven by a passion for social justice, left an impressive legacy for all Muslims. A proud graduate of the school of Muslim Brothers, Shaikh Muhammad al Ghazalli earned acclaim as a leading Sunni intellectuals of his time and beyond.

4

Shaikh Muhammad al Ghazalli

The People's Shaikh

The shuttered van passed through Cairo's deserted streets in the early morning hours.[1] The year was 1948. Egypt was ruled by the monarchy. The security forces of the palace had rounded up young activists of the Muslim Brotherhood. The police burst into homes just before dawn. They punctuated forced entry with loud shouts and blinding flashlights. Those caught in the dragnet included the youthful Shaikh Muhammad al Ghazalli (1917–1966), who provided an account of the experience.

There would be dogs. There would be beatings. However, while in transport the apprehended savored their moment of freedom. They used it to chant of "the greatness of God." The youth followed Shaikh Ghazalli in sounding this unifying Call to Islam. Over and over again, Muhammad Ghazalli had already proven himself to be that natural leader who was able to organize the resistance possible in even the most impossible circumstances. Even as a young man, Ghazalli sounded the calm but assertive voice of reasoned appeal to justice and opposition to tyranny. He always did so in Islam's name. Ghazalli gave confidence to his fellow youthful Islamic militants. He reassured movement activists that the path of assertive nonviolence to confront oppression and to struggle for justice was the path of righteousness. He helped them to summon the courage to face all the suffering that peaceful protests would bring them at the hands of the security forces.

Yusuf al Qaradawi (b. 1926), then also a student activist, was caught up in a similar activist round-up by the palace. On one such occasion, he found himself arrested along with Ghazalli. It would be their first personal encounter. Qaradawi was destined to join Ghazalli as a major twentieth-century Islamic scholar. Over his long and distinguished career, he has earned recognition as one of the most influential Sunni jurists of our time. At the moment of this first meeting with Ghazalli, he was still a student. Qaradawi tells of his impression of Muhammad al Ghazalli in these trying circumstances.[2] During a transport to prison camp in Sinai by ferry, chaos reigned among the detainees. Then,

Justice in Islam. Raymond William Baker, Oxford University Press. © Oxford University Press 2022.
DOI: 10.1093/oso/9780197624975.003.0004

Qaradawi reports, a young man suddenly began to speak. He did not shout. Yet, his confident voice rose above the din. His words "carried authority." His comments were "full of intelligence." Qaradawi describes how everyone stopped to listen to that voice that "brought resolve to the heart of the confusion." Qaradawi asked who was speaking. He was told the young man was Shaikh Muhammad al Ghazalli. Qaradawi had been given the opportunity to meet a figure whose reputation for learning and leadership, despite his youth, had already reached him. Qaradawi tells us that he had known Ghazalli from afar as a young man of impressive intellect who carried himself as an Islamic activist like "a soldier in battle." Ghazalli appeared to Qaradawi as a man who reasoned with care. He measured his words. He maintained focus. Yet, Qaradawi also came to know that Ghazalli's voice could "roar like a lion and his pen was a sword" in battles against tyranny. Meeting Ghazalli, Qaradawi soon discovered that "he was also was a man with a kind heart. Tears for the sorrows of others came easily to the young shaikh." Qaradawi reports that Shaikh Ghazalli's speech "was always eloquent, yet never pretentious." He was most often not the oldest in any group of prisoners in the camp in Sinai. Yet, Ghazalli was "consistently invited to act as Imam to lead the prayers and to give instructions in the faith." Much later, after the detainees were freed from the prison camp, Qaradawi recounts how Ghazalli was "the first to renew the active call to Islam." He was, or so it seemed to Qaradawi, always in the front ranks of those who both defended the faith and fought for justice.

Yusuf al Qaradawi had met the man whom he would embrace as his teacher for a lifetime. Qaradawi judged that Ghazalli's quiet strength came from the wisdom of the center. It flowed directly from the Qur'an and *Sunnah*. The holy book of Islam could not be clearer. Of Muslims, the Qur'an says "we have made you a centrist community, justly balanced, so that you might be a witness to the nations. . . ."[3] The Islam of the Qur'an deplores excess. The holy book of Muslims celebrates temperateness as the hallmark of lives rightly lived. The Qur'an describes the ideal Muslim community as one that cultivates judiciousness in all aspects of life. In parallel fashion, the Prophet Muhammad's example taught that moderation should mark activities as diverse as religious observations and resistance to tyranny in all its forms.[4]

Ghazalli, throughout his long career as a public Islamic intellectual, made himself the voice of Islam's call for justice. The active struggle for social justice in Ghazalli's vision defined the heart of Islam's Message. Over a long lifetime, he wrote some ninety-four books. In all of his writings, Ghazalli urged Muslims to act righteously for justice. There was no hint of passivity in Ghazalli's stance. At the same time, the shaikh underscored the difference between militancy and violence. Muhammad al Ghazalli was in all respects a *radical of the center*. He was a militant who abhorred violence. In his voluminous scholarly works, Shaikh Ghazalli frequently called on the legendary Abu Dharr al Ghifari as an exemplar of such an assertive *yet* insistently nonviolent stance. Ghazalli's writings bring the figure of Abu Dharr to life as both a man of action and a close observer of the Prophet's thoughts and actions in Islam's earliest years.

Muhammad al Ghazalli translated what he learned from the Prophet's example into a lifelong call for righteous action. Abu Dharr is remembered as a beloved companion of the Prophet. He also stands forth in Ghazalli's remembrance as an ascetic who loved justice more than the pleasures and comforts of the world. In his humility, Abu Dharr evoked the Muslim Jesus. The Prophet Jesus is remembered for his kind and gentle spirit that embodies the core Islamic value of a love for justice. There was, at the same time, more than a touch of the irascible in the character of Abu Dharr al Ghrifari. The Abu Dharr of legend consistently emerges as a figure who was unintimidated by great power or wealth. His sympathies were always with the most vulnerable. He spoke boldly for the poor. He acted fearlessly on their behalf.

Abu Dharr stepped out of Islam's fourteen-century history to stand with Ghazalli as a venerable symbol of justice *and* a caller to action in justice's name. He is remembered by Muslims as a beloved companion of the Prophet, a recorder of prophetic wisdom, and a lover of justice who at the same time evokes the gentle spirit of the Muslim Jesus. Whenever the venerable centrist Islamic trend has gained currency, the legends of Abu Dharr have come to life. This image of Shaikh Muhammad al Ghazalli as a radical of the center, inspired by Abu Dharr, is unavailable to the West. The Western imagination finds little space for either the venerable Abu Dharr or for Shaikh Ghazalli himself. Extremist intellectuals and movements receive the lion's share of attention. Reformist scholars, the movements they found, and the classical figures who inspire them are accorded only a faint presence. The focus is fixed instead on the retrograde and unchanging violent Islam of the Western imagination.

History tells a different story. Activist, forward-looking Islamic intellectuals like Ghazalli have fueled and led successive waves of reform in the Islamic world. The first took shape in the first half of the eighteenth century and extended until the second half of the nineteenth. The second appeared in the final quarter of the nineteenth century and lasted through the first half of the twentieth. The third wave arose after World War I and remained a vital force into the 1940s The fourth wave of reform arose in the late 1960s, gathered force in the early 1970s, and swept across Islamic lands over the course of the next four decades. Though waning in strength today, it is still with us.

Islamic scholars have designated this fourth historical wave of reform *al Sahwa al Islamiyya* (the Islamic Awakening). The early years of the Awakening defined a period when Muhammad al Ghazalli joined with Yusuf al Qaradawi and a small circle of other distinguished Egyptian Islamic intellectuals to speak and act for what they designated as the *New Islamic Trend*. They understood themselves to be the heirs of the nineteenth-century reformers Muhammad Abdou and Gamal Eddine Afghani in their efforts to advocate for a reformist Islam that supported nonviolent resistance. They cooperated in inventive ways as an *intellectual school*.[5] Their circle of Islamic intellectuals included distinguished lawyers, journalists, and judges, as well as accomplished Islamic scholars. They elaborated a contemporary vision of an Islam of rationality and spirituality that spoke to modern conditions.

These centrist Islamic scholars were defined above all by their insistence on an interpretive approach to all Islamic references. They explained that while the sacred texts themselves were fixed, the way in which they were understood was variable. Moreover, for the New Islamic Trend, while authentication of texts was important, interpretation always represented the crucial necessity. Islamic scholars had a duty to confirm the authenticity of texts. Yet, confirmation of the reliability of sacred texts was not in itself understanding of the meaning of those texts. Understanding how the Message spoke to one's own time required interpretation. Believers know that the Qur'an is the word of God. The certainty of that divine provenance in itself, however, did not assure that Muslim readers had attained a reasonable understanding of those verses. In parallel ways, particular *hadith*s (traditions) of the Prophet might be confirmed as reliable representations of what the Prophet thought and did. Such certainty did assure believers that the words or actions were those of the Prophet. That assurance in itself, however, provided no guarantee that they had fully grasped the meaning for their own circumstances of what the Prophet taught.

Shaikh Ghrazalli and his fellow intellectuals of the New Islamic Trend explained that human reason, God's great gift to humankind, always has an essential role in Islam. To be sure, reason itself and interpretations alone cannot attain to the wisdom of revelation. However, the intellectuals of the

74   JUSTICE IN ISLAM

New Islamic Trend did believe that human reason could act as an indispensable handmaiden to grasping the higher purposes of sacred texts that transcended time and place. They taught that revelation and reason must work in tandem. Above all, they warned of the danger of a failure to apprehend the inner kernel of laws and prescriptions. It was intolerable to them to mistake the external shell of a law or precept for the deeper meaning it carried. This critical interpretive project yielded an impressive literature that brought the venerable trend of midstream Islam into the twentieth and twenty-first centuries. These scholars and intellectuals of the New Islamic Trend produced an entire library of centrist scholarship on the arts, society, and politics. The influence of leading figures in the circle, like Muhammad al Ghazalli and Yusuf al Qaradawi, made itself felt throughout the Islamic world. In their engaging contemporary vision of Islam, the influence of Abu Dharr as symbol of reform in the name of justice played an important role. In the key centers of Turkey, Iran, and Egypt, reformist scholarship informed and enlivened the intellectual world. The scholarship of the intellectuals of the New Islamic Trend became a point of reference for centrist intellectuals and activists across the Islamic world. In their copious writings, these scholars put center stage an understanding of Islam with social justice at its core.

While their voluminous writings had central importance, the New Islamists never restricted their efforts to the realm of scholarship. The public intellectuals of the New Islamic Trend also modeled wide-ranging activist interventions on behalf of democracy, women's rights, human rights, and political freedom. In their public interventions, these activist scholars brought a contemporary experience of Islamic centrism to renewed life. In all their public work, they aimed to buttress the foundations of the balanced Islam of the Qur'an and *Sunnah*. They affirmed a "contemporary Islamic vision" that was inclusive.[6] Though they themselves were Sunni Muslims, their appeal and influence transcended the sectarian divide. Collectively, they aimed to bring a contemporary interpretation of the centrist Islam of the Qur'an and *Sunnah* into the modern era in the service of all Muslims. They named that venerable centrist trend, anchored by the Qur'an and *Sunnah*, the *Wasittia*. Their combination of scholarship and activism made the prominence of the *Wasittia* a critical feature of the Islamic Awakening.

To be sure, the centrist trend never stood alone. The *Wasittia* was always one trend among several. Retrograde Wahabbi Islam of the Saudis and a range of other violent extremist ideologies competed with the centrists for the allegiance of young Islamic activists. These noisy and destructive alternatives dominated the attention of Western audiences. Little attention was paid to the significant reformist gains of the New Islamic Trend. Today, this fourth wave of Islamic renewal in the modern era shows signs of receding. It is too early to pronounce that the wave has exhausted itself. History cautions that underestimating the capacity of Islam's center for renewal would be unwise. It would be just as unwise to imagine that we have seen the last of Abu Dharr al Ghifari.

Confidence in the resilience of centrist Islam does not alter the reality that today two very different interpretations of the faith dominate much of the Western scholarship on Islam and virtually all of the international media. Western publics are given little beyond the royal Islam of the Saudi monarchy and the terrorist Islam of al-Qaeda, ISIS (the Islamic State), and their shadowy progeny. Royal and extremist Islam have overshadowed the Islam of the Qur'an and *Sunnah* in the West. The Islam of the center has been rendered all but invisible. This displacement is stranger than it may seem. Both royal and extremist Islam represent strictly minority interpretations of Islam as faith and way of life. The Wahhabi Islam of the Saudi royals and the extremist Islam of groups like al Qaeda and the Islamic State combined represent no more than one or two percent of the world's 1.8 billion Muslims. The overwhelming majority of the world's Muslims adhere to centrist interpretations of the faith. Nevertheless, in the Western and especially American imagination, minority trends loom so large that they effectively define Islam. In reality, both royal and extremist Islam have very shallow historical and theological roots. Unlike the venerable *Wasittia* with its secure roots in the Qur'an and *Sunnah*, both trends emerged as the modern-day products of the Western-dominated modern world of nation-states and international capitalist markets.

Despite these clear limitations, royal and extremist Islam are taken together to define an inclusive continuum along which Islamic movements can be arrayed. This continuum is anchored at one end by "moderate" Saudi royals. Moderation in this context means no more than alliance with the West, particularly the United States. In fact, the Saudi monarchy has the distinction of being one of the few regimes on the planet that can match the Islamic extremists in the sadistic cruelties of its rule, stoning for stoning, beheading for beheading, and crucifixion for crucifixion. The second pole of this presumed continuum in Western thinking about Islam is secured by violent extremists of al Qaeda, the Islamic State, and their numerous offshoots.

76   JUSTICE IN ISLAM

The extremisms of that pole stand as violent enemies of the West, in general, and the United States, in particular.

This imagined "continuum" is not a continuum at all. It is rather a closed circle of extremism. The Wahhabism of the Saudis represents a harsh sectarian reading of the faith. It is as violent and retrograde as the Islam of the most extreme movements. Rigid and retrograde Wahhabi Islam legitimates the Saudi monarchy. Wahhabism represents the eighteenth-century marriage of a puritanical religiosity with an assertive tribalism. The movement originates as part of a first wave of Islamic reform that emphasized a return to fundamentals. By the twentieth century, however, Wahabism had lost its initial reformist and defensive dimension. It was reduced to the religious cloak for an antiquated and expansionist familism. The movement was fostered in the 1920s to serve the dynastic interests of the Saud family and the minor chiefdom the family dominated. Saudi Arabia today is less a modern polity than a family estate, essentially run by the numerous male progeny of the founder, Ibn Saud (1875–1958). An endless supply of "princes" assures continuity of the Saudi kingdom and the retrograde Islam it fosters. Successions always come with the gloss that the latest princely successor is a reformer at heart. In fact, the Saudi monarchs rule as demi-gods with absolute power. The sloganeering of the kingdom epitomizes theocratic authoritarianism. Their confected Islam sanctifies the regime's authoritarian purposes and often brutal character.

In strictly monotheistic Islam, only the one God is to be worshipped, not a ruling family. The Saudi clerical establishment nevertheless rationalizes the monarchial rule of the Saud family. Both of the holy cities of Mecca and Medina are located within the boundaries of the kingdom. The Saudi clerics clutch this simple geographical fact to give the royals an Islamic legitimacy. The family of Saud awards itself the historic title of "protectors of the two holy sites." The designation has been claimed by a succession of Islamic rulers, beginning with the Ayyubid and including the Mameluk sultans of Egypt and the Ottoman sultans. Mythology has it that the Saudi "royal" family owes its position to this critical role in Islam. In fact, the real source of their staying power is US intelligence and military support. The Americans arm and train the repressive Saudi police and military. Both repressive arms of the regime function to protect the royal family and guarantee American control over access to Saudi oil.

This misappropriation of a historic title was but one of the costs of Wahabbism. Not given to mincing words, Shaikh Ghazalli accused the

Wahabbi clerics of threatening to cause far more serious damage. He often pronounced that they were seeking to assassinate reason in the Islamic tradition. Ghazalli made it clear that the Wahabbi interpretation of Islam turns its back on the Qur'anic insistence on the role of reason in *ijithad* (interpretation). Instead, he argued that the Qur'an in the Wahabbi tradition is read in a highly selective and narrowly literalist way. At the same time, the very uneven body of *hadith* is given an importance that overshadows that of the Qur'an. What is left out of the Wahhabi reading of the Qur'an and Sunnah are the higher purposes of Islam. What is added from the selective reading of *hadith*s, in particular, is justification of obedient authoritarianism. According to Ghazalli, what is lost are the multiple ways the sacred texts cry out for social justice. What remains is a cruel and corrupt monarchy and its always meaningless promises of reform.

With the false continuum of the Western imagination in place, an unspoken conclusion inevitably takes shape: *Islam has no center*. There exists no golden mean in Islam. The very idea of a centrist Islam is effectively ruled out. Positioning Wahhabism as a moderate pole and the Islam of al Qaeda and ISIS as the extremist pole essentially makes the very idea of a centrist Islam unthinkable. The center, the natural space of the Islam of the Qur'an and *Sunnah*, is eliminated. The reality of the *Wasittia* as a historical force is denied. This massive distortion also means the negation of the space of appearance of Abu Dharr as a classic advocate for the Islam of justice, freedom, and compassion.

Contemporary centrist scholars, like Shaikh Muhammad al Ghazalli, have had their importance diminished by extremist versions of Islam. Alternatively, they are cast as "extremists in disguise" by the West that refuses to see the Islamic center. Islamic movements of the center are branded as "terrorist." They are pronounced indistinguishable in essentials from al Qaeda and the Islamic State.

Inevitably, the conception of an unchanging, violent, and retrograde Islam dominates. It is taken to be Islam in its essence. This Islam is everywhere and at all times the same. Genuinely historical accounts become impossible. Moderate scholars and movements are forced into this mold. They are *unmasked* as extremist at their core. Both Muhammad al Ghazalli and Yusuf al Qaradawi, as independent Islamic scholars, have suffered this treatment. Especially great harm is done when an essentially nonviolent mass movement, like the Muslim Brothers, is systematically denigrated and misrepresented with the same formula. A hostile West embraces these

78 JUSTICE IN ISLAM

misrepresentations. The larger point is made that there is something delusional about looking for moderation in Islam and in the social movements it inspires.

The Assault on Muhammad al Ghazalli

The *unmasking* of the revered Shaikh Muhammad al Ghazalli is particularly instructive in this regard. The assault on Ghazalli merits a closer look. It shows clearly how moderation in Islam is rendered unthinkable. The most damaging case against Shaikh Muhammad al Ghazalli rested on his peripheral and unfortunate involvement in a criminal case against the extremist assassins of a well-known secular intellectual. Farag Foda was a prominent professor, journalist, and public intellectual. He established himself as an effective, if provocative, advocate of secular liberalism. I read his commentary for years. I found his rhetoric at times exaggerated. However, his analyses were often incisive and his courage always undeniable. I saw Foda as a fearless and influential critic of the excesses of political Islam. His murder was a tragedy.

In the Cairo Book Fair of January 1992, the featured event was a debate on the secular versus the Islamic state. Shaikh Ghazalli represented the Islamic position. Standing with him but very much in his shadow was the head of the Muslim Brothers, Ma'mun al Hudaibi. With Farag Foda on the secular side was Muhammad Khalafalla, one of the founders of the Tagama', the official left opposition party. Khalafalla was a leftist thinker and activist with a strong Islamic coloration. From the time the program for the Fair was first printed in the national papers, the Egyptian political class was focused on this momentous encounter. It was my good fortune to be in Cairo at the time. I attended the three-hour debate. It was riveting.

Despite fears of violence, the hours passed without incident. Early on, there were some disruptive chants from youthful Islamic activists. Ghazalli's calm and authoritative voice spoke directly to them. He assured the youth that they would be heard. Their point of view would be represented. The noisy sloganeering faded. Things never got out of hand. The two formidable lead speakers provided Egyptians the chance for forceful articulations of Islamic and secular positions from the same platform. The public was given the rare opportunity to come face to face with alternative futures for their country. In articulating their respective positions, Ghazalli and Foda also provided exemplars of civility. The public dialogue modeled tolerance.

SHAIKH MUHAMMAD AL GHAZALLI 79

The terrible violence came several months later. Vitriolic cultural wars between Islamic and secular activists raged in the 1990s. The civil debate of Ghazalli and Foda was the exception. Animosity toward Farag Foda, as an outspoken advocate for secularism, had been building. At the same time, and far more ominously, incidents of extremist violence by subterranean Islamic groups were also on the rise. Escalation came from these extremist Islamic quarters. They charged prominent Muslim secularists with apostasy. Farag Foda became one such target. Along with other prominent secularists, he was falsely charged with disbelief. In a climate darkened by violence, the reckless accusation proved deadly. Shadowy Islamic extremists murdered Farag Foda on June 9, 1992.

The subsequent trial of Foda's assassins saw Muhammad al Ghazalli pulled into the controversy. The incident proved to be one of the most damaging in Ghazalli's entire career. His reputation recovered, but never fully, from the harm inflicted. The incident pushed the culture wars to their most hysterical and destructive levels. The prominent Islamic legal scholar Selim al 'Awa, himself a participant in the centrist New Islamic Trend, described the controversies that erupted as "unprecedented in our modern history."[7] The fears and apprehensions of secularists inevitably deepened. The deterioration had underlying structural causes. Material conditions had worsened. The grip of authoritarian rule had tightened. Opposition to Egypt's dictatorship found its most vocal and potentially most effective articulation from Islamic quarters. The government acted to "dry the springs." The slogan justified a generalized assault on all Islamic institutions and movements that in any way eluded government control. The targets for suppression included both centrist and extremist Islamic figures and movements.

The campaign also had the effect of silencing in public life the voices of responsible figures who spoke for the Islamic center. Consequently, the influence of the extremists was magnified. The prominent Islamic journalist Fahmi Huwaidi warned against "the spread of abnormal ideas among Muslim youth about the right to brand someone an apostate." He noted that these dangers are inevitably heightened in the absence of sound Islamic education and the suppression of legitimate means of public discussion of Islamic viewpoints. "Such deviationist ideas," he concluded, "flourish in the dark."[8]

Out of that darkness came the young men who in the summer of 1992 killed Farag Foda. He lost his life in a reprehensible act of murder simply for expressing his views. Foda's advocacy of the separation of religion and state had led to a condemnation by a committee of al Azhar clerics. Two members

80 JUSTICE IN ISLAM

of the extremist group al Gama'a al Islamiyya responded to this censure by assassinating Farag Foda on June 8, 1992. They murdered an unarmed and defenseless Foda in front of the Egyptian Society for Enlightenment that he had established.

Muhammad al Ghazalli had no role in the Azhar committee that unintentionally lent a measure of legitimacy to the unfounded charges of apostasy against Foda. Nor did Ghazalli have any connection to the terrorists of al Gama'a organization that murdered him. In his immediate public commentary, Ghazalli condemned Foda's assassination. Nevertheless, Shaikh Muhammad al Ghazalli and the entire project of moderate Islamic reform were drawn into the destructive and damaging storm of controversy that the murder precipitated.

The prominent journalist Fahmi Huwaidi, himself a leading figure in the New Islamic Trend, did not equivocate in the least in condemning the taking of Farag Foda's life. "It is a tragic end," he said in a compelling article written immediately after the murder, "and it can have no positive justification." Huwaidi added that "nothing in Islam allows a Muslim to kill an innocent person, whoever he might be.... Anyone who reads the words of the Prophet knows how greatly he stressed the sanctity of human life." To drive home the essential point, he added that "one is shocked when he finds a Muslim killing another Muslim or anyone at all, just because of a difference of opinion." In unequivocal language, Huwaidi concluded:

> In the case of Farag Foda, no one questions that the man was a strong adversary of Islamic activists. His attacks offended some and went further than most secular critics. However, despite all that it should be very clear that the man expressed himself in words. He did no more than state his opinions. I find no justification in logic or Islam for responding to his words with bullets.[9]

Huwaidi's powerful article was banned. The government muzzled the most widely read voice for the Islamic centrists at this critical moment. No Egyptian paper, whether government or opposition, could publish Huwaidi's condemnation of the murder. It did come out in Gulf papers, meaning that only a narrow stratum of Egypt's political elite had access to it when it was needed most. Only much later was Huwaidi able to publish the piece in a book that collected his censored articles.[10] Huwaidi's clarification of the position of midstream Islam came too late. The lasting but false impression was created that Islamic centrists had, at this crucial moment, failed to condemn the murder of an important intellectual for nothing more than the expression of his views. That damaging misreading of events persists to this day.

Demonizing Muhammad al Ghazalli

Great harm to hopes for national reconciliation came from the systematic mischaracterization of Muhammad al Ghazalli's role in the trial of Foda's assassins. There was room, as Fahmi Huwaidi commented, for "criticism of the performance of all sides" in the Farag Foda affair.[11] However, the frenzy of criticism that assaulted one of Egypt's most beloved Islamic intellectuals came close to moral assassination. It was undeserved by even the most critical reading of his shortcomings.

There were flaws in the role Shaikh Ghazalli played. The defense lawyers for the extremists charged with murdering Farag Foda called Ghazalli to testify. However, he did so only as a specialist in *Shari'ah* (the provisions from Qur'an and *Sunnah* to regulate human behavior). The court and Ghazalli himself made it clear in the course of the proceedings that the shaikh had no direct knowledge of the circumstances of the murder. He could not, therefore, testify in any way on the specifics of that case. While on the stand, Ghazalli was not asked to give his opinion on either Farag Foda nor on the guilt or innocence of the men charged with his murder. Questions focused on general *Shari'ah* provisions, without direct reference to this particular case. In his testimony, Ghazalli abided by these courtroom dictates.

The defense attorney asked Ghazalli a series of very precise but abstract questions about the application of *Shari'ah* provisions. The exchange focused on the punishment of any Muslim who questions the principle of the application of *Shari'ah*. Ghazalli responded succinctly and unexceptionably to all the questions. He explained that such a stance, if not repented when the accused was empowered to do so, would constitute apostasy. He added that it would be punishable as such. He further indicated that, although the consensus of scholars supported capital punishment to be administered by the constituted authorities as appropriate for apostasy, he personally advocated life imprisonment instead. Ghazalli then went further in the same vein by adding that, should the apostate flee abroad, no attempt should be made to bring him back for punishment. As expert witness, Ghazalli was asked one final question. If the authorities failed to punish the apostate and others took

82   JUSTICE IN ISLAM

it upon themselves to do so, were those who acted against the apostate guilty of a crime? If so, did Ghazalli know the penalty prescribed for such a crime in *Shari'ah*? Ghazalli responded that such action was indeed criminalized as "encroachment on authorities." As to punishment, he responded, "I do not know of one."[12]

This final response created an uproar. Ghazalli's answer was denounced as an exoneration of those who killed Farag Foda. Such a reading of Ghazalli's testimony is tendentious. Respecting the constraints on his testimony imposed by the court, Ghazalli responded to questions as an expert on *Shari'ah* only. He did so accurately. There is in fact no specification in *Shari'ah* for the nature of the punishment to be imposed on those other than the constituted authorities who act against an alleged apostate. Ghazalli's explanation that a Muslim's denial of the principle of applying *Shari'ah* would constitute grounds for a charge of apostasy reflects a consensus view of Islamic scholars. Furthermore, those who condemned Ghazalli ignored his clear explanation that anyone accused of apostasy must be given the opportunity to respond to the charges. Critics also overlooked Ghazalli's own clearly stated preference for life imprisonment over death as the appropriate penalty for anyone guilty of apostasy. In Ghazalli's judgment, there was no Qur'anic verse or strong *hadith* that prescribes death for apostasy.

The attacks on Ghazalli also paid no attention to his equally straightforward response that the usurpation of the right of punishment from the authorities was a crime, nor to the fact that all he had done was simply to acknowledge that he did not know of a penalty prescribed for that crime. He had explained accurately that no penalty is in fact clearly specified in Qur'an or *Sunnah*. If these views, as well as the context in which they were expressed, are kept in mind, it is impossible to read Ghazalli's testimony as an exculpation of those who killed Farag Foda as an apostate. There is room in Islam for judging his position on apostasy as harsh. However, it cannot reasonably be read as an exculpation of Farag Foda's killers.

Nevertheless, Shaikh Ghazalli does bear some responsibility for the outcry his testimony caused in secular quarters and for the damage suffered to his reputation as a centrist Islamic scholar. Though technically correct, his final response on punishment for those who take it upon themselves to penalize an apostate lacked nuance. Ghazalli missed an opportunity to challenge extremist views that were very much in the air. Ghazalli proved himself insensitive to the highly charged context within which this narrow legal question was posed. There is evidence that Ghazalli did have such latitude for a more expansive answer. Therefore, it is not unreasonable to hold him accountable for not using it. Earlier in the court session, Ghazalli did elaborate on the *fiqh* (Islamic legal reasoning) surrounding the issue of apostasy. He did indicate clearly his own opinion. He could have done so as well on the issue of the treatment of those who usurp legitimate authority and take it on themselves to take the life of someone charged with apostasy. What was at stake in the trial was precisely the fate of those accused of the murder of Farag Foda, as an alleged apostate. An elaboration of this issue would have been even more germane than the one he offered on a generalized discussion of apostasy itself. Ghazalli failed to take that opportunity. His reputation as a centrist Islamic scholar suffered. The wound was in part self-inflected.

Later, but only after the damage was done, Selim al 'Awa offered a balanced assessment of Ghazalli's testimony from a position that was essentially Ghazalli's own. 'Awa first affirmed the technical correctness of Ghazalli's testimony. 'Awa explained that the views Ghazalli expressed were in line with those of the majority of midstream scholars. However, he indicated three additional observations that could have been added to make it clear that centrist Islamic intellectuals, himself included, stood firmly against criminal usurpation of authority by violent extremists. First, 'Awa explained that a notion of "repentance," invoked but not elaborated by Ghazalli, has a precise legal meaning. It provides that any person charged with apostasy must be given the opportunity to hear clarifications and elaborations of the charges that his views were transgressive. Unless such opportunity is provided by qualified *'ulama*, consensus scholarship maintains that the case cannot even be filed, let alone judged. Ghazalli failed to clarify that the "repentance" he discussed carried this weight. Second, 'Awa also provided a useful elaboration of the *Shari'ah* notion that individuals may not themselves apply punishment. Ghazalli had explained the restriction as designed to prevent an encroachment on the prerogatives of legitimate authorities. 'Awa significantly added that it also afforded the person accused of apostasy protection against "violation of their human rights, especially the right to defend themselves before independent judges." Finally, 'Awa noted that the failure to specify a specific punishment for encroaching on authorities means that the crime is to be punished "in proportion to the seriousness of the consequences it entails and in accordance with the set of punishments specified by the state." It emphatically did not mean that the crime should go unpunished. Yet, this glaringly incorrect interpretation is precisely the view falsely attributed to Ghazalli.

84 JUSTICE IN ISLAM

Ghazalli's own clarifications after the trial were fully in line with these elaborations by 'Awa. However, Ghazalli also made clear his continued belief that in the context of the Western pressure against the Islamic world, a Muslim who contributed to the undermining of *Shari'ah* was subject to the charge of apostasy, analogous to treason. This judgment is harsh. However, it cannot reasonably be read as the same thing as justifying Farag Foda's murder. At no point during the trial and subsequent controversy in the press did Ghazalli ever intimate that the required cautionary procedures for treating apostasy should be suspended. On the contrary, he explicitly invoked the repentance provision. At no point did Ghazalli suggest that Foda's assassination should be condoned. On the contrary, he explicitly said that such a usurpation of legitimate authority threatened to "bring chaos to society."[13]

In the Farag Foda affair, Ghazalli occupied a centrist position that brought him little comfort. He was attacked from all quarters. To the dismay of secularists, Ghazalli had warned that there should be no questioning of the rightfulness of applying *Shari'ah*. At the same time, Ghazalli did warn of the more pressing dangers of Islamic militants resorting to illegitimate violence against alleged apostates. He saw both orientations as unacceptable in a just Islamic society. However, it is important to note that Shaikh Ghazalli made no false equivalency between the two positions. He explained clearly that the onus for resorting to violence rested on the Islamic extremists. For that reason, Ghazalli consistently supported the official use of force to contain Islamic radicals who resorted to violence. Ghazalli never in any way justified violence against secularists who simply expressed their opinions, as Farg Foda had done. Clearly violent extremists in the Islamic wave could find neither defense nor support in a dispassionate review of Ghazalli's opinions expressed before, during, and after the trial.

Many secularists dismissed all the nuanced dimensions of Ghazalli's position. They proceeded instead to demonize Ghazalli. They pronounced him indistinguishable from the extremists. In doing so, they lent credence to uninformed Western reporting that pictured Ghazalli as potentially an "Egyptian Khomeini." By that label, they meant a revolutionary not averse to violence. Ironically, years earlier a number of extremist books issued in Arab countries and widely circulated in Egypt and the Arab world made the opposite case. They charged that Ghazalli was himself an apostate and a threat to Islam, as the radicals understood it. The bases of the charges varied. Some stressed the dangers from Ghazalli's "socialism" because of his fight against poverty. Others emphasized his "pernicious" support for democracy and the rights of all, including non-Muslims, in an Islamic state. Still others charged that this "malicious" shaikh had blasphemed against the *niqab* (face veil). In their view, Ghazalli had adopted the call of Qassim Amin (1863–1908), the Egyptian pioneer for women's rights. They agreed on one thing: Ghazalli's views challenged their own deviant conceptions of Islam. For that, they charged him with apostasy. They wrote ominously that Ghazalli had committed "aggression against Islam and must publicly repent."[14] In the wake of the Farag Foda affair, attacks by secular extremists meant that by the end of his long and distinguished career, Ghazalli had come to represent the besieged Islamic center as no other figure. Extremists assaulted him relentlessly from all sides.

Critics of political Islam seized on Ghazalli's role in the Farag Foda case as confirmation of their conviction that, in the end, all Islamic intellectuals and activists were alike. They all represented an undifferentiated extremist threat to civilized society.[15] A template emerged that was systematically deployed by secularists to weaken and undermine their centrist Islamic adversaries. It rested on an essentialist denial of the very possibility of an Islamic center.

Muhammad al Ghazalli represented midstream Islam as no other. The discredit inflicted on Ghazalli by the Farag Foda case, however undeserved, did great damage. The argument gained traction that Islam, when stripped to essentials, has an inherently violent nature and little in the way of intellect or heart. A far-reaching conclusion took shape that Islamic movements all have a mindless and heartless violent agenda. Hizbullah should not be seen as a movement of legitimate resistance to a foreign occupation. Hamas should never be recognized as an expression of legitimate Palestinian national resistance to a regime of settler colonialism. Both were simply organizations of terrorists, *tout court*. The apparent moderation in Islam that Shaikh Muhammad al Ghazalli represented is always simply as a cloak for extremism. Recognized rights under international law, such as self-defense or self-determination, can be systematically denied the slightest relevance to Islamic movements. In many ways, the treatment of the Muslim Brothers provides the most egregious application of this ahistorical and falsifying formulation Shaikh Ghrazalli rose above it.

Ghazalli stood with the Brothers but also apart as an Islamic intellectual of world-class stature. Ghazalli always feared that criticism of the Muslim Brotherhood, at times fully warranted, might shade into unjustified criticism of Islam itself. His scholarship gave witness to a sharp and discerning mind. He blended sophisticated scholarship, meaningful social activism, and

86   JUSTICE IN ISLAM

unmatched rapport with *al nas*. Muhammad al Ghazalli, with deep roots in the Brotherhood, gave the mind and heart of midstream Islam tangible expression. Ghazalli's social activism gave testament to his deep compassion and legendary kindness. Together, his record of activism and his lifetime of scholarship made Muhammad al Ghazalli an Islamic scholar for the ages.

Ghazalli rose above movements, regimes, and sects.

5

Sa'id Nursi

Jihadist of the Word

Sa'id Nursi, the most revered of Turkish Islamic scholars, died on March 23, 1960, after a brief illness. The story of Nursi's passing did not end there. In a steady stream, thousand on thousands made their way to the site of his tomb in Urfa in southeastern Turkey. There should have been nothing surprising in the massive and emotional outpouring. At the time of his passing, it is reliably estimated that Nursi's followers numbered well over a million. It rapidly became clear that Nursi's burial site would become a shrine. His tomb served as the focal point for homage to Sa'id Nursi, revered for his immense contribution to the survival and revitalization of Islam in Turkey.

Turkey's secular rulers were alarmed. The army was called in. On July 12, 1960, tanks moved into Urfa. Soldiers used sledgehammers to break into the marble tomb to remove Nursi's shrouded body. An army truck spirited the body away for reburial in a secret grave. Activist followers of Nursi searched for the new site for years. When it was finally found, it was reportedly decided that the secret of the location would be shared with only two of the most trusted followers. If one of the two died, it was agreed that a second devotee would be chosen to guard the secret. Even in death, Sa'id Nursi's hold on his followers continued to exercise its extraordinary effect.[1]

Warrior *and* Ascetic

There was, in fact, very little of the ordinary in Sa'id Nursi's life. Unique figures populate the Islamic historical imagination. The warrior with aspirations for a political role finds a place in many cultures. So, too, does the ascetic who withdraws from public life to an austere private space of reflection and spirituality. More unusual is the Islamic fusion of the two in one persona. The Prophet's irascible companion Abu Dharr al Ghifari (d. 652) created an Islamic prototype of the assertive fighter who is at the same

88 JUSTICE IN ISLAM

time an ascetic and a *hadith* scholar (recorder of sayings of the Prophet). Sa'id Nursi represents the most important modern exemplar of this distinctive Islamic fusion. References to Abu Dharr, as symbol of justice and surrogate for the Muslim Jesus, have an important role to play in the Turkish scholarly literature. The seventh-century companion of the Prophet speaks to contemporary Turkish Islam. The core message of Abu Dharr is blunt. Islam is addressed to *al nas* (the common people). Islam is not to be owned by the rich and powerful, or by a clerical caste that serves them. This message reached Sa'id Nursi.

The three great ethnicities of Arabs, Iranians, and Turks populate an Islamic strategic triangle in the heart of the Islamic world. In the popular imagination, the gifts of the Arabs center on Arabic, the language of the Qur'anic revelation. The Iranians provide a reservoir of literary arts, most notably their incomparable poetry. The Turks have been the indomitable warriors. They expanded, protected, and governed the territories of Islam. Turkish military figures dominated rulership in all three of the last great Islamic empires.

Mustafa Kamel (1881–1938), the founder of the successor Turkish state, stood very much in the Turkish military tradition. In the standard accounts of modern Turkish history, this military hero and secular nationalist leader completely dominates. The stage for Kamel's rise was set by the Ottomans. In the twilight years of the Ottoman Empire, a coalition of Turkish reformers, known to history as the Young Turks, began the transformation of the Ottoman Empire in a reformist, modernizing direction. Kemal presided over the consummation of that process.

Mustafa Kemal was an Ottoman officer who distinguished himself in the critical battle of Gallipoli in 1915–1916 when the forces of the empire turned back an attempt by the Entente powers of Britain, France, and Russia to take their capital. The military assumed a dominant position. General Mustafa Kemal took power. He successfully built the modern Turkish republic on aggressively secular foundations. The words for "father" and "Turks" were combined to create his title. Mustafa Kamel is honored by the Turkish people as Mustafa Kamel Atatürk, "Father of the Turks."

With the volume turned so high on this secular nationalist narrative, it has been difficult to hear any alternative version of modern Turkish history. It was hard to see how that history could have gone differently. Yet, from the very beginning, there was a compelling Islamic alternative that shadowed the secular nationalist story. Sa'id Nursi dominated that very different story. He did so just as completely as Atatürk held sway over the secular narrative.

Not unlike Mustafa Kamel, as a young man Sa'id Nursi appeared to fill to perfection the role of the classic Turkish warrior. Nursi distinguished himself in World War I battles. The Ottomans entered World War I on the German side, against the British, French, and Russians. The consequences of that decision were severe. The dangers were real. At one point during World War I, forces from five foreign armies occupied Turkish territory. The empire was invaded from the south by the British, from the east by the Russians, and from the west by the Greeks. At war's end, only the Anatolian highlands remained under the control of Turkish forces. The invaders were poised to carve up the Turkish territories of the Ottoman Empire. They would do exactly that to the Arab lands of the empire.

Sa'id Nursi stood first with the Ottomans. The Young Turk revolution of 1908 had initially won Sa'id Nursi's support for its reformist thrust. His relationship with the Ottoman authorities did cloud, however, when their ambivalent attitude toward Islam became clearer. Nevertheless, Nursi fought for the Ottoman Empire on the Caucasian front during World War I. On the battlefield, he earned a reputation as a fearless fighter. He demonstrated exceptional personal bravery as a commander. To stiffen the morale of his troops, Nursi would go into the trenches with his men while they were under heavy shelling. By plunging into the fighting, Nursi made himself vulnerable. He was wounded and taken prisoner by the Russians. Stories of Nursi's subsequent escape from Russian detention added luster to his warrior image. His valor earned Nursi a medal for bravery. It was this Sa'id Nursi, as Ottoman fighter, who first garnered wide public attention.

The end of the Ottoman Empire and the onset of the struggles to birth the modern Turkish state created radically new conditions. Nursi adjusted. He returned to Istanbul as a war hero. It was presumed he would have a political future. Nursi expressed vocal support for the military figures who spearheaded the drive for a Turkish successor state. During the Turkish War of Independence from 1919 to 1922, he had aligned himself with the Turkish national resistance movement, led by General Mustafa Kemal.

The military leader, for his part, was aware of Nursi's record as a fighter. Moreover, he recognized the impressive following he was winning as an Islamic intellectual. He welcomed "Minister" Nursi's support. To consolidate that support, Kemal offered Nursi a very lucrative position as Minister of Religious Affairs for the eastern provinces of Turkey. The position carried

90 JUSTICE IN ISLAM

a generous salary, a deputyship in the Assembly, and a scholarly post that included a residence.[2]

However, by the time the offer was made, Kemal's vision of a secular state with a circumscribed role for Islam had become clearer. It contrasted sharply to Nursi's strong commitment to strengthening Islam in Turkey. Nursi turned down the official position. The relationship between the two men never recovered.

Sa'id Nursi withdrew from public life. That decision was a defining one for his life story. Two distinct chapters were marked. The first chronicled the brash adventures of a soldier and prominent public figure. The second told the subtle story of the prodigious scholar and spiritual ascetic. Nursi's retreat from the capital and return to Van Province initially brought the tranquility he sought. However, his peace did not last. Nursi was arrested in 1925 on charges of fomenting rebellion in eastern Turkey. He was sent into exile to Barla, an isolated village in the east that subsists in the shadow of a mountain with the same name. The rebels had indeed asked Nursi for support, although he had repeatedly spoken against armed internal revolts against the Kemalist regime.[3] In his revealing response, Nursi explained that "the Sword is to be used against the outside enemy; it is not to be used inside." Nursi sent the rebels an exhortation to "give up your attempt, for it is doomed to failure and may end up in the annihilation of thousands of innocent men and women because of a few criminals."[4]

Complexities and Contradictions: The Life of Sa'id Nursi

This blunt and unexpected response pointed to a consistent pattern that could be discerned in all phases of Nursi's life. In truth, Sa'id Nursi was never quite what he seemed. From the start, there was always something more to Sa'id Nursi than the exemplar of the Turkish fighter. The pattern of complexities emerged very early. First of all, this emblem of the Turkish warrior was not Turkish at all. Sa'id Nursi was ethnically a Kurd, a member of a linguistic and cultural minority community. He was born to Kurdish peasants in the village of Nurs in the Bitlis province of the Ottoman Empire. Nursi was the middle child of seven. His devout and humble parents raised him in a sun-dried brick house, typical of Kurdish villages.

However, it did not take long for this Kurdish peasant child to elude the future that should have been his. Nursi received his early education from a

Nagshbandi circle. The Nagshbandi is a major spiritual order of Sufism. In his formative years, these Sufi influences coexisted for Nursi with the effects of the example of an Ottoman administration that modeled itself on Western Europe. At a very young age, his intellectual gifts of the highest order also set him apart in unexpected ways. The boy had a photographic memory. While still a child, this son of peasants could read pages of complex religious works and reproduce them from memory later. By age fourteen, Nursi had committed to memory substantial parts of the major religious texts. More impressive still were his exceptional analytical skills. Nursi in his youth could do more than memorize. He reasoned with skill and confidence. By age sixteen, the adolescent Nursi would hold his own in vigorous dialogues with religious teachers in the wider circles around his village.

Word of the Kurdish prodigy spread. Tahir Pasha (1847–1913), the governor of Van Province in eastern Turkey, was intrigued by the stories. The governor invited the Kurdish youth to take up residence with him to continue his studies. In these privileged circumstances, Nursi first acquired Ottoman Turkish. Mastery of religious texts initially defined the intellectually talented young man. He seemed destined for a career as a traditional religious scholar.

However, just when that future seemed safely predictable, Nursi made yet another sharp turn. He came to understand that the most telling criticisms of a religious outlook were grounded in the sciences. In the library of Tahir Pasha, Nursi gained access to a trove of books and articles on the natural sciences that he had not encountered before. Nursi immersed himself in their study. This gifted auto-didact achieved a mastery of math and science that distinguished him once again. Core elements of Nursi's complex intellectual formation were at this point in place. It was clear that no unitary image would ever capture the distinctive and multifaceted intellectual profile of Sa'id Nursi.

The historical landscape through which Nursi navigated his 84 years was no more successful in offering a singular and consistent framing for his life story. Sa'id Nursi moved through life against the backdrop of a world fractured many times over and in multiple ways. He did so in the contradictory manner of an impassioned participant who was at the same time an astute observer. Nursi lived through tumultuous transformations that all left their mark on his development. He witnessed the encroachments of Western imperialism on the Islamic world, the decline and ending of the great Ottoman Empire, the global conflagration of World War I, and the disruptive eruptions of modern nationalisms. Importantly, Nursi saw firsthand the rise of the secular Turkish national state.

92   JUSTICE IN ISLAM

Confident and assertive, Sa'id Nursi plunged into all of these monumental developments. He found his footing at every turn. The Young Turk revolution of 1908 initially won Sa'id Nursi's support for its promise of reform of the empire. Nursi early on identified with the Ottoman Empire and suffered with its decline. Nursi's relationship with the Ottoman authorities did cloud, however, when their ambivalent attitude toward Islam became clear. Nevertheless, as we have seen, Nursi did fight for the empire on the Caucasian front during World War I. In the turmoil of World War I, he battled in the defense of the Anatolian heartland from virulent Western imperialisms.

However, the arresting narrative of Sa'id Nursi as engaged warrior was never the whole story. Nor was it by any means the central one in his long life. From the start, Nursi was a brave fighter with a difference. In the fighting on the World War I Caucasus front, Nursi was known to go into battle with a scribe at his side to record his thoughts. Whatever his circumstances, Sa'id Nursi was always registering his reflections. Those endless writings were consistently of Qur'anic inspiration. They were also early signs that the figure whom the Turkish people first came to know as a warrior was destined to become the greatest of Turkish Islamic scholars.

Unexpected turns consistently redefined Sa'id Nursi's life. The figure first known as an intrepid fighter made himself over the course of his life a world class advocate of nonviolence. As an Islamic scholar, Nursi built the intellectual foundations for nonviolence as a resistance strategy. Moreover, Nursi taught that nonviolence was much more than simply a strategy. It was a way of being in the world. A consistently positive and always compassionate message was the heart of the nonviolence that Nursi embraced and taught to his followers. It was where his nonviolent struggle always led.

From the margins, Nursi watched as the new secular state took shape. He witnessed the radical transformation of Turkish society. Atatürk moved quickly to weaken Turkey's Islamic identity. He demolished Islamic structures. Religious education was banned and replaced by secular curricula. The government seized control of religious endowments. Sufi lodges were closed. Judges of Islamic law in the country were fired. Attacks on manifestations of Islam were not limited to official structures. More personal domains were targeted as well. Hats were ordered in place of turbans or the traditional *fez* for men. The female *higab* (headscarf) was ridiculed and banned in public spaces. The calendar based on Islamic dating was replaced by the Gregorian calendar that referenced the birth of Christ. Even Friday as a Muslim holiday was abandoned in favor of the Western Saturday and Sunday weekend. The new regime ruled that daily calls to prayer could no longer be sounded in Arabic. The call was translated into Turkish. The Turkish version was imposed on mosques across the entire country.

As the coup de grâce, Atatürk engineered a radical revision in the way the Turkish language itself was written. Arabic letters were replaced by Latin letters. The Turks converted to Islam in the 900s. From that time on, their language had been written for hundreds of years with the Arabic alphabet. Familiarity with the Arabic script made it easier for the Turkish people to read the Qur'an and classical texts written in Arabic. Their Islamic identity was strengthened. The secular regime acted to break that link. Atatürk made the ultimate objective of the assault on Islam perfectly clear. The founder's secular commitment expressed itself in utter disdain for religion. Science, he believed, should replace religion. He famously mused that "I have no religion, and at times I wish all religions [would find their place] at the bottom of the sea." Atatürk condemned the faith as a "symbol of obscurantism." Islam, he averred, was the "enemy of civilization and science." He pronounced the faith a "putrefied corpse that poisons our lives."[5]

In the face of this sweeping assault, Nursi singlehandedly devised and advanced a resistance strategy that, over the long term and against the odds, preserved Islam in Turkey. It was an astonishing achievement. Yet, it should not be taken as the final characterization of Nursi's theory and practice of nonviolence. For Nursi, nonviolence did have a strategic importance. Yet, ultimately, nonviolence for Nursi was a principled rather than instrumental concept. It was in the final analysis an end rather than a means. It was a consistent choice of the humane and the positive over the expedient and negative. His vision as scholar and teacher aimed to bring his followers to the point where they could embrace and act according to this demanding precept when facing all of life's challenges.

The story of this distinctive Turkish conception of nonviolence is now largely forgotten. Sa'id Nursi is its chief protagonist. That oversight demands correction. With Atatürk ascendant, Islam as faith and culture was viewed as standing against progress. The Ottoman Empire, the last of the great Islamic empires, was reduced to *the sick man of Europe*. Islam itself was viewed as no more than the reactionary ideological cement that just barely held together fragments from a retrograde past. In this dominant narrative, the great drama of the early history of the Turkish republic centered on battles to overcome the backwardness that Islam had visited on the Turkish people. Islamic personalities and Islamic institutions were all cast as obstacles to be

94 JUSTICE IN ISLAM

overcome. The cold logic of Western Enlightenment thought provided the ideological energy for an unrelenting assault on Turkey's Islamic legacy.[6] In the West, this suppression of all manifestations of Turkey's Islamic past was uncritically celebrated.

The secular Turkey of Atatürk was the Turkey that first came into view for me in my Middle East graduate studies. Turkey in this framing had two dimensions. First, Turkey under Atatürk was projected as *the* exemplar for development theory, very much in vogue in the 1960s and 1970s. Second, a Westernized Turkey was cast as a bridge between East and West. In the Western political development literature, Turkey so understood could do no wrong. Even the troublesome coups that punctuated the early years in the political history of modern Turkey were magically transformed into a positive feature of the historical narrative of the making of the Turkish republic. I distinctly remember the peculiar talk in my political development courses at Harvard of Turkey's *modernizing coups.*

Atatürk was credited with creating the prototype for a larger category of important historical figures. He defined a class of *anti-Western Westernizers.* These conflicted figures included most notably Gamal Abdul Nasser of Egypt (1918–1970). As a type, such rulers combined a pro-Western civilizational orientation on key issues of domestic development with an independent nationalist and often anti-Western political stance.

Nursi's reaction to Atatürk's assault on Islam could not have been predicted. He made it clear, to the surprise of his followers, that he regarded the destructive work of the new secular order, including the hardships he suffered, as signs of God's blessings. From his unique angle of vision, he judged the dismantling of the structures of official Islam as a positive development. Nursi explained that the unintended consequence of the assault left popular Islam as the only extant form of belief that resonated with ordinary Turks. The popular Islam that survived, Nursi went on to note, was also the Islam most amenable to reshaping to meet the new demands of the age, as he understood them.

Through all the turmoil, Nursi remained the astute observer. He recorded his observations and the deep reflections they prompted. Under the most difficult circumstances, he gave priority to his writing. The *jihad* that most engaged him, as he himself expressed it, was the Qur'anic understanding of the *jihad of the word.* Few Islamic concepts have been more consistently distorted than *jihad* in Western parlance. The term is most often used, particularly in journalism, to refer to violent and often murderous actions by certain Muslims. Midstream Islamic intellectuals like Nursi understand the concept quite differently. They resist extremist appropriations of the concept. The noun *jihad* is derived from the root verb *jahada* which is best translated as "to exert (oneself) strenuously." With that fundamental meaning, the word *jihad* can properly be used for self-defense, as in the legitimate use of physical force in Islam. Nursi understood the term to refer as well to the greater spiritual and more personal struggles against one's own failing of heart and mind and societal shortcomings such as moral lapses and ignorance. The Qur'an points out myriad ways to struggle righteously and peacefully on the path of God.[7] Nursi's usage was insistently nonviolent in this Qur'anic sense.

This Qur'anic inspiration shaped Nursi's *jihad of the word* that gave expression to a set of core ideas that he elaborated over the course of his lifetime. He believed that the prolonged tumult that surrounded him indicated that the world was entering a new era in human history. This new period, he concluded, would require new ways of thinking and new forms of knowledge.

Nursi went deeper. He sketched in outline what general form the new thinking would take. Above all, he concluded it would be imperative to move beyond the presumed clash between religious and scientific worldviews. Nursi would have none of the blanket attacks on faith by extreme secularists. Nor would he tolerate the denigrations of science from retrograde religious circles. Nursi looked to a melding of religion and science as the hallmark of the required new thinking. Even as he deepened his own knowledge of the sciences, Sa'id Nursi reaffirmed his personal commitment to Islam in unequivocal terms: "I shall prove and demonstrate to the world that the Qur'an is an undying, inexhaustible Sun by updating it to meet modern life requirements![8] Nursi, the divine wisdom of the Qur'an would be indispensable to successfully navigating one's way through the new world that was coming into being. At the same time, Nursi understood fully that the emerging world would be shaped in critical ways by scientific advances. Nursi's fervent embrace of the guidance of the Qur'an did not in any way diminish for him the truths of science. To the contrary, Nursi believed that the wisdom of Qur'an and the teachings of modern science were fully compatible. He treasured both.

Science, in Nursi's view, made it possible to grasp more fully the truths of the Qur'an. He advanced the idea that what was needed to meet the needs of the new world was an unseamed fusion of religion and science. In his eyes, religion and science were complements that shaded into one another. They were not alternatives. With characteristic succinctness, he averred

96 JUSTICE IN ISLAM

that "the religious sciences are the light of the conscience; the modern sciences are the light of the mind; only on the combining of the two does the truth emerge."[9] In 1909, Nursi explained that "all believers are charged with upholding the Word of God, and at this time the most effective means of doing this is material progress. For the Europeans are crushing us under their tyranny with the weapons of science and industry." In conclusion, he wrote that "we shall therefore wage *jihād* with the weapons of science and industry on ignorance, poverty and conflicting ideas, the worst enemies of upholding the Word of God."[10]

There was a strong programmatic dimension to Sa'id Nursi's writings. In the *Risale*, he laid out three stages to guide the effort to give Islam an updated social expression. The initial and most critical stage looked to buttress *iman* (faith) of the individual Muslim. The second sought to enhance expressions of *iman* in *hayat* (social life). The third emphasized the implementation of *şeriat (Shari'ah)*. While the majority of Islamic activists and intellectuals focused on efforts in stage two and three, Sa'id Nursi made the first stage of *iman* his primary focus. He believed that with the *iman* of individuals strong, the rest would fall into place.

Nursi's way forward diverged profoundly from the path of advocates of political Islam. He did not aim to change or capture rulership for Islamic actors. Nor did he set the implementation from above of *Shari'ah* as the most pressing goal. Nursi inspired a faith movement, rather than a political one. Nursi looked most insistently to the deepening of the faith of individual believers. His grand abstractions found their clearest and most grounded expression in the projects for educational reform that he prioritized. He called for the teaching of the religious sciences in schools organized around the natural sciences. With parallel insistence, Nursi pronounced that the natural sciences must be taught in religious schools.

Sa'id Nursi understood that transformations on a massive scale would be necessary to realize the future of the Turkey he envisioned. New structures would be essential to guide the changes. The capstone of Nursi's educational reforms was to be the establishment of a university that he named *Medrestu'z Zehra* (the Resplendent Madrasa). Nursi characterized his work for the university as a prime example of his concept of *müsbet hareket* (positive action). Such action always aimed for building anew or repairing what was broken or corrupted. Even in the most difficult and contentious circumstances, Nursi urged constructive actions.

Nursi regarded this dream of a new university as the most important project of his life. He drafted the outlines of a university curriculum. It featured both scientific and religious instruction. The curriculum represented a distillation of his own prodigious learning. The students of *Medrestu'z Zehra* would be the architects and builders of the transformed Turkey that Nursi envisioned. To realize his vision, certain conditions would have to be bet. Islam itself must be available for renewal. A mass movement would be necessary to provide popular support for the revitalization of the faith. Equally important, there must be sufficient political freedom to allow for the remaking of societal structures in line with the re-envisioned Islam. Commitment to Islamic reform and realization of political constitutionalism would be the engines of transformation Nursi envisioned.

Initially, real progress was registered. In 1917, Nursi succeeded in bringing his ambitious dream to the receptive attention of the Ottoman Sultan Abdul Hamid II (1842–1918). Plans were ratified. Funding flowed. Construction began on the main university building. Then, World War I intervened. Only the cement for the foundation had been laid when the project was overwhelmed by the priorities of the war. The need for a mass movement was set aside. Nursi feared that he had failed in his most important life project.

Sa'id Nursi was wrong, although the successful outcomes were not the ones imagined. The edifice for his reforms had simply, by force of circumstances, taken a different and unanticipated form. The university as originally conceived was never realized. However, Nursi's enforced removal from public life did not by any means signal the end of his productivity. During the long years that followed, Nursi turned his enormous energies and talents inward. He retreated to a private realm of spirituality and reflection on the Qur'an. He suffered difficult conditions of periodic imprisonments and decades of exile. Yet, no matter the circumstances, Sa'id Nursi never interrupted his writings of Qur'anic inspiration. He completed *Risale i-Nur*, his 6,000-page plus Qur'anic commentary, under these adverse circumstances.

Risale i-Nur structures the legacy of Sa'id Nursi. It serves in multiple ways as the university he had been unable to build. *Risale* also inspired the mass movement to spread the message that his master work carried. It became the magnet that drew massive numbers to Sa'id Nursi. Out of those devotees, a mass movement took shape in an utterly unanticipated and essentially spontaneous and entirely distinctive way. Nursi's seductive writings were innovative in both content and style. Their effect was unprecedented. Nursi did not

98 JUSTICE IN ISLAM

follow any of the usual formulas for Qur'anic commentary. His reflections did not fall within the province of a *tafsir bi-al-riwaya* (commentary that relied primarily on the inherited classical sources). Nor did he follow the usual conventions for the alternative *tafsir bi-al-diraya* (commentary that relied on reason and interpretation). The usual patterns for all such familiar commentaries either followed the order of the chapters and verses of the Qur'an to offer elucidations of their meaning, or they provided more open-ended assessments of general Qur'anic themes.

In contrast to these standard approaches, Nursi offered a cascade of eclectic and often highly personal reflections in no easily discernible order. The collection of writings included counsel for his youthful followers, answers to questions they posed to him, philosophical analyses, theological speculations, and very intimate psychological insights into the human condition. Readers took from Nursi what they needed. What they needed was always there. The effect was intoxicating.

To this day, Nursi's complex writings provide this same intellectual and moral guidance. The thousands upon thousands who have looked to Nursi reached the master through the pages of his massive work. *Risale-i-Nur* became the lodestar of a mass movement, known as the *Nurcu*. In prison or exile, Nursi had no access to printing. His works were banned. The writings that would comprise the *Risale-i-Nur* were all handwritten by the master. They were then hand-copied by the legions of his followers. The *Nurcu* movement did not acquire copy machines until 1956. It is estimated that by then copies of *Risale* in the range of 600,000 had been made by hand and circulated.

Reading and discussion circles across Turkey spontaneously formed to study the smuggled pages of his master text. The delivery system for the hand-copied and hand-carried pages sent to the circles created a unifying network. It came to be known as *nur postacıları*, or "postmen of the Light." This delivery network established informal linkages between the independent reading and discussion circles. The unplanned result was the coordination of a movement. The connections were lateral and without a centralized hierarchy. It is no accident that Nursi often referred to his followers drawn together in this way as *öğrencilerin* (students). They in turn spoke of him with the honorific title of *ustaz* (teacher). Sa'id Nursi's *jihad of the word* succeeded in generating a university without walls. It also inspired a self-organizing, faith-based mass movement to bring to life an unconventional university.

The Islamic Alternative

In the Western development literature of my graduate training at Harvard, Atatürk stood out as the modernizer par excellence. It was quite impossible to conceive of an alternative path for the new Turkish state. I do, therefore, remember the precise moment and the exact location when the spell of that dominant narrative was broken for me. The year was 1980. I was on my way to the Turkish Republic of Northern Cyprus. This small Turkish-speaking country occupies just over one-third of the island of Cyprus. The remainder has a Greek character. When Greek and Turkish populations on Cyprus violently clashed, Turkey intervened in 1974 to protect the smaller Turkish populations and assure them of a territorial base in a divided Cyprus. That support enabled the Turkish Cypriots to establish a small state with a Turkish character. That state has never received international recognition. Today, you can enter Northern Cyprus only through Turkey. Over many years, I regularly joined an international group of progressive intellectuals, both Middle Eastern and Western, who met once a year in Northern Cyprus. All had an interest in the Middle East.

On the way to Northern Cyprus, there was always a layover in Istanbul. In the summer of 1980, I felt the full force of the grandeur of an imperial Islamic city. I admit to being completely transfixed by the splendor of the Blue Mosque. I had visited the mosque before. This time I experienced it. In that moment of transport, I learned something important. I came to fully appreciate one dimension of the dark genius of Atatürk. The "Father of the Turks" understood that it would be unnecessarily difficult to build a secular Turkey in the shadow of such spectacular architectural monuments of the capital city of a great Islamic empire. Atatürk wisely shifted republican Turkey's capital from dazzling imperial Constantinople to bland republican Ankara.

Paradoxically, I suspect it was immersion on a personal and intimate level in Nursi's work for psychological and spiritual insights that delayed my appreciation of his larger social and political importance. Turkey's modern history is most often told as the story of the triumph of the secular national narrative that appears to provide a comprehensive definition of Turkish identify. That definition masks as much as it reveals. Over time, the obfuscating haze of the secular nationalist narrative lifted, and the imposing figure of Sa'id Nursi come fully into view for me as both a transcending spiritual as well as a grounded national figure. With him, came appreciation for what

100 JUSTICE IN ISLAM

Turkish figures have contributed to Islamic mysticism. That experience had the character of a rediscovery of something that was there all the time.

Nursi had occupied an important space in my intellectual and emotional life for years. I immersed myself in his writings that focused on the personal rather than political level. The wisdom and penetrating psychological insight of Nursi's mystical writings made him a central figure in shaping the way I looked at the world. I initially paid little attention to his political role in Turkey, or his even place in the larger universe of Islamic mysticism. The relationship was personal. Nursi lived at first only in those interior and very private spaces, notably where the secrets of sexuality, friendship, and psychological distress reside.

No other figure, secular or religious, taught me more about what violence does to our humanity, especially violence in childhood. Through my intimate connection to Nursi, I engaged the dark mysteries of violence and its transcendence, as they are understood in Islam. Unlike Christianity, Islam does not harbor a wordless wish for a world without evil. Islam fully accepts the presence of evil in the world. In fact, the Islamic moral calculus, as Nursi brings it into view, centers on the idea of choice. For the warrior ascetic, the choice between good and evil has an indispensable place in the human world. Nursi teaches how the mind and spirit can be taught to develop awareness of moments of critical choice. Meaningful choice requires the presence of evil. Nursi offers guidance on the ways to lean to the good and away from the evil when the opportunity to make such choices arises.

What became clear to me in that moment of reflection in the Blue Mosque was that the story of Turkish Islam, dominated by Sa'id Nursi, deserves more attention than my restriction of Nursi to the private realm allowed. However, I very quickly discovered that there was no available script in the Western literature for telling Nursi's remarkable and multifaceted story. Historians with an Islamic viewpoint, in contrast, judge Nursi to be a major Islamic thinker with an importance that goes beyond Turkey. He thought deeply and wrote prolifically about educational and cultural reform in the Islamic world. He feared that secular thought was threatening not only Islamic cultural roots but the essentials of Islamic faith as well.

In Turkey, the practical movement that Nursi inspired focused on education and *tarbeyya* (upbringing). His followers founded countless schools with a strong Islamic character.[11] Nursi also single-handedly orchestrated a strategy of resistance that successfully shielded the faith from the violent onslaught of Turkey's secular founder. The Turkish experience under Nursi's guidance modeled the ways a protective shield against corrosive secularism could be created across the Islamic world.

Secular Extremism: The Dark Twin

There is no denying that the successes of Turkish secularism were real. Under Atatürk's leadership, the foundations of a modern economy and polity were built. There were significant and lasting advances in the social sphere, including stunning educational achievements and across the board gains for women. Atatürk is rightly celebrated for those exceptional accomplishments. However, it is nevertheless true that they also carried heavy costs. Those costs are not always acknowledged as fully as the successes. The striking gains were shadowed by painful excesses. Methods and timing often pushed the limits in extreme ways. Turks in the secular camp saw only the advances. Western observers, too, paid little attention to the unnecessary and painful exactions.

Secular extremism is the phantom figure of Western studies of the Islamic world. It is rarely engaged. It is as though extremism expresses itself exclusively in Islamic terms. In the Islamic studies literature, endless attention is lavished on violent Islamic movements. That spotlight is not without justification. The criminal deeds of Islamic extremists do rightfully command condemnation. Yet, the one-sided focus has unintended consequences. For one thing, the exorbitant attention comes much to the delight of Islamic extremist recruiters. The strength of their movements is consistently exaggerated. Their appeal is systematically enhanced by the massive coverage in the global media of their criminal depredations.

Meanwhile, with attention directed elsewhere, the dark twin of secular extremism remains in the shadows. In the standard accounts of modern Turkish history, it rarely receives careful study. Typically, the achievements of the secular nationalists are projected as the whole story. The very idea of extremism expressed in secular times is pushed into the background. The crimes of secularists in the name of the nationalist project that Atatürk advanced are not given anywhere near the attention they should have. Secularists are cast instead as heroic fighters for modernity. Their excesses are understood as the unintended consequences of the march of progress. Cast as collateral damage, those crimes are left to fade from memory. Fade they do.

Centrist Islamic scholars have rejected outright this standard Western treatment of violent secular extremism. The condemnations of extremism by

102 JUSTICE IN ISLAM

Islamic scholars are inclusive. The Qur'an sets the standard. Islam's holy book looks askance at all excess. Islam notably applies the same standards to both secular and Islamic immoderation. Islamic scholars persuasively conclude that both variants in their most extreme manifestations risk stains from the blood of innocents. In Islam, extremism is understood to have the potential of intruding into the most sacred activities. Even exaggerations in performing religious rituals come in for sharp criticism.

There are advantages to the Islamic perspective. Islam recognizes that one can be extreme in sexual restraint or even in prayer. Extremisms of this variety can most often be rectified, provided they are recognized and confronted. For example, an argument on firm Islamic ground can be made against celibacy as a violation of human nature that has little intrinsic virtue. It is for that very reason judged un-Islamic. Even excessive time spent in prayer or other external rituals of the faith can be rightly criticized as an excess with negative social consequences. In Islam, such behavior is judged to drain energy from the productive work for the common good that Islam encourages.

Costs of the Secular Nationalist Triumph

The toll of Atatürk's secular nationalist strategy is more shocking than generally acknowledged. The number of victims of Atatürk's vision of an ethnically homogeneous Turkish state on the classic Western model is staggering. It is reasonably estimated that more than one million Armenians perished in the effort to purge minorities and homogenize the population of modern Turkey. At least a quarter of a million Assyrians also died in the making of a secular Turkey "cleansed" of large minority populations. These mind-numbing tragedies were compounded by the expulsion of more than a million Greek Orthodox Anatolians. Kurdish identity in Turkish lands was also harshly repressed. Turkey's founder understood that for ordinary people, massive transgressions on this order are almost impossible to imagine. They are so beyond comprehension that perpetrators can repeatedly deny or simply ignore them with impunity.[12]

While homogenizing the population of the new secular state demographically, Atatürk launched a frontal cultural attack on Turkey's Islamic identity. Acidic characterizations of the faith prepared the ground for the abolition of the Islamic Caliphate in 1924. The caliphate had from the year 632 legitimized the Sunni community as the direct descendent of the Prophet Muhammad.

That venerable institution symbolically unified the Sunni world. It did so in aspiration, though not in actual practice.

Still worse was the psychological harm deliberately inflicted on believers. Atatürk forced the Turkish people to see themselves through the deprecating eyes of the West. He identified as objects of Western ridicule the most intimate and treasured aspects of their collective lives. Objects of denigration notably included distinctive elements of their traditional dress, their language, and their Islam. In Atatürk's view, the historic institution of the caliphate could only have been "a laughingstock in the eyes of the civilized world enjoying the blessings of science."[13] Hurtful actions matched the viciousness of these words. Mosques were not simply abandoned. They were turned to demeaning purposes. Sacred spaces where Turkish Muslims had sought guidance to live in accord with their highest moral aspirations were turned into stables and warehouses. The conscious aim to degrade those spaces could not have been more clearly expressed. For the Sufi Muslim minority, the assault was even worse. Sufi rituals and gatherings were outlawed. Sufi lodges, monasteries, and meeting halls were seized.

Sa'id Nursi stood undaunted by the calculated contempt of Atatürk's violent secular onslaught. He acknowledged the overwhelming material strength that Atatürk commanded. However, he did so with the insight that the fight for the faith was ultimately an internal one. Nursi reasoned that Islam's real strength in the world would depend on its living presence in the hearts and minds of ordinary Turks. He understood that the struggle to preserve the faith could be waged successfully in spaces out of the reach of superior secular military and political power.

Sa'id Nursi addressed all of his writings to these critical interior struggles that he identified as primary. Whatever the external imbalance of forces, Nursi taught that Turkish Muslims as individuals could triumph by simply guarding and nurturing the faith in the interior of their lives. By doing so, he expressed the conviction that al nas (the common people) could secure Islam's presence in Turkey, despite the superior material power of the secularists.

Apostle of Nonviolence

On a broader canvas, Sa'id Nursi pioneered a distinctive *nonviolent* Islamic resistance strategy. It had deep spiritual underpinnings. Those Turks who

104 JUSTICE IN ISLAM

rejected the blood-and-soil nationalism of Atatürk and sought to protect Turkey's Islamic character found a way forward with Nursi's guidance. For them, Nursi was as important as Gandhi was for Indians who fought for independence. He stands alongside Martin Luther King, Jr., who led black Americans and their allies in struggles for racial equality. Nursi, like both Ghandi and King, taught lessons of love and nonviolence. Like them as well, his ideas, for all the strength of their contextual roots, had universal signif-icance. Nursi deserves a place at their side as a *great soul* and champion of nonviolent resistance. For many, it will be unthinkable that an Islamic resistance leader could have made such a contribution. The confected po-larity of violent Islamist and progressive secularist screens that possibility from view.

Nursi's approach rested on two concepts: the *jihad* of the word and *positive action*. Resistance would be nonphysical. It would always include a struggle *for* something. Adversaries were understood in theological terms. They represented derivations from philosophical materialism and the atheism it engendered. Nursi offered his writings as providing the spiritual means to counter these negative forces. Relying on a distinctive blend of rigorous logic and abiding faith, Nursi sketched a path to advance in the face of the daunting power of secularism mobilized by Mustafa Kemal.

Enemies would be engaged. However, battles with them would not be fought on the grounds that secularism defined. Nursi insisted that the way of Islam was inherently nonviolent. Nursi's admonitions to those who sought to enlist him in violent struggles were blunt. He simply refused to endorse them.

Nursi called always for *positive action* rather than a resort to force to combat the damage that materialism and its ideological offshoots caused. In an age of science and civilization, he looked to a long-term strategy that relied on a commitment to *both* faith and scientific logic. Nursi generated two resources for the realization of his vision of change. First and most im-portantly, his writings, collected in *Risale-i Nur*, elaborated his message of spirituality and nonviolence, with some 6,000 pages of nuance and detail. Secondly, Nursi's works inspired the *Nurcu* mass movement. The movement would serve as a repository and guardian of Nursi's thinking. Nursi placed the task of rational interpretation at the very heart of Islam. Activists of *Nur* would bring distillations of his ideas to ordinary Turks.

The *Nurcu* movement had spread rapidly in the wake of the dissolution of Sufi brotherhoods in 1925. They sought—and seek—to revive Islam in Turkey by reconciling the faith with modern sciences. Activists of the *Nurcu* are adept at using mass communication as a vehicle for Nursi's ideas. The *Nurcu* movement does not hesitate to embrace many concepts associated with the West, including nationalism and democracy. At the same time, adherents give special emphasis to the concept of the Islamic community as both a national and global reality.

The animating idea of the movement is conviction that the unchanging Qur'an must be continually interpreted anew to understand its meaning for endlessly changing human circumstances. Activists protect that commitment, whatever challenges they face. The secular state harassed the movement in the 1960s and 1970s, even as its membership grew. Fragmentation set in during the 1970s and 1980s. Of the offshoots, the most prominent is the Gülen movement, that has recently clashed with the Turkish government of Recep Tayyib Erdogan as an alternative moderate Islamic movement of reform.[14]

The aggressive secular nationalism of Atatürk harnessed the powers of the nascent Turkish republic for a full-scale assault on Islamic institutions. Faced with unrelenting attack that extended to Islam itself, Sa'id Nursi made a difficult strategic judgment. He instructed his followers that the physical forces Islamic activists could mobilize would be no match for those the secular nationalists already commanded. Moreover, a civil war in the wake of all that the Turkish people had suffered in World War I was intolerable to Nursi. In place of confrontation, Nursi called for a strategic retreat into the spiritual realms of human experience. He reminded Turkish believers that the real citadels of their faith were within. Islam would find its most important protection in the hearts and minds of the faithful. Attacks on the external manifestations of Turkish Islam, such as the countless Turkish mosques, would not cause the crippling damage that secularists imagined. Turkey's justly famed mosques, large and small, were not core constituent elements of Islam itself. Nursi understood that Islam could thrive without them. He reminded followers that the teachings of the Qur'an and Sunnah instruct Muslims that all the earth is a mosque.[15]

Nursi projected confidence that the faith could flourish in the recesses of minds that knew the Qur'an and hearts that embraced its core value of justice. Sa'id Nursi understood that in those protected interior spaces, all of Islam's highest values could find refuge. The guardians who would matter most would be *al nas*. Ultimately, Nursi understood that prospects for the success of resistance resided with ordinary Muslims. The common people would defend Islam with their everyday spiritual commitments and practices.

106 JUSTICE IN ISLAM

Enter the Muslim Jesus

The spirit of the Muslim Jesus played a major large role in Nursi's argument for a strategic retreat to the spiritual realm in the face of the superior power of Atatürk's secularism. The Muslim Jesus looms large in Nursi's long-term thinking. The material superiority of the secularists, he believed, would not be permanent. The imbalance would be rectified on the spiritual plane. To explain that transformation, Nursi set before his readers the picture of the Muslim Prophets Muhammad and Jesus joining hands in a march to an era of transcendent piety and peace. In his theological writings, Nursi discussed at length the importance of the "second coming" of Jesus. Nursi's complex theology centered in important ways on a notion of the melding of Christianity and Islam made possible by the second coming of Jesus. The Muslim Jesus would return to earth as a just ruler in partnership with Islam's Prophet Muhammad. That hope transfixed Turkish believers.[16]

Turning to the Qur'an, Sa'id Nursi found reassurance for his followers that God would surely answer the call of His creations who desperately needed His help. Nursi taught that God would open a pathway to save people from the injustice of all systems of disbelief. God would bring them to a richer understanding of the Message.

Nursi's view of Islam's spiritual power was expansive. He projected that the Islamic world would find a way to prevail over worldly corruption and tyranny. Sincere believers, he taught, would communicate the values of Islam to the whole world. They would do so in the spirit of the humility and kindness of the Muslim Jesus. The example of the Prophet Jesus, son of the venerated Mary, would guide humankind from darkness to the light.

To develop his vision, Nursi drew on the Qur'anic characterization of the Prophet Jesus. Jesus's virgin birth is affirmed in Islam's holy book. So, too, are the miracles of healing attributed to the son of Mary, as Islam's Jesus is known in the Qur'an. The Qur'an explains that the Muslim Jesus was not crucified, as Christianity teaches. Rather, Mary's son was raised unscathed to heaven.[17] Nursi also reminded his followers that the Qur'an speaks clearly and in detail of Jesus's return to earth. This second coming would be in the first instance a sign of end-times.[18] Nursi positioned his treatment of the consequences of Jesus's return at the very heart of the contributions that made him the greatest Turkish Islamic scholar of the twentieth century.[19]

In the *Risale-i Nur* collection, Nursi places Jesus's second coming in the context of the cosmic struggle between belief and disbelief. The threats to

Islam and Christianity from materialist and naturalist thinking are judged perilous. The triumph of secular belief systems, Nursi warns, would cause profound disorder on earth. In their most extreme expressions, ideologies of disbelief represent a complete rejection of God as creator. The unbelievers hold that all life forms, including human life, result from accidental interactions of nonliving matter.

Sa'id Nursi looked to a union of Islam and Christianity to triumph over such dangerous disbelief. He taught that the strengthened faith would draw on the spirit of the Muslim Jesus. Nursi understood the second coming of Jesus as a *divine mercy*. He taught that Christianity in its merger with Islam would be cleansed of all superstition and distortion. A purified Christianity would meld with the truths of Islam. Nursi saw in the Muslim Jesus the figure of the "protector" and "helper" from God of whom the Qur'an spoke in answer to the calls of those oppressed by unbelievers: "Lord, take us out of this place whose inhabitants are oppressors! Give us a protector from You! Give us a helper from You!"[20] Nursi explained that Jesus, standing hand in hand with the Prophet Muhammad, would be that protector and helper. Nursi drove home the core lesson that neither Islam nor Christianity could triumph alone. As a unified force, however, they would emerge victorious in the cosmic battle with disbelief.

Nursi reasoned that together, Christians and Muslims represented the majority of humankind. United, victory over secularism would be possible. The triumph would have immense theological significance. The convergence of the two faiths would yield, in Nursi's stunning phrase, *the true religion*. Nursi's conception of that fusion was brought to life by the image of Muhammad and Jesus, hand in hand. Nursi explained that this union would be achieved because Jesus would rule with the Qur'an, God's final message to humanity. Christians who fused Islam with their own beliefs would serve in the front ranks with Muslims in the battles against the forces of disbelief.

On the momentous occasion of the second coming, Nursi foretold that God would uplift those Christians who struggled at Jesus's side to bring the values of the "true religion" to all humankind. With this unique spiritual strength, they would rout the unbelievers. Nursi believed that Jesus would then be recognized by all as the blessed "mercy" sent to all humankind. Just as Jesus would protect and guide all believers, the believers would also give wholehearted support to Jesus in his work on behalf of God. These believers would provide the answer to Jesus's haunting question recorded in the Qur'an: "Who will be my helpers [in my work] for God?"[21] Nursi reminded

108 JUSTICE IN ISLAM

his followers that the Qur'an promises that warriors in this epic struggle would be rewarded in a most uplifting way:

> God has sent down a reminder to you, a Messenger reciting God's Clear Signs to you to bring those who have faith and do righteous actions out of the darkness into the Light. Whoever has faith in God and acts rightly, We will admit him into Gardens with rivers flowing beneath them. He will remain in them for ever and ever. God has provided for him excellently.[22]

Nursi concludes his elaboration of the meaning of the second coming with an expression of gratitude to God for giving believers this opportunity to serve the higher purposes of his final message to humanity. They would find their reward both in this world and in the world of peace and piety to come.

What made Nursi's message of nonviolence so extraordinary was the ferocity of the assault on the faith waged by the army of secular extremists that Atatürk mobilized. To this day, whenever Islam is under attack, one can hear the mocking words of Atatürk and their echoes from the legions of his secular followers. Few have matched his vituperative attacks on the faith. Contemporary Western Islamophobia, for all the hurt it causes, comes nowhere close to the viciousness and deadly disrespect of Atatürk's assault on Turkish Islam. Yet, Islam in Turkey survived. It is strong today. That improbable survival owes an immense but only rarely understood debt to the complex figure of Sa'id Nursi. The importance of his remembrance, it should be remembered, extends beyond the Islamic world.

The Complexities of the Life of Sa'id Nursi

Sa'id Nursi himself created the most instructive template for all subsequent biographies of his own life. There were, he announced, two Sa'ids, the old and the new. The old Sa'id was the soldier and ambitious public figure. The new Sa'id would become the Islamic ascetic and prodigious scholar.

It was the new Sa'id who would define Nursi's legacy. In the end, it was the richness of Nursi's inner life that allowed the new Sa'id Nursi to withdraw from the world into breathtaking scholarly productivity. Nursi's massive commentary on the Qur'an was the single factor most instrumental in rescuing Turkish Islam. Nursi's insightful record of the interior battles he engaged and the choices he made represented his most durable life achievement.

It was Sa'id Nursi, mystic, scholarly ascetic, and apostle of nonviolence, whose influence reached across Turkey and the Islamic world beyond. A strong tradition of the Prophet calls Muslims to the belief that in every century God will send a religious figure as a *mugadid* (an Islamic scholar who is thought to appear to renew Islam). The Prophet had warned that the Word of Islam would suffer distortion after his passing. Like the other great monotheisms, the faith of the *ummah* would witness a fading of its message. In response, God would act once every century to provide a figure to rescue the faith from this anticipated decline.

Many Turks and non-Turks as well have identified Sa'id Nursi as the modern-day Islamic figure with the strongest claim as *mugadid* for the twentieth century. All prophets, the Qur'an instructs, have equal weight. They all take their place as invigorators of religious law. Turkish scholars, influenced by Nursi, argued that the special closeness between the Prophets Muhammad and Jesus, the son of Mary, merited greater emphasis. It was Nursi's striking image of Jesus and Muhammad hand in hand that captured the imagination of Turkish believers.

The Theology of Choice: Nursi's Fiction

The Qur'an was Nursi's constant companion in his long years of exile. Nursi was generally deprived of all books, except for the Qur'an. Islam's holy book proved more than sufficient to stimulate his creativity. In addition to his celebrated Qur'anic commentary, Nursi generated a body of fiction, primarily in the form of short stories. Study of the Qur'an filled the deep wellsprings of his spirituality. Words mattered to Nursi. The words of the Qur'an mattered most of all. They were the words of God. Sa'id Nursi lived all his life in their thrall. From that place of transcendence, he spun endless stories.

Nursi's short stories have the character of simple tales *and* grand myths. Nursi's fiction flowed freely from Qur'anic inspiration. Cryptic words and phrases were lifted from the sacred text in what only appeared to be a random way. These Qur'anic fragments triggered Nursi's very personal reflections on the ways the divine touches the human. Some of the phrases had become so much a part of everyday life that they received little conscious attention. Nursi rescued such phrases from the ordinary. He restored the spiritual force the Qur'an had given them.

110 JUSTICE IN ISLAM

Nursi's reflections most often took the form of what seemed to be very accessible short stories. It did not take readers long, however, to understand that the fiction offered more than an engaging surface simplicity. The stories provided a window on the underlying complexities of life itself. Those complexities found clearest expression at moments of choice. Nursi explored some of the most troubling dimensions of human experience. One could learn from Nursi how violent trauma, especially in childhood, left debilitating scars for a lifetime. The lessons Nursi taught applied equally to the traumas of the individual and to the trials of a nation. Damaging humiliation, Nursi made clear, took a variety of forms. A child could be ridiculed and physically abused. An occupied people could be humiliated and even casually murdered by settlers. Such was the history of the indigenous peoples of North America. Such was the fate of the Palestinian people. Those who dominated, for their part, could suffer the debilitating consequences of uninvited remembrance of their own crimes of genocide and enslavement. Nursi understood how such dark shadows could corrode dreams and trouble the soul, long after their apparent passing.

Nursi wrote with understanding of the lingering pain of past trauma that torment the individual and national psyche. Sa'd Nursi also celebrated the curative power of awareness. He worked to bring humanity to an understanding of the healing power of exertions of the conscious human mind. Left without healing intervention, he explained, past trauma could reverberate for the lifetime of an individual and the history of a nation. The wounds of the past are reopened each time fresh assaults occur. Nursi showed how, in this way, the present takes on the dismal coloration of the tormented past. As always, Sa'id Nursi went deeper. He clarified the ways that simple awareness of that damaging cycle of haunting memories could itself be the beginning of transcendence. Awareness could be the first step to blocking the endless recycling of past blows to the spirit. Very much in the mystic tradition, Nursi used his simple stories to instruct on the ways the conscious human mind could be taught to contain the echoes of past suffering.

At the heart of Nursi's teachings was the insight that an engaged and aware spirituality could move one beyond past wounds. God gave to humanity the capacity to choose. Through his short stories, Nursi insisted that one could make the choice to live in the present. He called on the wounded to make the decision to insist that the present be a platform for a future that would rise above, rather than replicate, a damaged past. Through his "simple" stories, Nursi reflected on the ways a changed history of tomorrow could be written by the conscious choices made today. Simple acknowledgment of the continuing effects of past harms had the effect of opening the possibility of acting to break the cycle of their damaging reverberations. He taught that the present provided the only site from which pain could be assuaged. The past is too late. The future is not yet here. Nursi helped his readers to rescue the fertile present from the sterile phantoms of a crippling past and a future not yet within reach.

Nursi urges the conscious embrace of wounds suffered. Awareness of the reality of the damage done must be registered. It must not, however, be reified and treated as a permanent fixture. The effects of past wounds could not be undone. They could, however, be transcended. In Nursi's view, there were always new and different choices that could move one beyond a debilitating past and truncated future. For new possibilities to work their palliative effects, Nursi insisted, they must be imbued with compassion for one's own suffering. One must learn to use the present to sit with one's own pain.

Yet again, Nursi plumbed deeper. He suggested how appreciation for the suffering of the self could be made a prism to better understand the pain of others. To see pain as inherent in the human condition is to be relieved of the debilitating sense that one has been singled out for suffering. Nursi's fictional treatment of these truths was realistic about the human condition. It was at the same time hopeful about the human capacity to acknowledge and rise above suffering.

The key elements of Nursi's fictional engagements with the history of tomorrow drew on the deepest springs of the theology of Islam, apprehended in a mystical mode. In Islam, Nursi reminded his readers, the realities of choice, conscious decision, and the striving for righteousness are at the very heart of what it means to be human. The Islamic theological tradition, as interpreted by Nursi, teaches that our experience in this world is a time of testing. The existence of evil is essential if that testing is to be fully meaningful. At the same time, the core Islamic value of freedom insists that humankind always does have critical choices to make between good and evil. The Qur'an does provide, after all, that even belief in divinity is a choice open to humanity.[23] The choice of the good, he taught, is most righteous when it is made in the presence of such evils as tyranny and corruption.

Nursi's fiction best captures his understanding that for an awakened mind and responsive soul, there is always a fork in the road forward that opens to radically different ways of being in the world. All of Nursi's fictional stories are structured by this core template of human experience. The idea of choice

112 JUSTICE IN ISLAM

for Nursi finds both pragmatic and speculative expressions. Nursi teaches that the Islam of the Qur'an teaches that where there is the prospect of darkness, there is also the possibility of light. Where there is evil, there is good. Where there is pain, there is well-being. Navigation of these choices gives each individual life its distinctive character. Small decisions have their influence in the ways they contribute to the creation of the larger patterns of one's life. They may relate to the practical, such as the choice of a profession or the acceptance of such a choice made by others for us. They may pertain to our emotional selves, such as the choice of a friend or a life partner. They may be more abstract and represent the modes of thinking we characteristically and most often subconsciously choose to deploy. Nursi insists on self-reflection. He asks that we question what distinctive blend of reason and emotion characteristically shapes our own choices. At the most basic level, where do we choose to look? On what do we choose to focus? What can our choices tell us about the history of tomorrow we are crafting?

Conclusion: The Power of the Conscious Mind

Sa'id Nursi taught that a critical effect of the centrality of choice to human experience is the cultivation of awareness of the power of the conscious mind. Awareness of the workings of the mind in exercising our scope for freedom opens to a heightened awareness of the power of the human mind more generally. Inevitably, the discovery is made that the mind is susceptible to complex processes of learning. Awareness and understanding of the possibilities of learning illuminate the ways the powers of the mind can be harnessed to the process of the autonomous self-creation of an individual and a community. There is a psychological dimension to the work of all the major scholars of the Islamic Awakening. However, Nursi most effectively claimed and explored that shared territory as his own. These psychological reflections are the gateway to the writings of Sa'id Nursi. For many, those explorations are the most enduring part of his legacy.

As a bold and courageous fighter, Nursi in his young manhood mastered the arts of war. That image lingered. As a thinker, he explored not only the Qur'an, but the complex workings of the human mind and the depths of the human spirit to which the Qur'an spoke. These interior explorations gave his theological work a psychological and spiritual dimension that markedly extended its reach. Nursi's interior life was as dynamic and creative as the persona of a fearless fighter that first defined Sa'id Nursi in Turkey and the Islamic world beyond. With remarkable self-awareness and understanding, Sa'id Nursi shared this interior life with his legions of followers and admirers. Sai'd Nursi had the mind of a rationalist committed to the sciences. He also had the spirit of an Islamic mystic who understood the limits of reason. It was the unfettered and meticulously recorded explorations of that mind and that spirit that earned Sa'id Nursi his title of "Wonder of the Age."

6

Grand Ayatollah Muhammad Hussein Fadlallah

Poet to Strategic Visionary

Failed assassination attempts played a substantial role in enhancing the mystical charisma of the Grand Ayatollah Muhammad Hussein Fadlallah. There were many. The most deadly came in 1985. Saudi money and CIA expertise came together to plan and execute the plot. A powerful car bomb, modeled on the work of Islamic extremists, was strategically parked in front of the Ayatollah's residence. A final tally of the victims was delayed due to the extent of the damage. Best estimates place the number of dead at just over 80. The Ayatollah was not among them. The victims were primarily women, children, and other innocents from the neighborhood. The Ayatollah himself missed his appointment with assassination. He was delayed by a stop to pray at a small mosque on his way home. Conversation with those who prayed with him slowed the Ayatollah further.

Saudis and Americans cooperated in the failed plot. The Saudis supplied several million dollars as funding. The CIA, led by William Joseph Casey (1981–1987), took operational responsibility for implementation.[1] A 440-pound car bomb was placed along the short route between Fadlallah's residence and a nearby mosque where he often prayed. Fadlallah's very vocal and highly influential support for the Iranian Revolution and Iran more generally provided all the motivation the Saudis needed. The justifications for the Americans to murder the revered Ayatollah came down to unsubstantiated accusations of support for terrorism. The Ayatollah was blamed for involvement in the taking of hostages in Beirut in the early 1980s and the bombing of marine barracks in Lebanon on October 23, 1983, that killed 307 people, including 241 US and 58 French military personnel, six civilians, and two attackers.

The Ayatollah denied these accusations. In lieu of hard evidence, American accusers relied on the record of the Ayatollah's frequent denunciations of

Justice in Islam. Raymond William Baker, Oxford University Press. © Oxford University Press 2022.
DOI: 10.1093/oso/9780197624975.003.0006

Israel as a colonial settler state and the United States as its major backer. Overlooked by the plotters was the simple fact that, in the eyes of much of the world, the Ayatollah's descriptions were accurate on both counts. Moreover, denunciations, no matter how public, frequent, and fervent, do not even come close to evidence. They are provocative and they did heighten frustrations for a nuclear-armed regional hegemon and a superpower with a massive nuclear arsenal and essentially unchallenged conventional military forces. In the event, frustrations overwhelmed legal restraints and rational thinking. Followers of Fadlallah can be forgiven for seeing the hand of God in the forces that saved their beloved Ayatollah.

The Lebanese Setting

The Grand Ayatollah Muhammad Hussein Fadlallah (1935–2010) appeared as a giant in Lebanon. Short in stature, he was a towering spiritual and intellectual presence in that small and beautiful land. It is hard to imagine a more perfect setting for the Ayatollah than the country he made his home for some four decades. Lebanon is at once international and traditional. Coastal Beirut is perhaps the most cosmopolitan city in the Middle East. It is no less important that the spectacular Lebanese mountainsides shelter very traditionalist village communities of all colorations.

The Lebanese population of roughly 6 million has a kaleidoscopic quality of stunning complexity. Religion is the most useful metric for the ultimately impossible task of succinctly describing the Lebanese people. The Lebanese constitution recognizes some 18 religious groupings. Lebanon is Muslim. Lebanon is Christian. Lebanese Muslims are Sunni, except for those roughly equal or more in number who are Shi'i, like the Ayatollah Fadlallah himself. Lebanese Christians are often thought of as Maronite, except for those who are not. Those others identify themselves as Eastern Orthodox, Melkite Catholic, Protestant, and diverse other Christian denominations non-native to Lebanon like Armenian Orthodox, Armenian Catholic, Syriac Orthodox, Syriac Catholic, Roman Catholic, Chaldean, Assyrian, and Coptic. Taking a wide view, the Lebanese are 95% either Muslim or Christian of some sect, except for the important and distinctive Druze community that is neither. The Druze self-identify as *al Muwahhideen* (believers in one God). The Druze community, comprising just over 5% of the Lebanese population, is centered in the mountainous areas to the east and south of Beirut.

116 JUSTICE IN ISLAM

The Ayatollah Fadlallah's own multifaceted identity suited perfectly the complexity that is the Lebanese people. Iraqi by birth, the Ayatollah established his base in Lebanon's neglected Shi'i communities. He brought with him the luster of a family lineage directly descended from the Prophet Muhammad. Fadlallah was impossible to ignore. From Lebanon, he cast an imposing shadow across all the Arab lands of the Middle East and beyond. The Ayatollah always projected a confident and engaged presence. At the same time, he somehow held himself just out of reach.

Lebanon was the land of his family origins. However, Najaf in Iraq was the place where Fadlallah was born and grew up. Both Lebanon and Iraq maintained a lifelong claim on the Ayatollah. Such duality provided a template for contrasts that were threaded through all of Fadlallah's life. The surface accessibility that the Grand Ayatollah Fadlallah projected screened a multifaceted and ultimately elusive persona. Over time, Fadlallah revealed himself as poet, Islamic scholar, and humanitarian, He also completely owned the very different roles of political actor and world-class strategic thinker. Fadlallah himself offered no grand synthesis of these contrasting and at times clashing identities. They simply coexisted under the canopy of a charismatic Ayatollah of great personal charm.

In 1928 Fadlallah's father, the religious scholar Sayyid 'Abd al-Ra'uf Fadlallah, migrated to Iraq from the small village of Aynata in southern Lebanon. He aimed to pursue advanced Islamic studies in the great Iraqi centers of Shi'i learning. The family settled in Najaf, south of Baghdad. Fadlallah was born there on November 16, 1935. He spent his childhood and adolescence immersed in the deeply religious atmosphere of this Shi'i holy city. Ties to Lebanon, however, were never severed. Fadlallah at times returned to the family homeland with his father. On those visits to Lebanon, Fadlallah presented himself as a theology student from Najaf. However, he left an impression that went beyond his impressive command at a young age of the core religious texts. Those who met him also remember the youthful Fadlallah for his recitations of original and inventive poetry.

Fadlallah was, even in early manhood, an Islamic scholar with a difference. From an early age and in a great many dimensions, Fadlallah consistently stepped forward as a figure defined by dualities held in creative tension. The Ayatollah's seductive playfulness as a poet and orator owed most to his Lebanese roots. Najaf in Iraq, on the other hand, gave Fadlallah's character its gravitas. The scholarly religiousness, so central to his mature personality, took shape in an organic way from his years of Islamic studies in Najaf. The tension between Fadlallah's identity as poet and orator and his deep religiousness was generative. It sparked his creativity.

As a speaker, Fadlallah was transporting. His sermons adhered to an organizing template replicated in the larger body of his scholarly work. Each sermon opened with citations of God's words from the Qur'an or commentary of the Prophet Muhammad from the *Sunnah* (record of all the deeds and words of the Prophet). Verses of the Qur'an and selections from the *hadiths* (sayings of the Prophet that illuminate his thoughts and actions) always grounded the message of his sermons, just as they anchored his scholarship. The sacred texts were given superb expression in Fadlallah's incomparable speaking voice. Fadlallah's exquisite classical Arabic had a captivating effect. His recitations of the sacred texts seemed to bring the inaccessible within reach. Followers in the thousands flocked to his Friday sermons. Listeners reported finding themselves carried to a place of otherworldly beauty and embracing spirituality.

Apposite Qur'anic verses and *hadith* showcased Fadlallah's masterful command of Islam's foundational texts. As soon as that impression was fixed, a shift would occur. With the sacred texts still sounding in their ears, listeners were invited to engage major issues of their own time and place. Fadlallah gradually allowed colloquial Arabic to take over. The subject of the sermon would shift full force to the real-world challenges of everyday life. Fadlallah knew the nuances and dramas of those stories of ordinary Muslims as well as he knew the sacred texts. He treated them with a parallel respect for the joy as well as the pain and disappointment they carried. He preserved their integrity in the retelling. That sonorous voice became the voice of an Ayatollah as witness and healer. As a master of the Islamic tradition, Fadlallah demonstrated that the sacred texts offered not only soaring spirituality, but also the practicality of down-to-earth guidance to meet everyday challenges.

The Muslim Jesus as Inspiration and Guide

With this duality of the sacred and the worldly, Fadlallah invoked the spirit of the Muslim Jesus. As noted earlier, the humble Jesus of the Muslims is revered as a prophet. He is also the fully human son of Mary. Jesus gives Islam's worldly dimension its most empathetic expression. The gentle Jesus is known in Islamic tradition for his boundless love, spirituality, and reverence

118   JUSTICE IN ISLAM

for justice. References to the Muslim Jesus run throughout Fadlallah's most important works. More often than not, the references to Jesus in Fadlallah's works are coded. The Prophet Jesus is only occasionally mentioned directly by name. Most references are made instead to Abu Dharr al Ghifari. For Fadlallah, the Prophet Muhammad's companion served as a representative of the Muslim Jesus.[2] Fadlallah consistently introduced Abu Dharr into the narrative as a figure with a deep knowledge of Islam in both its most spiritual *and* more mundane dimensions. Abu Dharr grasped not only the essentials of the faith, but also the ways it worked its uplifting effects in compromised social worlds and murky political settings.

Fadlallah's deep and resonant voice held the key to his ability to enhance spiritual messages in ways that spoke real-world experiences. His pronouncements were grounded and yet, at the same time, the vehicles to express an intense spirituality. Analytically, it was possible to identify a thread that explained how this union of opposite effects was achieved. The Islamic prophet Jesus stood at the heart of the mystery. An explicit invocation was often unnecessary. The distinctive character of the Islam for which the Ayatollah spoke achieved precisely that effect. Fadlallah's Islam was always the Islam evoked by the spirit of the Muslim prophet Jesus. It was as well the Islam of Abu Dharr al Ghifari.

Abu Dharr expressed Islam's truths in terms accessible to ordinary people. Abu Dharr's example taught that all one had to do to be a faithful Muslim was to listen to one's own conscience while engaging the sacred texts feelings of fellowship naturally inhabit the human heart. Those who found Islam in their own hearts, Abu Dharr's example suggested, would inevitably express their faith by standing with the poor. To be a Muslim was to be mindful and loving toward the least in the human community. At the same time, Muslims who grasped the deeper meaning of the Message would naturally be the enemies of corruption and tyranny. Abu Dharr heard in the incomparable language of the Qur'an an insistent call to heed the yearnings of the human heart. Hearts whispered to believers that oppression in all its forms was to be resisted.

Lest this meaning of Fadlallah's coded references to the Prophet's beloved companion be overlooked, the Ayatollah authored a brief study on Abu Dharr's importance.[3] He explained forthrightly how central the figure of Abu Dharr was to his own understanding of the faith. Fadlallah characterized the beloved companion as a venerable symbol of the core Islamic value of justice. In the Qur'an, the word for "justice" occurs almost as frequently as the word for "God." Refinements of the meaning of justice pervade the Qur'an. The frequent references allow complex elaborations of this core Islamic concept. They bring to the fore an integral connection between justice and freedom, on the one hand, and compassion, on the other. Seen through the person of Abu Dharr, justice most clearly unites the sacred and the worldly. Fadlallah explained how love of justice was a hallmark of Abu Dharr's complex character. He explained how this quality, along with constancy and asceticism, marked him as a figure in whom believers would recognize a spirit akin to that of the Muslim Jesus.

Engaging Fadlallah

The Grand Ayatollah shifted effortlessly among his very distinct personas. Interlocutors could never be perfectly sure just who was so intensely commanding their attention. Each Fadlallah persona was fully realized and intensely present. Engaged with any one of them, it was inconceivable that there were others. It was inconceivable, that is, until one or another stepped forward to redirect the conversation in what often seemed to be a completely new direction. The sudden shift would reshape both context and interaction. Fadlallah immediately engaged his interlocutor in the new dimension. He did so with a level of concentration that matched the original interaction. The Ayatollah's seamless attentiveness made the often abrupt but always purposeful shifts in the persona projected seem natural.

These performative dimensions of Fadlallah's public role made clear his confident and sophisticated awareness of the heterogeneity of his own persona. An astute journalist once asked Fadlallah where he "found himself" among the very different roles he played as poet, scholar, humanitarian, political actor, and strategic thinker. The Ayatollah accepted the premise of this unusually thoughtful question about the multiplicity of his roles. Without hesitation, Fadlallah responded with precision that each persona brought its own gifts: "I find myself in poetry where I experience emotional and psychological calm. In religion, I find myself spiritually closer to God." The Ayatollah's characterization of the gratifications of his political role revealed most clearly his core motivations. He explained that he experienced his greatest satisfaction "in drawing people's attention to their situation with the aim of guiding them to a better way of life."[4] Fadlallah's response reveals the depth of his own awareness. It was the self-awareness of a poet.

The Poet

In a land that accords great respect to the literary arts, the Grand Ayatollah proved himself a gifted poet. With his haunting voice and compelling presence, Fadlallah performed his poetry. His poetic recitations allowed him to offer his insights in succinct form. For many, myself included, the initial encounter with Muhammad Hussein Fadlallah come through his widely recorded and published poetry. I happened on the first recitation quite by accident in a chance meeting with a friend who was listening to the Ayatollah. The effect of that encounter was electric. The emotional and intellectual impact was transformative. It was immediately obvious that I had stumbled on a treasure.

In his poetic voice, the Ayatollah explored questions of the vagaries of human existence and the timeless nature of religion. Paradoxically, he did so by plunging in uninhibited ways into the political and social controversies of the day. He did so consistently from a midstream Islamic perspective. Fadlallah registered immediately as a poet who thinks and feels deeply about large issues. The first verse I encountered was his celebrated *To Be Human*:

> To be a human being,
> To get out of the prison of yourself,
> To be a human being,
> To be all the fresh air
> That gives the space around you its vitality.
> To be the sun that bestows on the universe its brilliance.
> To be the flowing spring
> That does not ask the nature of the soil through which it flows,
> Whether fertile or infertile
> To be human
> To live the meaning of humanity in your life.
> To be human is to feel you are part of humanity
> Throughout the existence of man on earth
> To give, to invest, to discover and to generate
> A new earth through what you plant, make, and create.[5]

The Ayatollah had the gifts of expression to convey in accessible ways the complexity and depth of Islam's message to humanity.

GRAND AYATOLLAH MUHAMMAD HUSSEIN FADLALLAH 121

Like many Arab young men, Fadlallah wrote poetry from adolescence. Unlike most, however, the Ayatollah earned a reputation as an accomplished poet. He authored dozens of published verses. He infused them with a unifying tone that gave them at once a transcendent quality and an insistent worldly relevance. I was not alone in my susceptibility to his gifts for recitation. The noted Egyptian Islamic thinker Selim al Awa, himself a leading Sunni Muslim legal scholar, met often with the Shi'i Ayatollah. After one such meeting, he commented that "it is impossible for me to imitate his beautiful voice. He speaks with perfect tones that are always closely attuned to his message. His intense delivery captivates."[6]

Well before I became aware of the Grand Ayatollah's importance as an Islamic scholar and political figure, I found myself haphazardly immersed in a whole library of videos and tapes of the Ayatollah's poetic recitations. My initial and most lasting impressions of the man were all auditory and deeply emotional. I was captivated by Fadlallah's performances. I experienced his deep and sonorous voice almost as entrapment. It was not the first or last time I would fall in love with a poet.

Gradually, I did learn that the Ayatollah frequently engaged political issues of the misrepresentations of Islam in Western media and scholarship. He tackled complex political questions with directness. Fadlallah insisted, for example, that Islam's worldly success had far less to do with the sword than was generally assumed in the West. Through his poetry, he explained that in winning converts to Islam, honest merchants had historically achieved more lasting gains for the faith than even the most fearless fighters.[7]

Muslim merchants who refused the chicanery too often prevalent in the market proved to be the most attractive representatives of Islam's character. Fadlallah believed that just behavior represented the heart of Islam's message. In his poetry, Fadlallah celebrated the compelling vision of a reign of peace that justice would bring. Like the venerable Abu Dharr and clearly under his influence, the Grand Ayatollah had reached a clear understanding of the centrality in Islam's message of the call for justice. Over his long and productive lifetime, Fadlallah would teach that the greatest source of Islam's power and appeal was its insistent call for social action on behalf of the poor and weak.

Initially, I reserved a space for the poet Fadlallah among the Islamic mystics who have moved in and out of my life since I first discovered their work in graduate school in the mid-1960s. In his psychological explorations, he reminded me most of the Turkish mystic and scholar Sa'id Nursi, whom readers got to know in Chapter 5. I have read Nursi for years for personal

122 JUSTICE IN ISLAM

guidance. Both Nursi and Fadlallah celebrate the human capacity to transcend given context. They do so in very different ways. Yet, both men insist that there are always better choices to be made than those circumscribed by one's immediate environment. I found their message liberating. Nursi and Fadlallah teach that there is always more freedom to make one's own choices than most realize.

Both Fadlallah and Nursi also understand the power of large dreams. Both grasp as well the importance of connecting expansive visions to modest and accessible actions. They understand that only in this way can large dreams come alive for ordinary people. They also reassure that dreams that must be deferred by circumstances can be safeguarded within for a time when their realization might be possible.

Fadlallah has the courage to dive into the deepest waters. He reflects in creative ways on fundamental questions of what it means to be human. His poetry explores as well how the excesses of unchecked power and exorbitant wealth could be kept at bay. Love, compassion, and simple kindness are the Ayatollah's weapons of choice in a world that fosters hatred and systematic cruelty to the most vulnerable. That underlying message of his poetry also animates his prolific scholarship.

The Scholar

Fadlallah's reputation as a scholar earned him a following across the Islamic world. His prolific writings were widely disseminated through networks of his followers. Fadlallah also tamed the new communication technologies as very few other Islamic intellectuals of his generation. Taped speeches and videos of all kinds carried his evocative voice far beyond Lebanon's borders. Shi'i traditions afford scholars a measure of financial independence more secure in many ways than that of their Sunni counterparts. Fadlallah had impressive means at his disposal. Contributions from followers in far-flung Shi'i communities provided generous and reliable income to fund his multifaceted social work. Fadlallah used these means with great wisdom as an independent "caller" to Islam.

The passage from the poetic recitations to Fadlallah's scholarly writings is a smooth one. Many of the more abstract themes are the same. At the same time, Fadlallah's lifetime was one filled with intense communal engagements. Yet, the Ayatollah never neglected his poetry or his scholarship. In his extensive writings in the Islamic sciences, the Grand Ayatollah brought the words of the Qur'an and the example of the Prophet to life in exceptional ways. In Fadlallah's exegesis of the sacred texts, the poet shines through. The Ayatollah is alert to the power of sensitively chosen words and phrases. He understands the demands and rewards of skillful recitation. Throughout his commentaries, Fadlallah engages emotions and dreams. His commentaries show the sophisticated attention to subtlety and nuance that reveal the poet behind the religious scholar.

The Ayatollah's voluminous writings in the Islamic sciences earned him the rank of *marja'*. That designation is the highest in the Shi'i clerical hierarchy. All Shi'i Muslims choose a *marja'*, whose teachings they follow and to whom they regularly give alms. Fadlallah won adherents beyond Lebanon, with particularly large concentrations of followers in Pakistan, Afghanistan, and Iran, as well as in Arab nations. Though the Shi'i sect provided his training and platform, Fadlallah nevertheless wrote consistently as an inclusive *Islamic* scholar. He expressly addressed both Sunni and Shi'i Muslims. Fadlallah's openness to influences from Sunni scholarship, in particular, did not always please his Shi'i critics.

It is too early for definitive assessments of Fadlallah's scholarship. However, highlights of his work can be presented here with some preliminary evaluations. It is already clear that the Ayatollah's embrace of inclusive centrist Islam gives coherence and weight to his work. The Grand Ayatollah is insistently and consistently a theological centrist. Fadlallah aims to contribute to the building of an inclusive scholarly foundation for *all* Muslims to contribute to reforming their faith and finding their rightful place as believers in the modern world.

In the book *Islam and the Logic of Power*, perhaps his most important theoretical work, the creative tensions that characterize Fadlallah's characteristic way of thinking as a scholar are in clear evidence. Thoughts never come to Fadlallah in isolation. There are always at least two voices at play in his texts. He addresses his study of power in the first instance to those who are weak and hesitant. He counsels that, with focus and a willingness to sacrifice, they can build their strength. At the same time, the Ayatollah speaks in a cautionary way to the over-confident. He does so with a message of restraint. Fadlallah advises that desirable caution would flow naturally from having clear and reasonable objectives. The Ayatollah advises that activist energy without thoughtful planning may simply dissipate and achieve nothing of lasting value.

124 JUSTICE IN ISLAM

Fadlallah's theoretical work on power reflected his direct experience of a total of five Israeli invasions of Lebanon. The Israelis have given their assaults anodyne labels. They have also described each of the five as defensive in nature. In 1978 the Israelis launched the South Lebanon conflict, with an Israeli army of 25,000 invading Lebanese territory up to the Litani River. In the 1982 Lebanon War, labeled by the invaders as Operation Peace for Galilee, Israeli forces again invaded southern Lebanon. Operation Accountability in the summer of 1993 brought a week of renewed attacks on Lebanese territory. Some two dozen Israeli civilians suffered wounds, while an estimated 120 Lebanese civilians perished and over 500 were wounded. The fighting displaced massive numbers of Lebanese civilians, most likely in excess of 300,000.[8] In 1996 Operation Grapes of Wrath brought further military strikes. The fierce fighting registered three Israeli military and some two dozen fighters from Hizbullah killed. Isreali civilians wounded reached 62, while Lebanese civilian killed may have been as high as 170, with an additional 350 wounded. A staggering number of civilians suffered displacement, with estimates as high as half a million. The Lebanese suffered devastating damage to infrastructure, including destruction of major bridges and power stations and over 2,000 homes in the south.[9] The 2006 Lebanon War saw renewed military actions in Lebanon, northern Israel, and the Golan Heights. By the end of the war in August 2006, nearly 1,200 Lebanese had been killed; over 4,000 were wounded, about one million displaced, and nearly 15,000 homes destroyed. Meanwhile, the Israelis also suffered casualties with a reported death toll of 43 Israeli civilians in addition to 116 soldiers and the displacement of almost 300,000 Israelis, particularly in the northern part of the country.[10] The Lebanese experienced some eighteen years of direct Israeli occupation of southern territories of their small and vulnerable state.

The Lebanese endured very damaging military engagements that grounded the Ayatollah's abstract thinking about power relations. There was direct experience behind Fadlallah's consistent advocacy of balance between debilitating hesitancy and damaging recklessness. Legend has it that the Ayatollah composed his book *Islam and the Logic of Power* by candlelight during a siege of Naba'a during the Lebanese civil war that began in 1975. Conditions of the harsh fighting dictated realism. Shi'i residents of the besieged neighborhood ultimately surrendered on August 6, 1976. With the end of a long siege, some 400 wounded were evacuated by the International Red Cross. Remaining civilians were relocated to West Beirut and the Beka'a Valley. Fadlallah read the Naba'a siege as sending an unambiguous message.

To survive as a community, the Shi'i of Lebanon would have to organize to defend themselves.

Fadlallah's abstract argument for balance found pragmatic applications. The Ayatollah's views of Palestinian activism makes the essential point. The Ayatollah argued that neither reckless assertiveness nor endlessly conflicted hesitancy would serve the Palestinian cause. In the body of his work, the Ayatollah traced in parallel fashion the evolution of Shi'i activism out of a pointedly quietist tradition. Characteristically, he urged a progression to a balanced and reasoned Shi'i activism that carefully avoided excess.

Fadlallah's insightful and original scholarship established his reputation with leading Shi'i intellectuals, including the important scholars based in Iraq and Iran. Recognizing his place in the influential Najaf network, the distinguished Iraqi Ayatollah Baqir al Sadr (1935–1980), who is the subject of Chapter 7, aptly summed up Fadlallah's stature in scholarly circles. He invoked an often-cited phrase that when most scholars left Najaf the focus was on what they lost by leaving that holy city. In Fadlallah's case, however, he explained that the issue was rather what Najaf lost when Fadlallah left Iraq for Lebanon.

Tawhid and Theological Grounding

Like all Islamic scholars, Fadlallah took *tawhid* (the oneness of God) as an unquestioned premise for all his thinking. The core theological meaning of *tawhid* is God's unitary nature. Islam pronounces that there is but one God and that God is one. The Grand Ayatollah Fadlallah put forward grounded interpretations of this traditional starting point. In a bold move, Fadlallah gave this foundational theoretical principle a temporal political meaning. For Fadlallah, *tawhid* should be as worldly as it was theological. *Tawhid*, the Grand Ayatollah reasoned, demanded no less than the unity of Muslims of all sects in sounding the call to global Islam. In the first instance, he understood that the call would demand that unified Muslims face aggressive Western imperialism and post-imperialist intrusions. To that end, Fadlallah's work aimed notably to build the scaffolding for a scholarly bridge between the Shi'i and Sunni communities.

In the Islamic world, Fadlallah's ideas on *tawhid*, interpreted to mean the unity of the *ummah* (Islamic community), proved highly controversial. Fadlallah typically argued for unity in both moral and power terms.

126   JUSTICE IN ISLAM

The fundamental principle of *tawhid*, he believed, summoned all Muslims to embrace one another as members of one Islamic family. Fadlallah made the underlying power logic of his position clear. A unified Islamic world represented strength. Islam's enemies worked assiduously to exacerbate or create schisms. Centrist scholars from both Sunni and Shi'i communities did support his general commitment to a unified Islamic world. However, their support was theoretical rather than practical. Meanwhile, fringe and extremist elements in both communities vigorously demurred. They at times acted forcefully on their objections.

The classic imperial strategy of divide and rule worked particularly well in Islamic lands when launched in sectarian terms. The Sunni-Shi'i sectarian divide has consistently been the most debilitating. It has also been the easiest to manipulate. Islam's enemies have understood that fostering sectarianism is their most powerful tool to loosen the bonds that unified Muslims. Communal memories often exaggerated historical enmities between the two communities. They were at times compounded by ethnic differences. These inherited cracks in unity were subject to manipulation. New hostilities could be generated. Heightened sectarianism could be fostered quite consciously by outside forces for the purposes of exploitation and domination.

For his argument on the imperative of the unity of Muslims, Fadlallah evoked the figure of Abu Dharr al Ghifari. To Fadlallah, Abu Dharr represented common ground for Islam's two most important sects. The Prophet's companion was a venerable and trusted symbol of justice for *all* Muslims. There is variance in the way Abu Dharr is remembered in Sunni and Shi'i communities. These are differences in emphases and not essentials. Sunnis focus on Abu Dharr's love for the Prophet. Shi'i give greater attention to his closeness to Ali and his support for Ali's claim to succession. Both, however, see in Abu Dharr reminders of the spirit of the Muslim Jesus. Both recognize Abu Dharr as a lover of justice. Fadlallah stressed this common ground. He insisted that Abu Dharr's example showed that the sects could, with good will, find accommodation on major issues of importance to all Muslims. In Fadlallah's views, Abu Dharr demonstrated that struggles for justice were shared *Islamic* struggles.

The Ayatollah was acutely aware that the regional and international press followed and recorded his every move. He turned that visibility to his own ends. Fadlallah made a point to meet in very public ways with important Sunni scholars. He aimed to give living examples of transcendence by Islamic scholars of the Sunni-Shi'i divide. One such particularly important occasion in Teheran in brought Fadlallah together with Shaikh Muhammad al Ghazalli and Muhammad Selim al Awa, two prominent Sunni scholars from Egypt. Awa is an Egyptian professor of international law and a leading member of the *intellectual school* of Egyptian centrist intellectuals to which Ghazalli also belonged.

The Grand Ayatollah Fadlallah was universally regarded as one of the most highly regarded Shi'i scholars. Shaikh Muhammad al Ghazalli had a parallel status in the Sunni community. Their meeting was momentous. Al Awa has provided a detailed account of their encounter in Tehran that he records from the very early 1980s. He made it available to the general public. The opening conversation of the two religious leaders centered on how best to contribute to resistance to Zionism. The three left their meeting and went to the place where Fadlallah was staying to continue the discussion. They shared a meal. Their extended dialogue across the sectarian divide centered on the broader theme of strengthening shared resistance. Awa reports that he and Ghazalli felt that they had met an *Insan Allah* (man of God) in Ayatollah Fadlallah. Awa remarks that from Fadlallah's first sentence, it was clear that "he was a man who knew what he was saying and said what he knew." A connection was established that was never broken. "I can't tell you how many subsequent meetings we had. After that connection, I never went to Lebanon without seeing Fadlallah, sometimes for hours on end. Our subsequent dialogue focused often on the challenge of Islamic unity." Awa reports that Fadlallah took for granted "the unity of the *ummah* as a whole."[11]

In Fadlallah's understanding, the value of justice was radically inclusive. All of Islam's core values rise above sect, ethnicity, and nation. The Islamic conception of justice, he explained, had the spiritual dimension that the Muslim Jesus had ascribed to it. The practical implications of this thought were far-reaching. Fadlallah's scholarly writings treat the Iranian Revolution as an *Islamic*, rather than a Shi'i upheaval or an Iranian nationalist event. Support for occupied Palestine was an *Islamic* cause for all Muslims, the most salient of such unifying causes. The repair of ravaged Afghanistan represented another.

Fadlallah celebrated Abu Dharr's unifying legacy in his extended essay on the Prophet's companion.[12] Through the lens of Abu Dharr's life, Fadlallah emphasized that Islam's core value of justice, along with its corollaries of freedom and compassion, were to be treasured by Muslims everywhere. It is particularly noteworthy that the Ayatollah refused any efforts by Shi'i activists to make Abu Dharr as symbol of justice a wholly owned captive of

128   JUSTICE IN ISLAM

the Shiʻi sect. Like all Shi'i scholars, the Ayatollah did emphasize Abu Dharr's closeness to the Prophet's nephew and son-in-law Ali. Like all Shi'i scholars, he took for granted the role of Ali as a foundational figure for Shiʻi Islam. At the same time, Fadlallah made it clear that although Ali of his account did have signal importance for Shiʻi Muslims, he was also a classical figure who belonged to both Sunni and Shiʻi communities.

The reconciliation of Islam's two most important sects will come one day. When it does, it will find safe passage through the thinking of the Grand Ayatollah Muhammad Hussein Fadlallah. It should also be noted that the inclusive thrust of Fadlallah's writings extended beyond Islam's permeable borders to all shades of moderate and progressive secular trends. The banners raised for battles of resistance and social justice were justice, freedom, and compassion. To Fadlallah, what mattered was that those values be held aloft. He paid less attention than most to the question of who raised them. The Ayatollah reminded even the most fervid sectarians that the core Islamic values resonated across Islamic lands and beyond.

The Humanitarian: An Empire of Kindness

For all his accomplishments as poet and scholar, the Ayatollah was as well known in the Islamic world for his social work as a Shiʻi community leader. The pioneering accomplishments of the Sunni Muslim Brotherhood provided the model for social activism under an Islamic banner. Fadlallah's extensive social projects in that mode extended his importance beyond the realms of literature, theology, and politics.

Fadlallah's network of social and cultural projects uplifted Shiʻi communities, stretching from Lebanon to Pakistan. Those projects provided a progressive social welfare dimension to the revered Grand Ayatollah's poetic, scholarly, and political reputation. The core of the Ayatollah's following came from Lebanon's depressed Shiʻi communities. These areas included poor urban neighborhoods outside Beirut and the too often forgotten Shiʻi villages of southern Lebanon. In these difficult circumstances, the Grand Ayatollah created a sprawling empire of kindness. The Ayatollah undertook his social activism explicitly in the name of the Muslim Jesus and his representative, Abu Dharr al Ghifari. The Ayatollah opened social centers. He established health clinics. He created safe spaces for abused women. All of Fadlallah's social justice projects were suffused with an Islamic spirit of compassion. Abu

GRAND AYATOLLAH MUHAMMAD HUSSEIN FADLALLAH   129

Dharr as symbol of justice was frequently invoked in Fadlallah's addresses from these sites of his social activism. Islamic legitimatization greatly enhanced the impact of the Ayatollah's numerous social projects. Abu Dharr took his place in messages sent from these sites as a representative of the Muslim Jesus and symbol of Islamic social justice. Abu Dharr's presence facilitated acceptance with dignity of all that was offered to those in need.

Fadlallah's literary and scholarly commitments found their activist complement in these struggles for justice in an unjust world. In a life work of social service, the Grand Ayatollah as humanitarian leaned on the scholar. Fadlallah's status as a *marja'* made his extensive humanitarian work possible. As a Shi'i *marja'*, Fadlallah stood at the pinnacle of the Shi'i clerical hierarchy. That status gave the Ayatollah the financial resources to fund his social projects. In Shi'i practice, followers of a particular *marja'* donate annually some 20% of their net worth to support his communal work. The steady flow of these substantial contributions provided Fadlallah with resources independent of the supervision of governments for his work for those in need.

In his communal social work, the Ayatollah aimed to teach the meaning of living in the way of the faith. To do so, he repeatedly invoked not only the words, but more importantly the exemplary actions, of Abu Dharr al Ghifari. For Fadlallah, Abu Dharr as the classic Islamic figure was the keeper of the values of social justice and compassion. In the spirit of the Muslim Jesus that Abu Dharr represented, Fadlallah taught that Islam was a faith to be lived through acts of righteousness. Islam offers no easy escape from the obligations that the value of compassion imposes. Fadlallah taught his followers that their holy book explicitly warns against escape into empty rituals in place of constructive social engagement. He called his follower to express their faith in work for the community. With the Qur'an in hand, the Ayatollah delivered his demanding message of social service. Islam's holy book, he endlessly insisted, calls believers to good works.

To be caught in the thrall of the Ayatollah means that there is always yet another layer of commitment to be fulfilled. The Ayatollah explained that "He has ordered me to love the poor and to approach them."[13] Fadlallah taught that it was the responsibility of believers to find ways to express the love they felt in concrete acts of kindness and succor that would be most pleasing to God.[14] Fadlallah's perpetual smile softened the preemptory demand. It did not, however, diminish the strength of the injunction. He taught that Islamic work of social justice must be an active expression of compassion. The Ayatollah explained that, for an Islam of the heart, compassion

130   JUSTICE IN ISLAM

trumped ritual and textualism. Neither performance of the rituals of the faith nor even recitation of the sacred texts could ever be a worthy substitute for social action to advance justice and express kindness. Fadlallah taught that the most effective preparations for the world to come would take place in the space of compassion created by righteous behavior.

In Islam, religious commitments cannot be locked away in one's private relationship with God. In Islam, faith is shared. It is public. The language of the Qur'an is blunt and direct. Islam teaches that God's favor simply cannot be won by personal belief nor by faith alone. The Qur'an says that when Muslims face their final judgment, only the sum of their *acts* of goodness and kindness will merit reward.

Alongside its importance to the spiritual life of individual Muslims, social activism, for Fadlallah, represented a very practical means to strengthen Islamic communities. The Ayatollah was confident that when the material conditions of the poor improve, their inclination and capacity to embrace Islam would be enhanced as well. Fadlallah regularly cautioned that the means for resistance might not always be at hand. However, with hearts and minds committed to justice, freedom, and compassion, Muslims would be ready for just battles when those opportunities did present themselves. The Ayatollah excoriated the idea of postponing realization of justice to the world to come. He insisted that Islam is a faith for this world, as well as the better world to come. Fadlallah frequently invoked the Prophet's beloved companion as a model of immersion in life's struggles in the name of the faith.

Fadlallah taught that an Islam without compassion is not Islam. Yet, all too often the story of Islam is told in the secular West with compassion and love left out. No other world faith is treated in quite this way. It is little wonder that Western journalists and even scholars have been at a loss as to how to treat the complexities of the Grand Ayatollah. Fadlallah was a beloved figure with a heart of massive proportions. It proved impossible to gauge such a figure in the loveless register that prevails in Western studies of Islam.

In all his efforts to lighten the burdens of the poor, the Ayatollah Fadlallah exemplified a widely shared and distinctly Islamic code of behavior for the well-off in their interactions with less fortunate brothers and sisters. Fadlallah reminded his followers that wealth in Islam belongs to God. The men and women who have the good fortune to hold a surplus of resources are simply "trustees" of that surplus on God's behalf for their limited time on earth.[15] Fadlallah clarified that this Qur'anic notion of trusteeship over wealth imposed requirements not only on those favored by substantial means, but also on those in need.

The Ayatollah urged his followers to take with the utmost seriousness the Islamic duties that flowed from the exigency of alleviating poverty. For the privileged, assistance to the less fortunate defines a religious obligation, rather than simply an appeal to the generosity of their better selves. Islam summons Muslims of means in excess of their requirements to share a meaningful part of their surplus with the less privileged. In turn, the poor, by the simple fact of their genuine need, afford the privileged a meritorious means to fulfill the obligations their faith imposes. The privileged are provided the opportunity to perform their religious duties in ways pleasing to God. For that gift alone, Fadlallah taught, the poor are owed respect and gratitude.

Mindfulness of the conditions of others thus had very practical implications for the Ayatollah. He understood that basic needs must be met before the spirit could soar. Over and over again, Fadlallah explained that it made no sense to appeal to spirituality with a hungry person. Basic human needs must be met before the spirit could soar. Assistance in providing the essentials is owed to the poor as a religiously sanctioned *right* that enables them to rise above all-consuming necessities. Widows and orphans are always a priority. However, help should be given to all who need it. That injunction notably extends to those who ask for assistance. The Ayatollah explained that no shame should be cast on those who ask for help when genuinely in need. Those with more than they require have a religious duty to respond. Shame makes its debilitating appearance only when the well-off fail in these obligations. Shame always falls to the side of the privileged who do not meet their religious obligations to the less fortunate. Fadlallah taught that shame should never attach to the poor for the simple act of asking for needed assistance. They too are God's creations. In Islam, there is no "charity" either in the giving or the receiving of help. In Fadlallah's view, the generous heart of Islam rises above such small-minded notions.

The Prophet's venerable companion Abu Dharr al Ghifari set the precedent that the Ayatollah cited for understanding these Islamic obligations. He gave these Islamic teachings assertive expression. He personally set an example of an asceticism that was attuned to the lessons that poverty could teach. Abu Dharr also regularly reminded the poor of their rights. He reassured the less fortunate of the dignity that comes with rights bestowed by God. He joined them in the fight for their realization. Abu Dharr devoted himself to

132   JUSTICE IN ISLAM

the rigorous defense of the rights of the least privileged. In all these ways, the Prophet's companion of legend made himself *the lawyer of the poor*.

Political Actor

The Grand Ayatollah published volumes of poetry, produced an influential body of scholarship in the religious sciences, and devoted boundless energy to humanitarian work. These accomplishments were more than enough to establish him as a major Islamic scholar with deep roots in Lebanon and the Arab world. However, it was Fadlallah's role as political actor and strategic thinker that drew global attention. Lebanon's Grand Ayatollah came to the larger world's attention as a controversial political actor and bold strategic thinker. There were unintended and quite unexpected consequences of the attention he received in this way.

In the West, it was the Ayatollah's defense of Hizbullah that proved most provocative. The storms that Fadlallah raised found their fiercest expression over his defiant support for Hizbullah, including its martyrdom operations. In Lebanon and the Islamic world beyond, the Ayatollah's strong stand against extreme sectarianism and his unequivocal support for the rights of women made him equally controversial. Both domestic and international controversies contributed to the definition of his political activism and strategic thinking. They differed, but generated the same fury. Both contributed to the Ayatollah's global visibility.

Characterizations of the Ayatollah as a political figure in the international media were rarely balanced. In the global spotlight, the poet, scholar, and humanitarian faded from view. In their place, the *godfather* of a "terrorist" Hizbullah took center stage. Israelis and Americans sought to make the Ayatollah a nefarious character in their grand narrative of global terrorism as a threat to Western civilization. This interesting fiction had little to do with Muhammad Hussein Fadlallah. The charges, however, did bring the Grand Ayatollah to international attention. In the domestic and regional spheres, the Ayatollah was most provocative in his advocacy for women and his critique of all forms of fanaticism, notably including the excesses of Islamic extremists.

Once in the spotlight, the Ayatollah proved unexpectedly adept at turning the international attention to his own purposes. The uncompromising logic of Fadlallah's forceful positions on critical issues amplified his voice. The

Grand Ayatollah offered no apologies for his unwavering support for the internationally recognized and Islamically sanctioned right of armed opposition to foreign occupation. He saw righteousness as well in the assertions of an Islamic movement that resisted occupation and dispossession. The Grand Ayatollah took these positions in a spirit of matter-of-fact rectitude. His moral certitude and imperturbable equanimity infuriated his critics.

No matter the criticism, the Ayatollah provided full-throated rhetorical support for the internationally recognized right of resistance to foreign intrusions and occupation. He spoke out frequently against the violent interventions of the United States. He strongly condemned Israeli occupation of Arab lands. An Islamic political thinker with a sense of history and a clear-eyed assessment of contemporary reality could not have done less.

The Ayatollah refused all sentimentality in formulating guidelines for strategic thinking. He understood that history knew no resistance movements without flaws. He appreciated that this harsh judgment applied to the Lebanese struggle. Fadlallah at the same time argued that imperialism was always about the appropriation of resources and the exploitation of subject populations. The nature of the resources varied. Exploitation in its essence did not. Appropriation and exploitation meant theft and violence. There was no such thing as benevolent occupation and colonization.

The Ayatollah's verbal condemnations of American policy in the Islamic world inevitably earned him the label "anti-American." Even sharper criticism of Israel's prolonged occupation of southern Lebanon and the West Bank made him not only anti-Israeli but somehow anti-Semitic as well.[16] In fact, Fadlallah took rational and defensible political positions that responded to transgressions. It is hard to see how they indicate general antipathy for Americans or Jews. The Ayatollah was aware and appreciative of American domestic critics who shared his negative assessments of the endless US wars in vulnerable Islamic lands. He also took note that uncritical support for Israel in the United States was increasingly challenged, notably by a younger generation of Americans, including Jewish Americans. He was aware as well of opposition to official policies in Israel itself. It is quite implausible to regard his denunciations of Israeli policies as proof of hostility to Judaism or hatred of Jews. Stranger still is the way that the Ayatollah's critical denunciations of American and Israeli policies are taken in the international media as "proof" for the Ayatollah's terrorist credentials. Media commentators often make such claims while failing to mention the arrogant and arbitrary assertion of an American right to intervene with military force at will in Islamic

134   JUSTICE IN ISLAM

lands. It is often "overlooked" as well that Israel has militarily engaged all its Arab neighbors. Israeli expansionism is an undeniable reality. The powerful Zionist state has seized and occupied land of all its Arab neighbors. Israeli military occupied extensive parts of the Ayatollah's beloved Lebanon for some eighteen plus years. The character of the repeated military actions as defensive or offensive is open to discussion. However, simply ignoring these military realities is unacceptable. Such background "oversights" are discrediting. There may well be military incursions and occupations that do not justify resistance, but I know of none.

Such erasures of the historical record have been consistently characteristic of judgments on Israel in American political culture. A powerful myth of Israel as "embattled ally" has been dominant for the last half century. It screens the realities of Israeli strength and assertiveness. It has rarely been challenged. It was my good fortune to have an authoritative exposition of this durable myth as part of my graduate studies. In 1981 Nadav Safran, my mentor at Harvard in Islamic studies, published the classic work that gave the myth its definitive statement. It is unsurprising that Safran's book *Israel: The Embattled Ally* is still in print. Americans to this day wrap their overwhelming majority support for Israeli expansionism in the unreal image of a vulnerable and "embattled" ally, an essential strategic partner, and the only democracy in the Middle East.[17] Safran's book gave all these elements classic expression. To hear Fadlallah is to confront the argument that no aspect of this description is accurate today, if it ever was. I did not find this characterization of Israel persuasive as a graduate student, and I do not now. Israel is a nuclear power. It has a European-level military. Dispassionate analysis also suggests that the US role in the Middle East would be far less difficult without the entanglements of the Israeli alliance, however essential some judge that alliance on non-strategic grounds. The idea of a "model democracy" with a permanent underclass of second-class citizens, defined as such on ethnic and religious grounds, defies reason. It would be far more accurate to characterize US sympathy for Israel as the natural affinity of an established colonial settler state for a latecomer to the same club.

Of course, the circumstances and details of occupation and colonization are never exactly the same. Yet, the essentials of the power relationship are. Colonial settlement means that the overwhelming violence of the strong is unleashed on the weak. Moral justifications are always invoked. A divine promise to a *chosen people* resonates in perfect pitch with the hoary American notion of *Manifest Destiny*, in the name of which the prolonged genocidal assault on indigenous American populations was carried out. Settlers everywhere shamelessly invoke God's sanction for what is essentially violent dispossession and, very often, casual murder.

The American easy embrace of globalization owes more than a little to the very same idea of *Manifest Destiny*. Apologists for the limitless expansion of American power found it easy enough to project that American destiny worldwide. Globalization as an idea proved useful. Fadlallah's commentary on international affairs makes it clear that he had no trouble seeing through the fantasies generated to screen this soft version of American expansionism. Globalization, in his view, was simply the silken sheathing for the raw power of American empire. The Ayatollah would have none of the most seductive rationalizations that have deluded uninformed and interested Western publics. The Ayatollah rejected out of hand the string of fantastic grand narratives of a universalized and insistently abstract struggle of the *lexus* of modernity and the *olive tree* of tradition, the emergence of a *global village*, or *the end of history* with the coming of a homogeneous world of free markets and democracy.[18] The latest version portrays America as *the indispensable nation*. The notion of the United States as the beneficent guarantor of a pacific world order made no greater impact on the strategic thinking of the Grand Ayatollah than earlier justifications of empire.

The lived realities of military occupation by an American-backed regional hegemon shredded all such self-serving imperial rationalizations that pretend to be social science theories. The Ayatollah's regular flow of analytical commentary illuminates a realist world of clashing interests and shifting alliances, dictated by power balances rather than the interplay of unreal ideological constructs. Putting aside Islamic references, when reading Fadlallah's analyses of global politics, it is easy to imagine you are reading one of the important proponents of the American school of realist thinkers.[19]

Politics in the Domestic Arena: Extremism

Fadlallah's political activism in Lebanon evoked levels of controversy that paralleled those generated by the positions he took on contentious international issues. With his insistently Qur'anic perspective, the Ayatollah concentrated on combatting extremism and advancing women's rights. These Lebanese domestic issues resonated as both regional and international

136 JUSTICE IN ISLAM

concerns. Fadlallah treated both with sophistication and an unafraid audacity that attracted attention far beyond Lebanon's borders.

The Ayatollah's views on extremism took as premise the judgment that extremist positions did often originate with reasonable grievances and commitments. When neglected, they led inexorably to extreme responses. Such exaggerations crossed a red line for Fadlallah. He judged them un-Islamic. He treated them as such.

Fadlallah's engagement with what he regarded as the blight of sectarian "exaggeration" began with pointed self-criticism. He reasoned that all manifestations of excessive sectarian attachments, including those of his own Lebanese Shi'i community, risked endangering *tawhid*. Fadlallah reminded believers that, shortly before his death, the Prophet Muhammad had warned of the likelihood of sectarian fragmentation of the *ummah* after his passing. Invoking this prophetic warning, the Grand Ayatollah explicitly criticized the tendency to ceremonial excesses in Shi'i communities. Most notably, Fadlallah forthrightly pronounced as an unreasonable excess the ritual self-flagellation that bloodied believers in Ashura, the day the of mourning in Shi'i Islam for the martyrdom of Hussein, the Prophet's grandson. He issued his criticism of this sectarian extremism with the full force of his standing as a Shi'i *marja'*. The Ayatollah pointedly reminded his followers that Islam was a faith of reason rather than unbridled emotionalism. To often less than enthusiastic reception, the Ayatollah pronounced unequivocally that Islam provided no justification for ritualized abuse of the body.

Politics in the Domestic Arena: Women's Rights

Fadlallah addressed women's rights with a parallel audacity rarely encountered in the Islamic scholarly literature. He took as his unequivocal starting point the multiple Qur'anic assertions of the equal status of men and women as God's creations. In the Qur'anic vision, men and women share the responsibility of *istikhlaf* (the divine call to humanity to act as God's regent on Earth).[20] That shared mission, assigned to all humanity, provides the Islamic rationale for the egalitarian partnership of men and women.

Fadlallah brought to the fore powerful but neglected verses that highlighted this divinely sanctioned partnership of equals. He pointed out that the verses he cited only seemed to represent radical departures because they were systematically ignored or downplayed in centuries of traditional patriarchal *tafsir* (exegesis)[21] Pointedly, Fadlallah insisted that believers had the obligation to consider the implications of these neglected verses for their own lives. Whatever the prejudices of their inherited culture, the Ayatollah insisted that humanity does not have the option to select and choose from God's words only those that coincide with the prevailing customs of their own time and place. The Qur'an in its totality and as supplemented by the *Sunnah* was to be taken with the utmost seriousness. As God's word, Islam's holy book is the ultimate authority for all times and places.

Fadallah's bold exegesis set his extensive supportive commentary on women's rights against a long tradition of patriarchal interpretations. An avalanche of exclusionist interpretations that date back to the ninth century had all but buried the Qur'anic equalitarian and inclusionary texts. Fadallah audaciously set aside that record of historic chauvinism in favor of the clear injunctions of the Qur'anic verses he highlighted. Fadallah heard only the word of God.

The Ayatollah judged that the egalitarian message of verses like the following could not be clearer:

> The Believers, men
> And women, are protectors
> One of another: they enjoin
> What is just, and forbid
> What is evil: they observe
> Regular prayers, practice
> Regular charity, and obey
> God and His Messenger.
> On them will God pour
> His Mercy: for God
> Is Exalted in power. Wise.[22]

Fadlallah explained that even when such unequivocal verses are considered, their explicit meaning is distorted. The common misreadings claim arbitrarily that all such Qur'anic verses that project the equality of men and women refer only to the spiritual domain. Men and women are to be judged equal, if at all, only in religious obligations like prayer and the payment of *zakat* (religious obligation owed to support those in need).

Fadlallah dismissed this sophistry out of hand. In his commentary, he took the clear meaning of forthright egalitarian verses as the standard for

138 JUSTICE IN ISLAM

understanding the rightful relationship of men and women. The Grand Ayatollah explained that the Qur'an evokes *a partnership in faith* between men and women. More emphatically, he continues that the verse that he has explained reaffirms the egalitarian vision of the Qur'an that encourages women to be involved in all areas of social and political life. In frequent pronouncements, Fadlallah explicitly rejected traditional exclusivist understanding that restricted women to their function as wives and mothers. Fadlallah never denigrated those roles. However, he saw no reason to make them the sole horizon for women's lives.

The Ayatollah taught that the talents of both men and women for social and public work vary widely. Not everyone has the requisite skills and sensibilities to make positive contributions in the public arena. The Ayatollah pronounced that both men and women who did have such gifts should step forward to use their God-given talents to build their community. Fadlallah went so far as to pronounce that confining women to marital duties alone meant that marriage would be little more than imprisonment for women.

Qur'anic exegesis was not the only means of communication available to the Grand Ayatollah. To reach the widest possible audience, he elaborated his deep commitment to the personal, social, and political rights of women in less formal and often even more memorable public pronouncements as well. In a particularly striking formulation, the Ayatollah pronounced that women subject to the violence of the men in their lives would find support in a proper understanding of Islam. Fadlallah assured abused women that they had a religiously sanctioned right to defend themselves and their children against assaults by the men close to them. Fadlallah interpreted that right literally. *If physically abused, women had the right to strike back.* Islam, the Ayatollah insisted, in no way sanctioned the abuse of women. Passivity in the face of all forms of violence was not something Islam ever sanctioned. It mattered not at all if the victims were men or women. Their right of self-defense in Islam was the same.

On a whole series of equally controversial social issues, the Grand Ayatollah announced judgments in strong support of the dignity and fundamental rights of women. In striking contrast to prevailing views and customs, the Ayatollah pronounced that Islam condemns female genital mutilation. He also issued a stern opinion that pronounced so-called honor killings un-Islamic. The Ayatollah's strikingly progressive positions on the most controversial domestic matters regularly generated great turbulence and often a fair share of rage.[23]

Politics in the Global Arena: The Iranian *Earthquake*

The controversies that swirled around Fadlallah for his interventions on foreign policy issues were equally or even more consequential. Assassination attempts against the Grand Ayatollah became almost routine. The list of potential perpetrators of violence against Fadlallah was long. It included American and Israeli intelligence operatives. In the documented assassination attempt mentioned in opening of this chapter, the CIA placed a massive car bomb along the short route between his apartment and the closest mosque. Ayatollah Fadlallah, delayed by conversations with followers, narrowly escaped the explosion. Eighty innocents from the Ayatollah's neighborhood were killed.[24] Just as likely to act as assassins were enraged Shi'i sectarians who fiercely objected to the Ayatollah's inclusive and egalitarian Islam. At the same time, violent Sunni extremists feared his Islam of righteous social works and inclusion would undermine their call to violent *jihad* as the only way forward.

The Ayatollah's broad view of the deadly hostility of the West was given point by his forthright celebration of the Iranian Revolution of 1979. He supported Islamic resistance movements such as Hizbullah and Hamas with parallel logic and boldness.

The Ayatollah had immediately celebrated the global significance of the Iranian Revolution of 1979. He saw it as a mass social upheaval of Islamic inspiration that expressed as well as a refusal of Western intrusions. In Fadlallah's views, the revolution was a history-changing event, an *earthquake* with wide repercussions like the French or Russian revolutions.

Internationally, Fadlallah's unapologetic defense of martyrdom in resistance struggles drew especially sharp criticism internationally. The poet, scholar, and humanitarian all faded from view as the rhetoric heated. On the global plane, a radical apologist for the Iranian Revolution and the threatening *godfather* of a "terrorist" movement was brought center stage. These confections, whipped up by the United States and Israel, dominated the hostile assessments of the Ayatollah in the international media. Seemingly unfazed, the beloved Grand Ayatollah moved forward with an equanimity that only further enraged his critics. The numerous failed attempts on the life of the Grand Ayatollah enhanced his stature. The mystical air that came to surround the Ayatollah's public persona appeared to provide a protective shield.

Fadlallah's commentary mattered. It also evolved in response to developments on the ground. In his initial assessment, the Ayatollah did

140 JUSTICE IN ISLAM

celebrate the Iranian Revolution for its Islamic rather than national or sectarian character. Fadlallah did so by right. His scholarly credentials as a Shi'i *marja'* matched those of the Iranian scholars who emerged from the Shi'i centers in Qom and exerted great influence on the successor regime in Iran.

The Ayatollah strongly affirmed the Islamic sanction for the overthrow of the shah. The Iranian people, in his view, had suffered a full-fledged imperial assault. Their revolt against the regime of the American-imposed shah was legitimately defensive in its essential character. The CIA had engineered a coup against the democratically elected Iranian prime minister Mossadegh in 1953. Mossadegh's "crime" was the nationalist assertion of Iran's right to greater control over its territorial oil reserves. Mossadegh became prime minister in 1951. He achieved great popularity for his strong stand against the Anglo-Iranian Oil Company. He is to this day remembered for his pronouncement that "the moral aspect of oil nationalization is more important than its economic aspect."[25]

This British-owned oil company had made massive profits, while paying Iran at most only 16% of its profits. Mossadegh aimed to turn a greater share of these assets to self-directed Iranian development. Britain turned to the United States for help in aborting such efforts and removing the prime minister. A CIA-organized coup in August 15–19, 1953, ended Mossadegh's tenure and strengthened the dictatorial regime of the shah. Long years of repression followed.

Mass revolution to unseat the American-backed shah finally came to Iran in 1979 under an Islamic banner. It was the first world-class revolution inspired by a non-Western ideology. The Ayatollah Khomeini's leadership role assures him a distinctive and secure historical role in Islam's history. Fadlallah initially stood with the revolution understood in this way. When the nonviolent and spiritual dimensions of the Iranian Revolution began to give way to distressing clerical absolutism, the Ayatollah qualified his assessment of what the Iranians had accomplished. Fadlallah found particularly objectionable the inclination of Iranian clerics to claim to speak for all Shi'i. In his view as an Arab Shi'i *marja'*, the revolution, for all its importance, gave them no such right.

With time, Fadlallah emerged as a thoughtful and balanced critic of the longer-term Iranian revolutionary experience. He offered a sober assessment of the deteriorating course of events in post-revolutionary Iran. Fadlallah came to believe that the clerics of the new Islamic order in Iran departed over time from an inclusive Islamic orientation. The Islamic character of the

Iranian "earthquake" faded. Both ethnicity and sectarianism changed the original character of that momentous event.

Fadlallah did not hesitate to register critical qualifications to his support for the revolution on Islamic grounds. The Ayatollah sided openly with those dissenting Iranian clerics who regarded Khomeini's core notion of *wilayet al faqih* (rule of the jurisprudent) as an unacceptable innovation in Islamic thought. With particular clarity, Fadlallah categorically rejected the idea afoot in Iran that any one experience or leader should be sacralized. Fadlallah came to believe that Khomeini's justification for clerical rule was less Islamic than dictatorial. To advance such a theory of rule as Islamic, he came to believe, was to diminish Islam with *bida'* (unacceptable innovation).

Yet, for all the importance of his demurrals, Fadlallah never broke completely with the Iranian achievement. He did refuse, however, to accept the Iranian Revolution as the prototype for what an Islamic revolution *should* mean. Uncritical supporters of the Iranian Revolution, like Hassan Nasrullah and the leadership of Hizbullah, demurred. They took as the group's official spiritual guide Ayatollah Ali Khamenei, Iran's supreme leader. Fadlallah dissented. He insisted that, for all that the revolution represented, there were flaws in what the Iranians had achieved. Actions, rather than pronouncements, consistently mattered most to Fadlallah. Most importantly, he judged that the regime of Khomeini ultimately compromised the moral high ground by a record of distressing humanitarian abuses and repression as the regime acted to consolidate and maintain power at all cost.

The Ayatollah warned early and in blunt terms against these departures from the revolution's initial promise. At the same time, he refused to paint the momentous upheaval in all black colors. Fadlallah judged that there could be no question that Iranians had used force by right in overthrowing the harshly authoritarian regime of the American-imposed shah. Taking the long view, the revolution had sound Islamic justification. Islam is not passive in the face of aggression. There could be no doubt that the Iranian people had suffered grievously from violent American intervention.

To Fadlallah, that blatant intrusion of the "interested" American empire in 1953 could never be forgotten. Iranians had a right of resistance sanctioned by Islam. It was only when the successor Iranian regime itself took on a dictatorial character that Fadlallah mounted his stinging critique of what the revolution had become. Fadlallah's reassessment initially drew criticism from the Shi'i scholarly class. With time, however, influential ayatollahs both from within Iran and outside came to see the wisdom of Fadlallah's careful

142 JUSTICE IN ISLAM

reassessment.[26] Islam leans to nonviolence. However, the defensive use of violence is explicitly sanctioned. There is little trace in Islam of the theoretical passivism of Christianity. The Muslim Jesus does not turn his other cheek when struck. To do so in Islam would be a major moral failing. Muslims have an obligation to defend themselves and their community. However, the Ayatollah made it perfectly clear that the regretful decline of the revolutionary regime into a pattern of domestic tyranny was another matter. The Grand Ayatollah's disquieting assessment proved prescient. Leading members of the Shi'i religious establishment, including important Iranian scholars, have gradually come to share his critical views and to register their own dissent.[27]

Politics in the Global Arena: Hizbullah Resistance

From his vantage point in wounded and vulnerable Lebanon, Fadlallah saw clearly that the strength to resist against daunting odds must be the core of Islam's gift to beleaguered believers across Islamic lands. Fadlallah's unabashed advocacy of resistance as the essence of what political Islam means lies behind the intense hostility the Ayatollah generated in Israel and the West. In interviews with Western journalists and diplomats, he offered no apology for his part in inspiring active resistance.

There were distinct practical advantages to Fadlallah's vantage point in Beirut. Lebanon's capital hosted not only the diplomatic emissaries of the great powers. There were to be found as well the representatives of global banks and corporations. The city also perpetually teemed with the agents of the intelligence and military establishments of powers with interests in the region. In cosmopolitan Beirut, all these diverse international actors were close at hand. Outsiders to be taken into account included as well the international media with a constant presence in the Lebanese capital. Their attentiveness to the charismatic Ayatollah helped immeasurably to make the Ayatollah a global figure.

It has always been difficult to move around in that remarkable city without stumbling over international journalists or agents of the world's most powerful security agencies. Spies and reporters are everywhere. Beirut is home base. Their interests rarely center on Lebanon. These advantages also meant that there was no way to avoid or even minimize awareness of the hostile forces that incessantly pressed on him and his community.

GRAND AYATOLLAH MUHAMMAD HUSSEIN FADLALLAH   143

Despite the perpetual threats, often tinged with violence, Fadlallah insisted that Islamic resistance could never be narrowly militaristic. Nonviolence, as well as force, must be available in the armory of Islamic fighters. Islamic resistance judged violence as one means among many. Fadlallah opposed the blanket militarization of resistance. He made it clear that nonviolent resistance did represent a legitimate strategy. However, in his strategic thinking, nonviolence had no persuasive claim as the most moral form of resistance. Fadlallah was not a moral absolutist. Absolute commitment to nonviolence could not be a badge of righteousness for all times and conditions. He understood that the human social world is far too complex for such a rigid formula. Context, in his view, always matters. It is often decisive.

The inherent violence of occupation meant that righteous resistance could by right be violent as well as nonviolent. For Fadlallah, the choice was a strategic rather than a moral one. The angels did not always stand with nonviolence. The Ayatollah understood that nonviolence in particular contexts could have profoundly unjust consequences. It depended on the forces at play in any given situation, with the balance of those forces the key determinant. In Fadlallah's thinking, realism would define the available options. Pragmatism would guide choice to the strategy with the greatest prospect of success. Islam, in turn, would frame the battles, whichever form they took, as struggles for justice.

Fadlallah acknowledged without equivocation that the material forces arrayed against the Shi'i community in Lebanon would be overwhelming. More broadly, the Grand Ayatollah Fadlallah recognized the crushing power of the Western assault on Islamic lands. However, he also knew that the logic of power had a character more complex than a purely quantitative assessment allowed. Power resided not only in the numbers of fighters and weapons. The logic of power, the Ayatollah reasoned, was multidimensional. It had qualitative and even spiritual dimensions, as well as its obvious material elements.

History revealed that there was great strength in such modalities of inspired direct mass action such as street demonstrations and civil disobedience. To tap into these resources, it was required that incapacitating despair and fear be overcome. Here the Shi'i communities had the great resource of their Islamic faith. Belief in the righteousness of struggles in this world and confidence in rewards for sacrifice to come in the next could alter the cold calculus of quantitative power balance. *Spiritual power* would make the difference. The Ayatollah predicted that unafraid and committed fighters for justice and the defense of their homeland could ultimately force the withdrawal

144   JUSTICE IN ISLAM

of even the "invincible" Israelis. He was in time proven right. In the year 2006 Israelis did withdraw the last of its forces from southern Lebanon to end their prolonged occupation.

To explain Hizbullah's improbable role in the withdrawal of Israeli forces from Lebanese territory, Western analysts have at all cost avoided serious consideration of Islam's role. Instead, they have been quite willing to acknowledge the logistical support the movement received from the Iranians, identified in American and Israeli mythology as *the leading supporter of state terrorism*. They have also noted the remarkably innovative horizontal formations that the fighters developed on the battlefield. However, there has been revealing silence on the ways a revered religious scholar and poet brought Islam directly onto the battlefield.

The scales tipped. Fadlallah inspired Hizbullah, the Party of God, to make its critical contribution. Outnumbered and outgunned, Hizbullah fighters stood up to a nuclear-armed and American-backed occupying power. With Fadlallah as spiritual mentor, the movement dented the debilitating myth of Israel invincibility. The world had done nothing to end the outrage of almost two decades of Israeli occupation of Lebanese territory. The resistance acted explicitly in Islam's name. Iran's self-described Islamic regime provided support. This signal victory, against the odds and under an Islamic banner, galvanized resistance movements throughout the Islamic world.

It would be unwise to underestimate the importance to the improbable victory of the moral support Hizbullah fighters received from the spiritual giant who lived among them. For the daunting tasks he faced, Fadlallah found inspiration from a source that those who know the Grand Ayatollah only from the Western media will find unlikely. Awash in noisy negativity, the Ayatollah turned unnoticed to the quiet, affirmative spirit of the Muslim Jesus. Fadlallah's theological writings are replete with allusions to the calming and affirming figure of Islam's revered prophet Jesus. The humility, asceticism, and profound compassion of Jesus were precisely the qualities for which Fadlallah strived.

The success of Hizbullah did not come without controversy. Like all other resistance movements with which I am familiar, including those instrumental in founding the United States and Israel, there were excesses. They were too often criminal. They fully deserve condemnation for their crimes. There is nothing uniquely Islamic about that record. Fadlallah was acutely aware of the compromises and shortcomings of all movements of resistance, including those of Hizbullah. Nevertheless, the Grand Ayatollah offered no apologies for his critical support for the internationally recognized and Islamically sanctioned right of armed opposition to foreign occupation. The Ayatollah refused all sentimentality in formulating guidelines for strategic thinking. He understood that history knew no resistance movements without flaws. He appreciated that this harsh judgment applied to the Lebanese struggle. Fadlallah at the same time argued without contradiction that imperialism was always about the appropriation of resources and the exploitation of subject populations. The nature of the resources varied. Exploitation in its essence did not. Appropriation and exploitation meant violence and theft. There was no such thing as nonviolent occupation and colonization.

Fadlallah explained that to carry moral authority, defiance would evince mindfulness of the transcendent wisdom of the sacred texts, combined with attentiveness to the harsh contextual realities of power politics. The Lebanese resistance movement could not even dream of the level of material support that the Israelis received from the United States. However, the fighters of Hizbullah did not fight alone. "Spiritual power" became a palpable factor. The Grand Ayatollah called on Islam's agents of the past and the present to join the battle. The Ayatollah regularly reminded the fighters that their battle was part of an age-old Islamic struggle for justice.

Abu Dharr al Ghifari, the Prophet's companion, was frequently referenced in the corpus of Fadlallah's commentary. As a venerable symbol of Islamic justice, Abu Dharr would fight at their side. The "earthquake" of 1979 had also introduced an important new Islamic partner. Revolutionary Iran would stand behind the fighters of Hizbullah with material assistance. The legitimacy of the resort to violence in defense did not abrogate the over-riding commitment to the peaceful resolution of conflicts among God's varied creations. An interactive standard should be put forward for dealing with adversaries even when engaged in battle. If the enemy makes genuine peace overtures, they should be responded to in good faith. Fadlallah denied having a formal membership in Hizbullah or any direct leadership role in the movement. To the consternation of his Western critics, Fadlallah at the same time calmly explained that the commitments he stood by found their clearest and most laudable expression in the legitimation he offered for the armed struggle of the Lebanese people to drive out a foreign occupying power.

In this sense, some part of Fadlallah is rightfully identified as a movement intellectual. He was intimately engaged with Hizbullah. He recognized that Hizbullah, for all its shortcomings, represented the most successful Islamic resistance movement the Arab world had produced. His inspiration infused

146 JUSTICE IN ISLAM

the resistance movement with Islamic values that would strengthen a distinctive identity, enhance resolve, and set higher purposes. Fadlallah's support was both principled and pragmatic.

Fadlallah did not hesitate to attack the mythology of self-sacrifice in the form of so-called suicide bombers as something distinctly and perversely Islamic. He insisted that simple logic tells a different story. Is there really a nation-state on the planet, he asked, that does not ask the ultimate sacrifice? Is that not the measure of commitment universally demanded by modern secular nationalism? Willingness to serve in the military and ultimately risk death to protect the *homeland* is widely taken as the ultimate measure of citizen loyalty. Yet, when Arabs and Muslims engage in comparable behavior, it suddenly becomes the signature of a cult of death. That death cult is taken to stand in contrast to the exaltation of life that is said to characterize the West.

When faced with overwhelming power, principled resistance does often open to martyrdom. The phenomenon is not uniquely Islamic. There may well be a country or culture that has survived into the modern world without a tradition that celebrates martyrdom. However, one is hard pressed to think of one. Certainly, not the Americans with their celebrated call to "remember the Alamo." That incident saw the massacre of several hundred Texans who knowingly fought an impossible battle against the Mexican army of Santa Anna in 1836. Most definitely not the Israelis with their treasured narrative of Masada. A rock plateau overlooking the Dead Sea, Masada saw the mass suicides of over 900 Jewish rebels who welcomed death rather than surrender to the conquering Romans in 73 or 74 CE.[28] Yet, by some strange alchemy, the martyrdom of Muslim fighters is judged to mark Islam uniquely as a faith that celebrates death over life. The Israeli and American propaganda mills endlessly tell us that Islam encourages the worship of violence. The epic stories of the martyrs celebrated by Christians and Jews apparently carry no such message. The logic that makes Judeo-Christian martyrs one thing and Muslim martyrs another is elusive.

The Ayatollah's most daring positions went beyond the narrow focus on so-called suicide bombers to the broader issue of righteous violence more generally. In a context of peaceful relations, the Ayatollah clarifies that Islam makes a compelling case for nonviolence. However, under a violent occupation the case for nonviolent resistance weakens. The internationally sanctioned right of self-defense, recognized in Islam, assumes enhanced relevance. The Ayatollah understood that there is no such thing as the benevolent occupation of one people by another. The level of actual violence might vary. It might be psychological and cultural rather than physical. Whatever the case, foreign occupation always entails oppression and appropriation in one form or another. Appropriation is everywhere and at all times an ultimately violent and often deadly process, whatever justification its perpetrators provide.

The Qur'an stands unequivocally for the sanctity of human life. A celebrated verse, often cited by the Ayatollah, could not be clearer: "If anyone slew one person . . . it would be as if he slew the whole people."[29] Self-defense, moreover, is not to be understood as a license for reckless violence. Islam has no reluctance to enter the battlefield and set moral guidelines for behavior, even in the heat of battle. Islamic scholars, like Fadlallah, have updated the restrictions on the use of violence for conditions of modern warfare. They do not hesitate to condemn those who exceed these limitations.[30]

Fadlallah had little patience with the delusionary and self-serving American and Israeli thinking on "suicide bombers." He offered a clear and unsentimental engagement with the idea of martyrdom operations. Islam does not sanction suicide, he explained. In Islam, severe personal distress, whether psychological or material, can never justify taking one's own life. The very notion of ending one's life for personal reasons, no matter how dire one's circumstances or psychological suffering, is completely rejected. Life belongs to God and no human being is ever justified in taking a life, not even one's own. In contrast, the Ayatollah explained that the risk of one's life for the sake of one's community under foreign occupation is another matter. The sacrifice of one's life in defensive resistance is martyrdom, not suicide.

There is no inclination in Fadlallah's extensive reflections on Islamic resistance to celebrate violence for its own sake. He makes no argument for the therapeutic impact of assertions of violence, as can be found in some varieties of Third World revolutionary theory.[31] Alternatives to violence are strongly and consistently preferred. Yet, Fadlallah reasoned that there are circumstances when those alternatives are blocked. To sacrifice oneself in such extreme circumstance is another matter. Asymmetrical confrontations everywhere invite self-sacrifice. There is nothing exclusively Islamic in this systematic outcome.

However, to preserve their moral dimension, martyrdom operations, like other forms of resistance, must be evaluated by their efficacy. The costs they impose must be part of the calculus. Realistic measures of success and failure should guide decisions. Violence in itself should never be exalted. If the target struck is a youthful wedding party or gathering of adolescents in a

148   JUSTICE IN ISLAM

club, it makes little difference to the horror of the murder of innocents if the weapon is a human body or a drone.

For all the attention the Ayatollah's relationship to Hizbullah has received, there was always a great deal more to Fadallah as a public figure than his support for the movement. Fadlallah himself rightly insisted that there was a space between his efforts to provide inspiration for the movement of resistance and his larger role as a Grand Ayatollah for all Shiʻi Muslims. Not even the undoubted charisma of Hizbullah's leader, Hassan Nasrullah, could overshadow the larger-than-life Ayatollah. Remarkably, for all its celebrated prowess against the most powerful military in the region, Hizbullah never eclipsed Fadlallah's more expansive religious role as a Shiʻi *marja'*. Not even a remarkably successful resistance movement could swallow Lebanon's improbable spiritual giant whole. Fadallah's reach as a grand Ayatollah exceeded that of Hizbullah. His followers extended through the chain of Shiʻi communities that stretched like a string of pearls from Lebanon, through Syria and Iraq, and on to Pakistan.

The accomplished poet, tireless humanitarian, and the prolific Shiʻi scholar all did fall back when Fadlallah stepped forward as a political figure. Great controversies gave definition to the broader pattern of his often controversial political role. Fadlallah's poetry, social work, and scholarship can all be seen through an implicitly political lens. Islam itself has such an inherently political aspect. That political dimension was never the Ayatollah's whole story. However, when he did assume an explicitly political role, it did make a difference. The power features of all his work come into sharper focus. The quiet dissipates. Everywhere he turns, the Ayatollah is engulfed in contentious political disputes.

Politics in the Global Arena: The West and the Islamic World

The Grand Ayatollah was perfectly clear that, in his view, the greatest danger to the Islamic world came from the West. The American empire was most threatening. He judged that the historical record of Western depredations was perfectly clear. It could be taken for granted. In his view, the overarching commitment to *Westernize the world* was an inherently violent project. From the outset, the Islamic world has been a primary target of this sweeping transformational goal. The Ayatollah spoke pointedly of the lives ruthlessly taken and the destruction casually wrought by expansionary Western powers, including in the first rank the American empire.

Why do they hate us, asks a wounded and uncomprehending American public. Given the well-documented record of the depredations of Western, including American, imperialism, the Ayatollah considered such feigned innocence intolerable. The Ayatollah is not the only scholar ready to call out the faux innocence. A major American realist scholar provides a straightforward answer to that plaintive question. The Harvard political scientist Stephen Walt coolly estimates that the United States has killed somewhere between 30 and 100 Muslims for every American lost in the perpetual conflicts in Islamic lands. Total killed, he argues conservatively, could easily reach one million, if the deaths by Israeli forces are included, as they clearly should be.[32] With these statistics in mind, to question animosity to the West makes no sense.

Strategic Thinker

As a strategic thinker, Fadlallah made himself endlessly available to the international media. Yet, he consistently projected an impression of aloofness and ultimate inaccessibility. The mystery finds its explanation in Fadlallah's unusual combination of the imaginative powers of an empathetic poet married to the detached critical thinking of a scholar. Fadlallah drew on both his imagination as a poet and depth as a scholar to shape his strategic thinking. The Ayatollah's impressive gifts as a strategic thinker of both creative imagination and disciplined intellect allowed him to see far beyond his own inevitably constrained context. At the same time, he remained intensely engaged as a grounded political actor. The creative poet consistently pressed for the speculative exploration of what might exist. The disciplined scholar carefully assessed opportunities and dangers already at hand.

The Ayatollah distinguished himself by a disciplined mindfulness of self, other, and situation that had a decidedly global dimension. The Islamic mystical tradition cultivates this same quality of intense, yet nuanced awareness of situational context as it is to be transcended in mystical practice. His analyses are strategic in this distinctive sense. That effect is understood to partake of the divine. The Ayatollah regularly gave his strategic thinking an element of such transcendence.

150 JUSTICE IN ISLAM

Conclusion: The Passing of the Ayatollah

The death of a figure of such controversial and activist commitments should have had an abrupt and jarring quality. Yet, on July 4, 2010, the Grand Ayatollah Muhammad Hussein Fadlallah died a peaceful, natural death. Fadlallah's passing in such a way was extraordinary for a man at the center of seemingly endless disputations. Numerous potential assassins had all failed to silence his extraordinary voice. The Ayatollah's peaceful ending was instead one befitting a poet. It was quite miraculous given the provocative social and political positions the Ayatollah had regularly advanced in his own community, the region, and the larger world beyond. Neither the gift for poetic recitation, nor the prolific scholarship, nor even the inspiration he provided to struggles for justice sum up the Ayatollah Fadlallah's contributions in Islam's name. Not even awareness of the river of compassion that flowed through his network of social projects or the victories of his political activism complete the effort to see the Ayatollah whole. Fadlallah himself offered no synthesis of the roles he played. At his death, it became clear that there was in fact no such synthesis to be had. With Fadlallah himself gone, it has become clearer that there was never a master key to discern patterns in the kaleidoscope of commitments that marked his shifting engagements with the world.

However, there was a pattern. To his reading of Islam's sacred texts, the Grand Ayatollah brought an alert and responsive moral sensibility. That same sensibility was in evidence when the Ayatollah reflected on his own life experience. At those moments of self-reflection, it was always the voice of the poet that dominated. Only the poet could capture the complexities of discerning the meaning of unchanging texts for the constantly shifting realities of human experience. Only the poet could recognize the prior right of aspirations to righteousness while all too cognizant of the exigencies of survival. The Grand Ayatollah, as poet, could do those things.

For Fadlallah, awareness also often took on a consistently realistic and pragmatic character. Yet, those qualities did not define him. Both attributes were at the service of a beloved figure who was felt to have a heart of monumental proportions. To engage Fadlallah close at hand was to discover that his heart was never silent. On Fadlallah's death, it was left to the hardnosed and pointedly unsentimental British journalist Robert Fisk to find the words to capture that complexity. Fisk insisted that, for all the complications of Fadlallah's life and work, it was "epic kindness" that defined the greatness of the Grand Ayatollah Muhammad Hussein Fadlallah. Fisk pronounced that "Fadlallah was a very serious and very important man whose constant sermons on the need for spiritual regeneration and kindness did more good than most in a country constantly flooded in a rhetoric bath." Fisk concluded that "hundreds of thousands attended his funeral in Beirut on Tuesday. I am not surprised."[33]

7

Grand Ayatollah Baqir al Sadr

Martyred Theorist of the Islamic Alternative

Saddam Hussein was hanged for his crimes on December 30, 2006. Above the din raised at the public execution, one name resounded. Chants of *Baqir al Sadr* filled the air.[1] Ordinary Iraqis had not forgotten their martyred Imam. On April 9, 1980, Saddam Hussain's security forces had imprisoned and tortured to death the Iraqi Grand Ayatollah Muhammad Baqir al Sadr. "It was the crime of the century," lamented Lebanon's Ayatollah Muhammad Hussein Fadlallah. Reportedly, his murderers drove a nail through his skull. They burned his body. They ravaged his library. No trace was to remain of Iraq's most distinguished Islamic scholar.

Yet, Baqir al Sadr survived in the hearts and minds of the Iraqi people. The life story of Baqir al Sadr brings into view a man of impressive intellect and prodigious learning. Scholars matter in Islam. They matter in distinctive ways in Shi'i Islam. The Grand Ayatollah left his mark.

Iraq's Shi'i Scholarly Tradition

As scion of a venerable line of Shi'i scholars, Baqir al Sadr was born into a family that had deep roots in the Shi'i scholarly tradition. The family traced its lineage to the Prophet Muhammad through the seventh Shi'i Imam Musa al Kazim (745–799). Baqir's father, Haydar al Sadr, was a high-ranking cleric. His family roots in the scholarly tradition of Shi'i Islam assured that Baqir would have before him the model of scholar as activist.

Through the centuries, both Sunni and Shi'i scholars accepted Abu Dharr as the trusted recorder of a substantial body of *hadith*s (sayings of the Prophet that illuminate his thoughts and actions). They also remembered him as a strong advocate for the poor. Through the centuries, they came to regard Abu Dharr as a symbol for social justice. In the Shi'i scholarly tradition, Abu Dharr has a particularly strong influence. His closeness to Imam Ali

Justice in Islam. Raymond William Baker, Oxford University Press. © Oxford University Press 2022.
DOI: 10.1093/oso/9780197624975.003.0007

GRAND AYATOLLAH BAQIR AL SADR   153

(601–661) and his opposition to what he judged to be the worldly excesses of the third caliph Osman Ibn Affan (577–656) made him a figure of great reverence for the Shi'i. Beyond his base in Iraq, he is regarded as one of the four founding figures of Shi'i Islam.

By his scholarly and political work over his short lifetime, Baqir deepened his identification as a scholar who, like Abu Dharr, struggled boldly for justice. He did so in a culture that celebrated and even revered such activist Islamic intellectuals. A prodigy, Baqir augmented his inherited cultural capital by memorizing the Qur'an while still a child. He published his first scholarly treatise when barely out of puberty. At the preeminent Shi'i Najaf seminary, Baqir's teachers were the distinguished scholars Ayatollah Sayyid Abul Qasim al Khoei (1899–1992) and Ayatollah Muhsin al Hakim (1889–1970). While still a young man, Baqir became a major intellectual figure among Islamic scholars. At the age of twenty-five, when young scholars were typically just seeking admission to Dar al Kharij seminary, the precocious Baqir secured a teaching appointment there. He made himself a luminary of the Najaf network of Shi'i scholars. Baqir's scholarship earned him the rank of Grand Ayatollah. His meteoric rise in the Shi'i hierarchy culminated with attainment of the highest status of *marja' al taqlid* ("source of emulation").

Over his lifetime, the Ayatollah published an impressive corpus of commentary on Islam's sacred texts. He also authored widely read interpretations of the major systems of secular thought that competed with the Islamic orientation. What stood out in Baqir's work was the encyclopedic range of his writing, rather than particular scholarly breakthroughs. His writings showcased an impressive ability to facilitate access to the most complex ideas of both the Islamic sciences and secular learning.

Baqir and the Islamic Awakening

Baqir's prolific and highly regarded scholarship had a profound influence on the renewal of Islamic thought central to the Awakening. He significantly advanced the project of bringing the Shi'i scholarly legacy into the modern world. Study of the writings of the major intellectuals of the Islamic Awakening inevitably occasions an encounter with the work of the youthful Iraqi Ayatollah. References by Islamic intellectuals to his highly regarded revisions of classic theological works in the core curriculum of the Najaf seminary first brought Baqir's intellectual work to my attention. Most

154 JUSTICE IN ISLAM

notable was his updating of the standard text for the study of *usul al fiqh*, the fundamentals of theology. Baqir's *Halaqaat al Usul* represented a revision of the text used for generations at the Najaf seminary to teach advanced seminary students how to derive laws. Baqir's renewal of this indispensable work won the endorsement of the most senior seminary scholars. He succeeded in bringing a critical inherited text into the modern age. Baqir singlehandedly rescued aspiring young Islamic intellectuals from a barely penetrable but indispensable inherited text. The most senior scholars testified that he did so without compromising the integrity and rigor of the texts. Baqir's version of the indispensable classic on the derivation of laws became the standard for successive waves of students. This one book had an enormous impact on the training of a long line of Shi'i scholars in training who came in his wake.

Such highly specialized theological works were only the tip of the iceberg of Baqir's scholarly achievements. Over his lifetime, he wrote some three dozen books and countless articles. His work included significant contributions to Shi'i Islamic learning in jurisprudence, theology, Islamic culture, and Qur'anic exegesis. Alongside his highly regarded Qur'anic exegesis, Baqir produced volumes of contemporary social commentary that engaged the work of secular critics of the Islamic orientation. It was his comparative studies of materialist and Islamic worldviews that established his wider reputation among both Sunni and Shi'i intellectuals. Baqir authored works in philosophy, logic, history, and, to greatest effect, economics. Two books, in particular, made Ayatullah Muhammad Baqir al-Sadr not only a figure of note among Shi'i scholars but also a highly respected scholar across the Islamic world. His *Falsafatuna* (Our Philosophy) and *Iqtisaduna* (Our Economics) are celebrated to this day for bridging the gap between Shi'i classical learning and the contemporary scholarship of renewal. As a public intellectual, the Ayatollah also produced a small library of accessible philosophical studies that critically engaged contemporary secular thinking from a centrist Islamic perspective.

Baqir's closely reasoned critiques of socialism, communism, and capitalism were especially widely read. He took as the starting point for his work in contemporary social theory the conviction that the economy provides the foundation for all social systems. To reach this conclusion on the primacy of economics and the corollary of its immediate relevance to broader questions of social justice, Baqir had no need for Marxism. As an Islamic scholar, Baqir knew that some two hundred Qur'anic verses treat issues of the economy. Economic practices referenced in the Qur'an include *zakat* (religious obligation owed to support those in need), the generation and distribution of wealth, the regulation of transactions, and all manner of contractual relations. Greatest focus is given to the positive values that should be at work in any economic system. Justice looms largest. The Qur'an gives special attention to economic activities that bear on the protection of the vulnerable and the enhancement of social responsibility. Celebrated as well are the values of fairness and honesty. Negative values to be avoided include injustice, excess, stinginess, and greed.[2]

Baqir points out that prohibitions are an important part of the Qur'anic message on the economy. They are not, however, the whole story. Negative economic practices such as the imposition of exploitative interest or usury, misappropriation, hoarding, and gambling are all sternly condemned. Pointed economic verses inveigh against behavior that violates the core values of Islam. Explicitly prohibited actions include dishonesty, fraud, misrepresentation, and theft. The Qur'an calls those who commit such acts to repent. They are warned that failure to do so will mean suffering in this world and hellfire in the world to come. At the same time, Baqir emphasized that the Qur'an signals in clear language strong approval for mutually beneficial trade: "O you who believe, take not your wealth among yourselves in wrongful ways, but let there be trade among you by mutual agreement."[3]

Baqir's evaluation of materialism as economic theory opened with appreciation for the impressive productivity registered by economies structured by materialist worldviews. However, on Islamic ground, Baqir challenged the premise of such studies that overall growth in production was the appropriate standard for assessment of an economic order. In his celebrated comparative studies of the major contemporary economic worldviews, Baqir systematically elaborated the contrasting characteristics of socialist, capitalist, and Islamic systems. Clarifying his own views of Islamic economics, he argued that success in the economic realm should be evaluated by the standard of just distribution, rather than simply the volume of production. An Islamic framing would seek to assess the justice of economic outcomes by distribution that was attentive to not only individual well-being but also the general welfare of society. Baqir argued that the historical record demonstrated that high levels of productivity did not, in themselves, assure just outcomes.

Baqir identified the underlying failings of both major materialist systems. Their productivity, he reasoned, came at too high a cost. He judged that socialism as a worldview and organizing social principle was not consonant with inherent human nature. By downplaying the interest of the individual

156 JUSTICE IN ISLAM

for the sake of the collective, socialist thought dilutes the force of individualism. Baqir considered individual self-interest the most effective driver of creativity and constructive effort. As a result of this flaw, socialism requires the application of oppressive levels of political pressure to assure maximum output in the absence of the free play of self-interest. Such a top-down approach, by default, risks producing a dangerous concentration of political power at the political center. It tempts tyrants. Freedom and attention to the general welfare of society both inevitably suffer.

In parallel, Baqir explained that capitalism has its own distinctive failing. The capitalist believes that the values of hard work and social responsibility need not be taught. The market, capitalists judge, would automatically provide the incentives for maximum productivity and the realization of social interests. Capitalism is based on the belief that efforts to realize one's personal interests in a free society will in the long run promote the general welfare. Again, personal interest provides the strongest incentives for all manner of work. However, capitalism adds the notion that pursuit of personal interest is at the same time the surest pathway to the realization of social welfare. Personal strivings will improve production methods to assure maximum gains, while cutting expenses. Societies built on this conception of individual interest have the best chance for economic prosperity. By unleashing individual drive, capitalism is believed to automatically realize the social interest. Simply put, capitalism posits that, as the individual thrives, society gains. Therefore, in the capitalist worldview, individuals need not be motivated by social concerns nor even understand them. Market mechanisms are believed to assure their automatic realization.

Baqir rejects what he considers such exaggerated confidence in the market. He argues that historical experience has demonstrated the terrible shortcomings of market mechanisms in advancing the common good. Baqir paints a devastating picture of the glaring inequalities that characterize even the most "successful" capitalist societies. The American version of capitalism, in his view, provides a particularly egregious example. The very rich are awash in frivolous luxuries, while the mass of people struggle simply to meet basic needs. Worse still, the gap between rich and poor widens with each generation. Unearned incomes accelerate the uneven concentration of newly generated wealth in fewer and fewer hands.

By the early 2020s, it has become clear that America has entered a second *gilded age* of startling inequalities. The first lasted from the late nineteenth to the early twentieth century and ended with the Great Depression of 1929.

Maldistribution of wealth is even more dramatic today. The wealthiest 1% of families own wealth equal to that of the bottom 90%. The impact of this maldistribution is exacerbated by the destructive behavior of the top 20% of richest families. They engage in widespread hoarding that preserves the power their riches confer, while excluding others.

The Qur'an and the Economy

No Islamic scholar could fail to notice that these were precisely the outcomes against which the Qur'an warned. Two Qur'anic injunctions have a striking relevance to the American experience. Concentration and limited circulation of wealth are both excoriated in clear Qur'anic passages.[4] The Qur'an warns without equivocation of the dangers to a just social order of exorbitant and unregulated concentrations of wealth. American capitalism exemplifies the threat posed. A closely related Qur'anic notion teaches that in a just society, circulation of wealth must not be confined to the upper reaches of society. For an American scholar, the Qur'anic injunctions have a jarring relevance. By the early 2020s, anticipated inequalities had arrived with a vengeance. The glaring gap between rich and poor has not only persisted but widened, precisely as Baqir feared. Of advanced industrial societies, the United States has a strong claim as the one with the most unequal distribution of wealth. Such an unjust outcome arises from unearned incomes. Larger shares of the wealth naturally yield higher income. Meanwhile, an ever-growing percentage of the population faces the ravages of poverty in the wealthiest society the world has ever known.

Baqir concluded that the capitalist judgment that it was not necessary to teach values is undermined by such outcomes in the most developed capitalist societies. Market competition by itself cannot achieve humane balancing of individual and social interests. Baqir took note of the tyranny of exorbitant wealth. He judged, correctly, that accumulated wealth, rather than income disparity, posed the greatest threat to just outcomes. Market forces rewarded concentration of capital, while at the same time restricting the circulation of wealth to the highest reaches of society. Baqir reminded his readers that these were precisely the inevitabilities of which the Qur'an warned.[5] In the 1950s, when Baqir was writing, the worst excesses of the American example were not yet apparent. However, Baqir theorized correctly that, without moral guardrails, a system that concentrated capital in

158 JUSTICE IN ISLAM

fewer and fewer hands would inevitably be corrupting. He judged that the oppression of excessive wealth concentration toward which unregulated capitalism leaned was as devastating for freedoms as the tyranny of unconstrained political power.

Baqir argued that only a religious framework could curb the terrible distortions of exaggerated capital concentration and limited circulation of wealth to which a market economy was susceptible. It will come as no surprise that, in Baqir's view, Islam was the religion best suited to this tutelary role. Islam, he explained, was the religion of *tawhid* (the Islamic belief in the oneness of God). As a faith built on the principle of unity, Islam would reconcile the gap between individual interest and social welfare. A value-centered economic system could foster a disciplined and humane individualism that would consciously advance the social good alongside individual interest.

A common misreading of Islam argues that the faith provides no protection of individual rights. The dismal record of human rights in so many Islamic countries is typically offered as all the proof the argument requires. The facts are accurate. However, the explanatory reasoning is flawed. The disregard for the individual so much in evidence has more to do with despotism and corruption than Islam. The faith does have a place for the support of individual rights in the context of *istikhlaf*, the Islamic call to humanity to build just societies. Within the larger moral context of commitment to building a just society, Islam does not ignore human differences. The faith takes for granted the disparities in talent and commitment that mark human beings. However, there is a limit to celebration of these natural differences. Islam teaches that a common humanity and brotherhood should transcend emphasis on such distinctions. On the individual level, the Qur'an exhorts every Muslim to act as the protector and defender of every other Muslim.[6]

Baqir's work in social theory aimed in these ways to demonstrate the superiority of social systems explicitly based on moral and ethical principles. The value of his studies and their general appeal was greatly enhanced by his consistent effort to highlight the strengths as well as the weaknesses of the materialist orientations he critiqued. At the same time, Baqir recognized that extensive work remained to be done to elaborate the exemplary Islamic economic model he advocated. Baqir noted that the economics of socialism and capitalism could be studied empirically. Islamic economics, in contrast, would necessarily be a theoretical discipline. Baqir acknowledged that there were no "actually existing" Islamic social systems to be studied. He dismissed out of hand the self-proclaimed African and Arab "socialist" systems. In his eyes, they had little to do with socialism and most often everything to do with venal and despotic nationalisms.

Thoughts on Democracy

Saddam Hussein provided all the instruction in the dangers of corrupt and tyrannical dictatorship that Baqir and his readers could ever have required. While Baqir's contributions were most significant in economics, he also produced important political commentary. Consistently, he argued that democracy in Islam was possible and desirable. His work in economics was complemented by his call for an activist politics under an explicit Islamic banner. Baqir was fully aware of the appeal to Iraqi youth of Marxism, with its compelling critique of the unjust distribution of wealth in unregulated market economies. Baqir heard the call of progressive youth for a radical restructuring of society along equalitarian, socialist lines. He believed that such an end could be best realized within an Islamic centrist, rather than capitalist, framework.

Baqir fully acknowledged the at times dazzling productivity of the most advanced capitalist societies. However, he registered just as clearly their terrible flaws. As we have seen, Baqir saw clearly that the most advanced capitalist societies were plagued by terrible equalities between the rich and the poor. Most distressing for Baqir was the capitalist argument for the absence of any moral restraints on economic behavior. All indicators pointed to the increase in an unbridgeable gap between rich and poor without guardrails in place. Societies would be dominated by the economic and political power of billionaires. Within the capitalist framework, these failings appeared to Baqir to have no remedy. Capitalism interpreted any attempt to teach moral restraint as a damaging infringement on the workings of the market.

Baqir judged the very different flaws of socialist economics to be just as serious. His critique of the Marxist foundations of socialism emphasized the way socialist societies diminished the motivation for the individual to work harder than absolutely required. A socialist or communist society, for this reason, contradicted human nature. Only a religious society, erected on religiously informed values, could successfully resolve the tensions between

160   JUSTICE IN ISLAM

individual and social interest with freely embraced moral and ethical principles. Sadr explains how Islam reconciles the personal motivations of the human being with social interests by teaching an Islamically grounded morality and an ethics of responsibility. Together, in his view, they work their just effects with God's knowledge and permission.[7]

Abu Dharr and Islam's Activist Impulse

For all the attention that Baqir's intellectual work merited, there was more to the story of Iraq's distinguished Ayatollah than his prolific scholarship. From the outset, Baqir committed himself to serious social and political engagement. The Islamic Awakening challenged the quietism that had so often prevailed in Islamic lands and questioned the judgment that Islam was the source of the social passivism. Scholars of the Awakening insisted that, quite to the contrary, an activist impulse pervades Islam's sacred texts. In their collective view, Islam sounded a call to righteous action.

The Prophet's beloved companion Abu Dharr al Ghifari has, from Islam's earliest beginnings, amplified that call. When Muslims are called to accountability, the Qur'an makes it clear that actions will count most, rather than simply ideas or beliefs. In parallel fashion, the *Sunnah* of the Prophet Muhammad modeled community involvement. The Prophet Muhammad lived among his followers. He participated fully in all aspects of their collective lives. Spirituality and individual piety have their place in Islam. There have always been mystical and often quietist interpretations of the faith. However, to follow the Prophet Muhammad is to embrace activist involvement in the building of the just society.

Baqir heard and echoed that call. He is credited with providing the intellectual foundations for *al Da'wa*, a party of Islamic activists that was founded in 1958–1959 in Iraq. With Baqir's intellectual leadership, *al Da'wa* emerged by the late 1970s in the forefront of resistance to the tyrannical regime of Saddam Hussein. The party championed social justice. Party activists openly welcomed and trumpeted the Iranian "earthquake" of 1979 as an *Islamic* revolution. They proclaimed its relevance to struggles for justice not just in Iran, but across the Islamic world. The Iraqi regime reacted severely, with periodic campaigns of arrest, torture, and murder. Despite the heavy repression, the party survived and remains a force in Iraqi politics to this day.

Modeling the Scholar as Activist: Abu Dharr al Ghifari

In the Iraq of Saddam Hussein, the combination of stellar scholarship and consequential political activism brought Baqir al Sadr to martyrdom in 1980 at the age of forty-five. For an Islamic scholar, death at that age is tragically premature. More typically, scholars continue productive work through the seventies and often well into the eighties. Baqir's brutal murder while in his prime made his scholarly productivity and activist achievements over such a short lifetime all the more remarkable.

Activist Islamic scholars like Baqir al Sadra who are committed to justice have been the bane of tyrants through Islam's fourteen centuries. Abu Dharr al Ghifari, the Prophet's beloved companion, gave a human face and compelling voice to Islam's core commitment to social justice and resistance to tyranny. Baqir al Sadra made that commitment his own. Abu Dharr modeled the Islamic intellectual as an activist for justice. He is rightfully considered a scholar of weight as the author of over two hundred strong *hadiths*. However, for the most part, Abu Dharr is remembered in a more personal way for his close relationship with the Prophet Muhammad. His closeness to the Prophet allowed Abu Dharr to bring a spirit of righteous rebelliousness, coupled with enlightened learning, into the Prophet's inner circle.

Through the centuries, Abu Dharr's influence has been reinforced in endlessly elaborated myths and legends. For many, including the Prophet himself, Abu Dharr's asceticism, humility, and kindness evoked the spirit of the Muslim prophet Jesus. To the revered persona of Jesus, he added the contrast of a confident assertiveness that both complicated and enhanced his impact. Abu Dharr is beloved of the Shi'i for his connections to Ali. He is not, however, remembered as an easy figure. The Prophet's companion is admired for his bold challenge to the third caliph, Osman ibn Affan (577–656). Abu Dharr stood against what he saw as a drift to corruption under Osman. His actions reflected righteous rebelliousness in the name of justice.

Had Abu Dharr been simply a political activist, it would have been easy enough to consign him to oblivion. His *hadith* scholarship, however, protected Abu Dharr's relevance. The trusted *hadiths* of Abu Dharr authoritatively reported on the thoughts and actions of the Prophet in Islam's first years. A passion for justice, heartfelt compassion, and embrace of the poor are all important threads in the foundational *hadiths* he provided the community. The Prophet himself celebrated Abu Dharr's learning and

162   JUSTICE IN ISLAM

righteousness. That embrace has guaranteed the ageless relevance of the beloved companion.

Abu Dharr and the Islamic Awakening

Abu Dharr's contributions as a *hadith* scholar built a progressive understanding of Islam's core features into the textual foundations of the faith. He made his contributions in the spirit of the Muslim Jesus. Such a figure can be willfully ignored. His impact, in particular circumstances, can be minimized. His memory may dim. However, Abu Dharr and the progressive Islam for which he stood cannot be expunged. As a foundational figure, Abu Dharr retains the capacity to intervene in Islamic history.

Abu Dharr has done precisely that in our time of Islamic Awakening. He has had a clear and recurring impact on the leading Islamic scholars of the contemporary Islamic Awakening. He periodically appears on stages grand and small. He has traveled through time and space as far as the mosque in my Alexandria neighborhood, as the Introduction to this book reports.[8] Abu Dharr has a regularly renewed place in the storehouse of memories and legends of all Muslims. The Sunni majority and the Shi'i minority do remember Abu Dharr somewhat differently. Essentials, however, are shared. Muslims of both sects affirm his status as a close companion of the Prophet.

Baqir al Sadr, as a major Shi'i scholar, made himself a particularly worthy renewer of Abu Dharr's legacy. The circumstances in the Iraq of Saddam Hussein provided an exaggerated example of the dangers of which Abu Dharr warned. Brutal political tyranny and boundless corruption defined Hussein's regime. The Ayatollah Muhammad Baqir al Sadr had no illusions about the murderous brutality of the regime of Saddam Hussein. He fully understood the dangers that the pathway of Abu Dharr represented in a despotic setting like Iraq.

Baqir al Sadra saw clearly the specter of martyrdom in his future. He recognized that his activism in the name of Islamic justice would most likely lead to his death at the hands of the regime. While under house arrest, Baqir once confided to a confidant his awareness of the price his active opposition to Saddam would exact. Baqir expressed his belief that every nation must produce a *Hussain* for the revolution of justice to come. The reference is to the Prophet's grandson, Hussain ibn Ali (626–680). Hussain died fighting tyranny. He gave his life in a battle he knew he could not win. Baqir al Sadra believed that revolution in the Iraq of Saddam Hussein would require the blood of martyrs. Such figures would knowingly sacrifice their lives in the way of Hussain ibn Ali. Baqir al Sadr had come to terms with his own place in their ranks. The Grand Ayatollah cast himself in the role of the Hussain of the Iraqi revolution to come.

Islamic Intellectuals Do Matter

Western commentary on Islamic movements signals that midstream Islamic intellectuals like Baqir al Sadr have little to say of lasting importance. In the Western literature, the works of centrist scholars and activists are routinely given only minimal attention. Instead, the incoherent rantings of extremists are cited far more frequently to illustrate the thinking of Islamic intellectuals. The tirades of such figures are easily discounted. The murderous Saddam Hussein, in sharp contrast, knew it was the words of Islamic scholars of stature that mattered. The extreme character of Baqir al Sadr's murder makes it clear that the Iraqi dictator took very seriously the task of silencing Islamic scholars. The ritualized brutality of Baqir's murder was clearly intended to offer a gruesome warning to any inclined to follow his path.

In the West today, a parallel silencing of centrist scholars is achieved by very different means. In the context of a metaphysical war on "terror," the lion's share of journalistic and even scholarly attention is directed by the global corporate media away from midstream figures. Moderate voices in Islam are unheard. Baqir al Sadr, in particular, has suffered unfortunate neglect in Western commentary, despite the respect in which he is held by Islamic scholars. The scholarship of the youthful Imam has only rarely received the serious attention it deserves. In place of attention to thoughtful and committed scholars like Baqir, the most outrageous Islamic extremists provide the never-ending focus of the international media. The message of the extremists is threatening but without depth. Images of their violent actions are graphic but most often bereft of context. However, the hollow words and unbearably cruel images make exactly the attention-grabbing content on which a profit-driven international media thrives. The repetition of disturbing slogans and endless recycling of images of pornographic violence immeasurably magnify the extremist presence. The most violent among the extremists loom largest. Not surprisingly, extremists are taken

164 JUSTICE IN ISLAM

by many in the West as the most important representatives of Islam and the world's 1.8 billion Muslims.

The Ayatollah Baqir al Sadr represented as few others the alternative face of a centrist Islam of justice. He expressed his centrist thought as both *fiqh* (authoritative commentary on the sacred texts) and *fikr* (social theory and philosophy). To know Baqir al Sadr is to understand that the Islamic challenge to the West has always had a serious intellectual dimension. Baqir projected a confident scholarly command of core religious references. He emerged from the deepest layers of the Shi'i scholarly tradition. At the same time, Baqir al Sadra made himself a luminary of one of the most influential contemporary networks of influential scholars. In his scholarly work, Baqir al Sadra embodied both a repository of the collective wisdom of the past and a harbinger of the more just future Muslims were called to build.

Baqir's always carefully reasoned and researched criticism of secular alternatives went to the heart of their failings. At the same time, the youthful Ayatollah accurately reported their impressive material achievements. The full stature of Baqir al Sadr as a scholar is difficult to convey. His authoritative and prolific scholarship played an important role in grounding more securely the efforts of scholars of the Awakening to assess the strengths and limitations of secular accomplishments. Such realistic contrasts were essential to the effort to revitalize contemporary Islamic social theory. He contextualized the work of Islamic scholars as both a revitalization of the legacy and an advancement of contemporary scholarship.

The young Ayatollah dominated an Islamic cultural geography that is largely invisible to the West. Oceanography offers a suggestive parallel when it conjures up submerged seascapes. The precise measurements of science and electronic simulations bring towering mountains and the deepest valleys into detailed and precise view. Islamic studies, for its part, does have the power of descriptions. Carefully deployed words can evoke unseen realities. Words, to work their effects, must of course be articulated in a language that readers understand. Understanding means that they can be used to provide plausible interpretations of complex cultural worlds without which a grasp of situational meanings remains out of reach. Interpretations, unlike scientific representations, can make no claims to universality. They can nevertheless illuminate contexts beyond our reach. They cannot, however, transcend them. They must always be grounded. Their meanings are always contextual rather than transcendent. The demands on readers and listeners are far more exacting. Without empathetic understanding, both interpretations and the contexts that give them their fullest meaning are not easily brought within reach. However, with a modicum of goodwill and effort, the human imagination can conjure the minimal empathy necessary to bring a cultural context other than one's own into view. Cultural studies demand exactly that.

Once imaginatively glimpsed, the submerged Islamic cultural landscape opens the way to a grounded understanding of the unfolding of *Islam haraki* (movement Islam). The spiritual and organizational resources of an Islamic context come into view. Latent connections are brought into focus. Revitalization of historic networks sets a practical agenda. Inherited networks pass through national and ethnic barriers to offer safe passage for inspiration, ideas, and for the scholars and activists themselves. It falls to Islamic scholars to preserve and revitalize these indispensable resources for their own time and purposes.

Baqir al Sadr played exactly this role. He enjoyed access to the scholarly treasures of Najaf by birth. As a young and highly gifted scholar, he stood at the very center of the all-important Najaf network of Shi'i Islamic scholars. The Iraqi city of Najaf in central Iraq ranks among the most important of centuries-old Shi'i centers of learning. Located about 100 miles south of Baghdad, the city is widely believed to be the burial site of Ali ibn Abi Talib, the Prophet's son-in-law and the most revered figure of Shi'i Islam. From Najaf, leading scholars and their students have for generations radiated out across Iraq, Syria, Lebanon, the Gulf, Pakistan, and beyond. Najaf was Baqir's home for much of his early life. He lost his father at the age of two. At ten, his family moved him to Najaf, where he was raised and educated by scholars of the extended al Sadr family.

To immerse oneself in the Islamic scholarly traditions, it is not enough to appreciate the work of individual scholars. Understanding of the networks by which they are connected, such as the all-important Najaf network, should be given as much weight in efforts to assess their work. Often, the real importance of a scholar lies precisely in contributions to the strengthening of the networks through which they move. These linkages extend effortlessly across national, ethnic, and even sectarian boundaries.

Without the connections generated by such centers of Shi'i learning as Najaf, it is unlikely that the important Shi'i dimensions of the Islamic Awakening would have been so enlightening. The influence of Najaf affiliates loomed especially large in the two great twentieth-century successes of Shi'i movement Islam. Most important are the 1979 Iranian Revolution and the dramatic 2006 Hizbullah victory in ending the eighteen-year

166 JUSTICE IN ISLAM

Israeli occupation of southern Lebanon. It is noteworthy that Iran's Imam Khomeini, who led the Iranian Revolution, spent thirteen years in Najaf. Ayatollah Fadlallah, whose writings inspired Lebanon's Hizbullah, was himself born and trained for years in Najaf.

In parallel fashion, this venerable Najaf culture of Islamic learning nurtured the Grand Ayatollah Baqir al Sadr. Baqir's incomparable scholarly achievements seem impossible to imagine without the intellectual riches of Najaf that he absorbed from childhood. Baqir al Sadr's place as a major spiritual and intellectual link in the Najaf Shi'i network parallels in its weight that of the Egyptians Hassan al Banna and Sayyid Qutb and their roles in contributing to the Awakening. Both the Sunni Muslim Brotherhood as a transnational Sunni force and the influential Najaf Shi'i network served as orientating points of reference as the multifaceted, transnational Awakening took shape.

Baqir al Sadr drew strength from Najaf, even as he at the same time enhanced and strengthened the network that originated there with his prodigious scholarship and courageous political activism. The Ayatollah Baqir al Sadr joins Hassan al Banna and Sayyid Qutb as intellectual giants of *Islam haraki*. The sectarian categories of Shi'i and Sunni suggest an exaggerated separateness. In reality, influences from Banna, Qutb, and Baqir merged and flowed into all Islamic communities, whatever their sectarian coloration.

Sectarian differences did define borders and erect barriers. However, complex patterns of spiritual and cultural interactions regularly succeeded in penetrating them. Those points of connection included inclusive rituals that expressed love for the Prophet, shared political programs, or pilgrimages to holy sites held in common. Such border crossings ebbed and flowed in their frequency. They were, nevertheless, always there. Breeches of sectarian boundaries made possible creative enrichments. In the face of sectarian distortions, they expressed Islam's inherently inclusive spirituality. They buttressed its bold claim to universality.

For the most part, these submerged patterns of interactions have eluded Western perspectives on the Islamic Awakening. The failing is understandable. The West projects an interest in divisions that weaken the Islamic world. There is little inclination to pay attention to aspects of the Islamic tradition that foster the strength that unity brings. *Islam haraki* has been one such vehicle of transcendence.

The American security elite, in the wake of the Iranian Revolution of 1979, judged *Islam haraki* a serious threat. The shah's regime had served as a bulwark against radicalisms of all varieties. Its collapse before the Islamic wave proved traumatic. It continues to fuel an exaggerated and irrational hatred of the Iranian regime to this day. The Iranian Revolution did galvanize Islamic movements across the Islamic world. However, those movements were already in the field, with deep local roots of their own.

Nevertheless, the success of the Iranians represented a triumph for *Islam haraki* as a force for resistance to imperialism *and* local tyranny. In the worldview of the Western security establishment, it definitively reinforced ideas of movement Islam as a dangerous adversary. Those sentiments cast a pall over Islamic intellectuals in general. Henceforth, the West, particularly the United States, could be counted on to welcome the assassination of Islamic intellectuals, if not to participate directly in such outcomes. Saddam understood that murdering imprisoned Ayatollah Muhammad Baqir al Sadr would not contribute to any worsening of his relationship with the American government.

Muhammad Baqir al Sadr's distinguished lineage assured privileged access to the bountiful intellectual traditions of the Islamic heritage. Yet, Baqir did not lock himself within inherited modes of Islamic thought. Rather, from that secure base, Baqir explored alternative worldviews. The Ayatollah acquired an unusual familiarity for an Islamic intellectual with capitalist and socialist thought as the dominant materialist ideologies of the West. To be sure, in the end his aim was always to demonstrate the ways in which the Islamic vision of man and society was more compelling. However, Baqir escaped the trap of hollow and purely reactive apologetics. He established himself as a serious social theorist. He did so by demonstrating an impressive competence and familiarity with both Islamic and Western intellectual traditions. Baqir al Sadr attained a deep understanding of both. He treated both with respect.

In his philosophical studies, Baqir carefully reconstructs the alternative ideological positions he critically dissects. He does so with rigorous honesty. Baqir, for example, makes clear the ways socialism and capitalism have produced complex and seductive visions of man and society. Most importantly, he explains how they give abstract materialist formulations concrete expression in impressive societal progress.

Baqir's expositions of the Marxist foundations of leftist philosophies stand as perhaps the most coherent and attractive available in Arabic. His depictions of the materialist philosophies could achieve that level of authenticity only by passing through empathetic understanding. That route is

168   JUSTICE IN ISLAM

precisely the one Baqir consciously took. He sought to create the opportunity to understand socialism and capitalism in their own terms before he engaged in sustained critique. He succeeded. Leftist parties in Iraq were known to lift his summaries of their ideologies from his critical Islamic framing and present them as freestanding explanatory essays. With only minor editing, they could function for recruitment purposes.

Baqir produced his assessments of ascendant materialist ideologies in the 1950s. In those years, leftist ideologies were enjoying the peak of their influence among Arab intellectuals and the students they influenced. In Arab intellectual circles, widespread acceptance of the premises of alternative materialist ideologies meant that Baqir's work had to be well argued in both theoretical and empirical terms. To clear space for an Islamic alternative, Baqir had to do more than produce another recital of the familiar Islamic litany of socialist and capitalist failings and injustices. Such polemical rebuttals of materialist ideologies were well-known. They were guaranteed to have little effect.

Baqir instead set for himself the task of engaging critically the core theoretical notions that defined socialism and capitalism, respectively. The Ayatollah reasoned that at the heart of all varieties of socialism was the notion of class struggle as the engine of progressive social change. For its part, capitalism was energized by the workings of the market. Unfettered competition provided its driving force. Baqir as a major Islamic social theorist was called first to identify and critique these fundamental secular conceptualizations of the driving forces of social change. Only then did he undertake the task of elaborating an Islamic alternative.

Baqir embraced both challenges. As a social theorist, Baqir stepped out of the world of classic Islamic thought to elaborate a critique of class struggle and the market as the key drivers of the economy in socialism and capitalism. He did so from a centrist Islamic perspective that held a value-centered view of how a just Islamic economy should function. Baqir reported his findings most authoritatively in his classic *Our Economy*. This major work was premised on his view that the understanding of economics was central to all social theories. He argued that a value-centered Islamic theory of the economy would be grounded in the Qur'anic vision of a just social order and a moral system of governance. Understanding of the economic realm in Islamic thought would be imbued with the value of justice and other major Islamic values like freedom and compassion. Baqir announced forthrightly that the sources of that vision would be the Qur'an and the *Sunnah*.

In his work, Baqir made clear the relevance of the Qur'an to economic thinking. He pointed to the values, rules, and guidelines elaborated in the Qur'an that had direct relevance to economic life. Baqir reveled in the richness of Islam's holy book in its treatment of economic life. He took particular note of the over 200 Qur'anic verses that treat economic life. He highlighted that of the values emphasized, justice takes pride of place. Honesty, moderation, compassion, and simple kindness are also celebrated. Injustice, greed, extravagance, and both miserliness and extravagance are condemned. Actions in the economic realm are evaluated by value criteria. Major categories given attention include obligations of justice and social responsibility, guidelines for the acquisition and distribution of wealth, and regulations of transactions through contracts. There are also directives for the rightful management of wealth, ownership, trade, credit, and debt. The Qur'an signals that profitable production and fair trade are approved. Exploitive interest or usury is condemned, along with corruption and gambling.

Baqir acknowledged the great obstacles his efforts to elaborate an Islamic vision of economics faced. In particular, he signaled how efforts to move from Qur'anic theory to practice would be severely hampered by the absence of real-world economies that embodied these values. Islamic economics would inevitably have an abstract character. There were simply no already existing Islamic economic systems build on these sacred value foundations. He wrote forthrightly that Islamic theorists of the economy had only the experience of the Prophet's direct rule in Medina, where he arrived in 622 CE, and the subsequent period from 632 to 661 of the rightly guided caliphs, on which to draw to exemplify the practical ways the Islamic model would work. Baqir's treatment of the Prophet's example served to create a model to inspire the future rather than the reification of a prototype from the past. The clarity and blunt honesty with which these fundamental facts were acknowledged and presented greatly enhanced the value and impact of Baqir's comparative studies of major contemporary ideologies and the respective economic systems at their core.

The contrast to the situation of materialist economists could not be greater. Whether capitalist or socialist, they are awash in real-world models of working materialist economic systems. Examples drawn from them could exemplify a variety of materialist economic formations, notably capitalist, socialist, command, and market economies. Baqir understood that, for this reason, materialist theorists were, to their own satisfaction, able to transform economics into an almost exclusively empirical domain of inquiry.

170   JUSTICE IN ISLAM

He also grasped that acceptance of that premise would render deep critique impossible.

Economics as a Western social science rose on the accuracy of its careful recordings of closely observed economies. Studies in economics were marked by increasingly sophisticated mathematical mappings of the actual workings of complex economic systems. To step away from the most precise and replicable observations was taken to mean degradation of the social scientific status of economics. In the Western discipline of economics, historical and even comparative studies were suspect. Such reflective avenues of inquiry were relegated to the margins of the prized secular discipline of economics. Young scholars in the West were dissuaded from building careers on such marginalized foundations.

In contrast, Baqir explained that economics as a central part of an Islamic civilizational alternative would unavoidably be raised on largely theoretical foundations. In Baqir's hands, Islamic economic theory drew explicitly on the Qur'an and *Sunnah* of the Prophet. Baqir judged that, like socialism and communism, Islamic economics would have strong theoretical foundations. They could be referenced as part of a rational inquiry.

In sharp contrast, Baqir argued that capitalism had no such sound theoretical bases. Its foundations were almost exclusively empirical. Competition rather than compassion emerged as the driving force behind the success of all materialist ideologies, most pointedly in its extreme capitalist variants. Capitalist economic theory leaned on the "proof" of its practical successes. The dazzling empirical record of productivity and progress carried the day. Those foundations, Baqir warned, were far less secure and reliable than surface appearances suggested.

The Mystical Foundations of Capitalist Economic Theory

It was barely noticed, Baqir argued, that the brilliance of material achievements under capitalism rested on the weakest of theoretical foundations. Mystical notions of the rational actions of an *economic man* were conjoined with the vision of an imagined market of perfect information and fair competition. Baqir insisted that such a man and such a market are purely mythical. Most magical of all was the idea of an *invisible hand* that reconciled the crudest pursuit of self-interest with an anemic notion of the common good. Such were the core theoretical notions that undergirded capitalist thought. Baqir argued that few dared point out that the imagined rational actor in such a conjured world simply did not exist.

Baqir's inquiries from a centrist Islamic perspective generated intellectual critique with surprising relevance to ongoing debates on the meaning and limitations of capitalist success in the West. There is no denying that capitalist freedom of the individual fosters productivity alongside individual creativity for those who prosper. Baqir argued that hidden from view by the dazzling displays of material advance were serious shortcomings. Baqir explained in simple and compelling terms that what really mattered was not simply production, but distribution. Baqir pronounced that uneven distribution and massive and ever-expanding inequalities are the inevitable outcomes in capitalist economies.

The rationalization of a capitalist system rested ultimately on confident notions of the way in which individual and social interests could be reconciled. In capitalist theory, there was in fact no conflict. Unfettered individual competition would dramatically raise the overall level of production. The material foundations of the common good would be within easy reach. The resolution was automatic and value-free. Baqir pointed out that this vision did not, however, take into account the destructive impact of human greed and insatiable appetite for *more*. Unregulated competition inevitably exacerbated inequalities. He analyzed the ways accumulated and inherited wealth distorts both competition and the balance of information. Greater wealth inevitably solidifies ever-expanding inequalities. Baqir reasoned that unfettered competition that pitted the strong against the weak inescapably produced monopolies. Ultimately, powerful concentrations undermined the market. Staggering inequalities that dangerously weakened the bonds of social solidarity resulted as well. The automatic mechanisms at work were simple and powerful.

Value-Centered Islamic Economic Theory

Without values operative in the system, the economy would inevitably be despoiled by human shortsightedness, greed, and propensity to domination. The values to transcend these human failings could only come from a higher source. Humanity's great religious traditions all identified that source as the divine.

172   JUSTICE IN ISLAM

To Baqir, the remedy presented itself with great clarity. The core message of the Qur'an is the primacy of *'adl* (justice). The Qur'an calls for justice in all aspects of human life, but with particular emphasis on the economy. In the economic sphere, humanity is called to act honestly and in a spirit of cooperation. Both excessive concentration and restricted circulation of wealth are condemned. The Qur'an is clear: "wealth should circulate freely in society and not be concentrated in a few hands."[9] Those engaged in economic affairs are also admonished to act fairly, with honest descriptions of goods exchanged and fair measurements of their worth. Those who act in ways to contravene these guidelines for just behavior are warned to repent or face suffering in this world, as well as severe punishment in the world to come.

Qur'anic treatment of inheritance aims to discourage unhealthy concentration and to foster the expansive circulation of wealth. To the same end, hoarding and miserliness are condemned. Moderation and balance in all such matters is encouraged. Just outcomes are at the heart of the promise of Islamic economic theory. Value-free and unregulated competition has no place in the Islamic vision. In Islam, the human trajectory is centered on *istikhlaf*, the divine mandate to build just societies. Sources are the sacred texts and the singular example of the actions of the Prophet Muhammad as founder of the first Islamic community. In Islam, guidelines for economic behavior are both theoretical and practical.

Baqir did judge that socialism of Marist inspiration did have a reasoned philosophical foundation. In that sense, socialism could be compared usefully to the Islamic alternative he was elaborating in his own philosophical studies. However, in Bair's view, capitalism lacked such coherent theoretical moorings. Material success could screen theoretical failings. It could not, however, correct them. In Baqir's view, a string of disjointed notions did not attain the status of coherent theory. Rather, they simply provided rationalizations for a system of unbridled competition without moral moorings or constraints on the play of raw power.

Fragmented ideological formulations were given their practical coherence and force by the naked military power that backed them. The global triumph of capitalism was not the result of the persuasiveness of its ideology and the capitalist system that ideology justified. The most astute advocates of Western culture recognize that the West excelled above all in the destructive technologies of violence, rather than the attractiveness and coherence of Western ideologies or overarching value systems. The late Samuel Huntington, with rare honesty, acknowledged that "the West won the world not by the

GRAND AYATOLLAH BAQIR AL SADR   173

superiority of its ideas, values, or religion (to which few members of other civilizations were converted) but rather by its superiority in applying organized violence."[10] Instruments of extractive warfare and relentless repression made the impressive material prosperity of Western societies possible. Undoubted material success obscured the theoretical weakness of capitalism as an economic and social system.

Baqir al Sadr acknowledged that on those violence-soaked foundations there did arise the remarkable cultural and technological attainments of Western societies. The Ayatollah reasoned that to understand the West and the market economy as its preeminent institution, both the wondrous achievements and their equally impressive costs in unjust social outcomes must be brought into view. The costs, Baqir insisted, had most to do with capitalism's flawed philosophical foundations. Only with a fully rounded understanding of capitalism, Baqir reasoned, could a genuine alternative be conceptualized.

The costs of capitalist triumphs were both international and domestic. Baqir concluded that capitalism, bereft of secure theoretical moorings, offered no means of moral or even simply rational restraint. Capitalist societies, in Baqir's view, harbor the deadly possibility of consuming themselves. A culture of limitless consumption means that culture and nature are themselves vulnerable. Nothing is preserved from the jaws of consumption. Baqir theorized that, in the end, humanity in a world dominated by capitalism would find itself in the grip of massive cultural, social, and ecological disasters.

Baqir explained that the contrast with Islamic understanding of culture and nature could not be greater. In Islam, both nature and civilization are treated as living organisms that may one day experience destruction and death. As an Islamic theorist, Baqir took note of the signs that civilizational and natural resources for recovery have been severely strained by the profligacy of a careless humanity. In Islam, it is the mission of those who think, i.e., the educated, to recognize and respond to these dangers. Islamic economics, in Baqir's view, could not escape these profoundly moral responsibilities.

From this theoretical vantage point, the Ayatollah sought to ground more securely in theology and philosophy the efforts of scholars of the Awakening to revitalize contemporary Islamic social theory. The capacity for reasoned and measured assessments of competing ideologies characterized all of Baqir's work in social theory. For him, clarity and honesty in the critique of materialism in all its forms constituted a critical first step on the path of

174 JUSTICE IN ISLAM

elaborating a genuine Islamic alternative. His intellectual work is ultimately grounded in the divine revelation at the heart of Islam. Yet, it has practical as well as theoretical implications. Islamic thought refuses the Western polarity of the material and the spiritual. In contrast, the imagined Islamic communities that inspire Islamic economic and political thinking are viewed holistically. The spiritual is never banned from the material realm.

Precisely for this reason, political economy is front and center in all of Baqir's writings. His work in economics is motivated in the first instance by a sense of the unfortunate neglect of the study of the economic realm in the work of Islamic social theorists. Baqir finds this inattention to economic theory debilitating. He argues that the way the economic realm is understood is absolutely central to the reasoned evaluation of competing social theories. Alternative conceptions of the economic system capture the heart of the fundamental choices humanity faces. As we have seen, in capitalism, the driver of the economy is competition. In leftist materialist ideologies, like Marxism, class conflict provides the motivating force of history. In Islam, the economic realm is animated by values of divine origin. In the Islamic social vision, Qur'anic values, with a priority to justice, provide both the driving force for advancement and the standards for evaluating the results achieved. Islam refuses the Western notion of value-free social theory.

Baqir unequivocally rejects the Western model of the free market as the controlling structure for society. He is fully aware of the power and the stunning technological advances that market systems have made possible. He also understands how the market has been wed to a formal liberal variant of the democracy of elections. Such democratic market systems, Baqir frankly acknowledges, have registered undeniable and enviable advances in political and economic development. However, Baqir argues that all of these advances have come in a materialist framework that lacks coherent theoretic underpinnings and most importantly effective moral restraints. The practical results of the lack of theoretical guard rails to discipline competition, he insists, are devastating. Effective restraints of any kind on unbridled competition become impossible.

Baqir builds his critical vision of Western societies on these intellectual foundations. The picture Baqir paints of the future is severe. The gap between rich and poor inevitably widens. Wealth inexorably flows in greater and greater concentrations to the upper reaches of society. Nature suffers despoilation in the name of higher profits. Local cultures suffer devastation from homogenizing commercialism. Moral restraints are voided of their content by a ruthless and all-pervasive instrumentalism. The effect of inherited value systems is minimalized. All relationships are viewed as transactional.

Baqir judges that the price for progress in these terms is simply too high. To leave humanity, culture, and humanity itself to the mercies of a morally indifferent market produces predatory societies. In the end, such societies inevitably consume their own. The logic of capitalism undermines all mechanisms of humane forbearance. Baqir concludes that this Western model of man and society lacks the kind of secure philosophical foundations, moral restraints, and practical guidelines that would make it worthy of imitation.

In contrast, Baqir concludes that Islam holds out the promise of a preferred alternative that rests on two essential principles. The first is "general reciprocal responsibility," on the basis of which it is obligatory upon Muslims to help each other in times of need. The second calls for "social balance," on the basis of which it is the responsibility of the state to bring the different standards of people close to each other. Reciprocal responsibility and social balance will allow the Islamic commitment to social justice to be realized for humanity. The Islamic economic vision that Baqir elaborates reflects the compelling message of the Qur'an: "We sent Our Messengers with clear signs and sent down with them the Book and the Measure in order to establish justice among the people. . . ."[11]

8

Ali Shariati

The Believing Revolutionary

The most influential Iranian revolutionary intellectual was not in the streets when the Iranian people rose up in 1978–1979 to make their Islamic Revolution. Exiled to London, Ali Shariati had died a year earlier in June 1977. Those who took to the streets that summer in major cities across Iran acted to ensure that Ali Shariati his rightful presence. When the Iranian people moved, they brought with them their improbable revolutionary Islamic intellectual. Portraits of this non-cleric, with Marxist leanings, were everywhere when Iran's mass Islamic Revolution erupted. The Iranian people had heard Shariati's call for the overthrow of the regime. They reveled in the Islamic phrasing of his call, despite the complexities of his views. They accepted his notion of revolution as *a return to ourselves*. They embraced his commitment to the reassertion of the priority of Islam and Islamic culture in their lives. From the streets, millions shouted out Shariati's sobriquet as *mo'allem-e enqilab* (mentor of the revolution). Ordinary Iranians made sure that Ali Shariati kept his appointment with history.

The roots of the revolutionary impulse in Islam run deep. Abu Dharr al Ghifari, a beloved companion of the Prophet, pronounced himself "perplexed by a hungry person who has no bread in his house; why does he not arise from among the people, his sword unsheathed and rebel."[1] Abu Dharr sounded this heartfelt call to act for social justice in seventh-century Arabia. Through the centuries, his words have echoed across Islamic lands. In all times and whatever prevailing conditions, Islam's worldly presence assures the righteousness of struggles for justice,

The Islamic call to social justice has sounded with particular clarity in our own time of Islamic Awakening. From the late 1960s, the Islamic Awakening has made itself a transformative force in both Sunni and Shi'i communities across the Islamic strategic triangle of Turkey, Egypt, Iran, and beyond. The turn to Islam has everywhere become a fact of life. It has taken on distinctive meanings in diverse settings. In an Iran oppressed by the tyranny and

Justice in Islam. Raymond William Baker, Oxford University Press. © Oxford University Press 2022.
DOI: 10.1093/oso/9780197624975.003.0008

corruption of the shah's rule, the call for social justice sounded in the late 1970s was no less than a summons to revolution.

When Ali Shariati called Iranian youth to revolution, he did so in in the name of the Prophet's beloved companion. To anchor his revolutionary message in Islam's classic tradition, Ali Shariati insistently invoked Abu Dharr al Ghifari. The biography of the Prophet's companion that Shariati authored made it perfectly clear that Iran's revolutionary intellectual had made the Islam of Abu Dharr his own. "I took Islam from him," he wrote. "I absorbed his trials and his pains," he added.[2]

Shariati invoked Abu Dharr in a distinct way. It was at once intensely personal and broadly symbolic. The Abu Dharr brought to life in his writings and lectures stepped forward as a venerable symbol of social justice. Shariati added further definition. He gave Abu Dharr and the justice he symbolized a spiritual character. He did so by casting the Prophet's companion as a figure who mirrored the qualities of the Muslim prophet Jesus. He projected Abu Dharr as sharing with Islam's Jesus humility, piety, and love for the poor. The Prophet Muhammad himself had linked the two figures in just this way. A strong prophetic hadith advised "those who sought to know Jesus to look to Abu Dharr."[3]

There were, to be sure, differences in the way the two figures of companion and prophet were remembered. The Abu Dharr of legend was far less restrained and far more assertive than the humble and gentle Jesus. The legends that attached to the companion's name projected an aura of a colorful irascibility, quite unlike the prophet Jesus. What the two did share was the message that Islam in an unjust world fosters righteous resistance. Through the centuries, Abu Dharr has come to life as both an assertive symbol for justice and a figure who at the same time walked with the personal humility and caring for the poor that the prophet Jesus modeled. In lectures and writings, Shariati turned to the history and legends of Abu Dharr al Ghifari repeatedly to remind Iranians that Islam provided the essential building blocks for a vision of revolutionary change.

In Christianity, the divine Jesus as the son of God returned to heaven. In Islam, the Holy Qur'an as the word of God remained on earth. As noted earlier, that difference means that for Muslims the direct inspiration and guidance from God to build just communities are always close at hand here on earth in a tangible and accessible form. Existing circumstances may not always allow effective action. However, the call to justice nevertheless sounds in anticipation of that more promising moment yet to come.

178   JUSTICE IN ISLAM

The late 1970s in Iran proved to be such a time. Abu Dharr's seventh-century cry from the heart changed history when it reached the ears of Iran's twentieth-century revolutionaries. The revolution of 1979 was a mass revolution, as in France in 1789 and Russia in 1917. It shook the world. Ali Shariati emerged as a major intellectual force behind those momentous events. He tells us clearly that he was moved by the example of the Prophet's seventh-century companion to act for social justice.

Iranian youth, in particular, responded to Shariati's message, delivered in powerful oratory and elegant Persian prose. Abu Dharr stepped forward in his speeches and writings as an exemplary model of Islam's progressive promise. Most importantly, Shariati taught that the venerable Abu Dharr's example showed Iranian youth that they could be both believing Muslims *and* revolutionaries. Its Islamic inspiration meant that Iran's was the first world-class revolution of the modern era *not* prompted by a Western ideology. Shariati embedded a value-centered understanding of the faith as the foundation for Iran's ideology of revolution. Islam defined the very core of the Iranian radicalism that burst forth in the late 1970s. To refine that revolutionary possibility, Ali Shariati did absorb a great deal from Western and Third World radicalisms. He had made himself familiar with Western revolutionary theory, in general, and Marxism in particular. However, the deepest roots of his intellectual formation lay elsewhere.

Islamic Roots of Revolutionary Theory

Ali Shariati Mazinani was born in 1933 to comfortable circumstances in the village of Kahak in northeastern Iran. He was the son of Muhammad Taqi, a teacher and religious scholar from a family of Islamic intellectuals. His mother came from a modest landowning family in a small town near the city of Mashhad. It was Shariati's father who launched and guided his lifetime study of Islam. In 1947, his father opened the Centre for the Propagation of Islamic Truths in Mashhad. The Centre hosted an Islamic social forum. Members of the Centre were drawn by their social activism into the Iranian nationalist movement of the 1950s. The nationalist drive against imperialism centered on winning greater control over Iran's oil resources.

Raised on a blend of religious and nationalist sentiment, it should come as no surprise that Shariati matured into an Islamic activist as part of the broader Iranian nationalist movement. The city of Mashhad played a major role in Shariati's intellectual and spiritual formation. The city is the second largest in Iran, with a dense and diverse population. It also enjoys a measure of fame as Iran's *holy city*. Mashhad is the home of the tomb and shrine of the Shi'i Imam Reza (765–818), the martyred Eighth Imam of Shi'i Twelver Islam, known as the "Kind Imam." The Imam's shrine has a claim as the largest in the Islamic world.[4] It is renowned for the beauty of its blue tiles and elaborate mirror work. The shrine preserves the memory of Imam Reza. The Imam is celebrated for his commitment to reason and for his exemplary kindness. Among the Imam Reza's sayings, one of the most celebrated states forthrightly: "The friend of every man is his intellect and his enemy is his ignorance." The massive complex built around the Imam's mausoleum contains a mosque, museum, library, four seminaries, a cemetery, the Razavi University of Islamic Sciences, a dining hall for pilgrims, and expansive prayer halls. The shrine is a monument not only to the Kind Imam but to the glory of Shi'i Islam.

Ali Shariati grew up in the shadow of the Kind Imam's mausoleum. He completed his elementary and high school in Mashhad. Shariati then remained in the city to attend the Mashhad Teacher Training College. He concentrated the liberal arts dimension of his training on Arabic and French. In 1960 Shariati graduated with his secondary school teaching certificate.

From the start, these years of preparatory study in Mashhad had a political dimension. Shariati emerged early as a student leader. In 1952, Shariati founded an Islamic Students' Association. His robust activism continued while employed as a high school teacher. These critical years of adolescence and young manhood were punctuated by several long and arrests and always abusive imprisonments for spearheading protests.

Shariati's early academic studies and youthful student activism were not, however, the only critical learning experiences the city made possible. In Mashhad, Shariati directly encountered for the first time the Iranian working class and the poorest of the poor. He acquired a firsthand knowledge of what poverty meant close at hand. He began to develop his appreciation of the way extreme deprivation damages people. Those lessons lasted a lifetime. Images of the *wretched of the earth* would loom large in his mature studies.[5] They first came into view for Shariati in Mashhad. The brutal realities of extreme poverty did more than inspire his youthful activism. They haunted his thinking for all his life.

In late 1950s, the academically gifted Shariati secured a fellowship for advanced studies in France. On first arrival in Paris, the youthful scholar

180 JUSTICE IN ISLAM

plunged once again into political activism. Soon after arrival in the French capital, he became involved with the Algerian FLN, the major nationalist party in the Algerian resistance. On January 17, 1961, Shariati was arrested by French security for participation in demonstrations honoring Patrice Lumumba. Alongside his consuming activism, Shariati managed to continue his advanced studies. He received his doctorate in sociology and Islamic studies in 1964 from the Sorbonne. During his years in Paris, Shariati also became acquainted with several leading European thinkers. They included the Islamic scholar Louis Massignon (1883–1962) and jurist and sociologist Georges Gurvitch (1894–1965). The renowned sociologist Jacques Berque (1910–1995) acted as his academic mentor. In Paris, Shariati infused his Islamic intellectual moorings with deep engagement with Western Marxism and existentialism, as well as Third World radical theory. However, Iran remained the focus of his scholarly work, although his engagement with secular revolutionary theory encouraged a broadening of his reach. Shariati ultimately framed his studies with a sweeping intellectual project that aimed at nothing less than the development of a progressive Islamic ideology. His ambition for his intellectual work was boundless. He sought to provide the theoretical foundation for Islamic movements to transform existing Muslim societies.

In 1964, Shariati returned to Iran with his doctorate from the Sorbonne in hand. The new PhD was greeted almost immediately by Iranian security with arrest and imprisonment. He faced accusations of participation in political activities while concluding his advanced studies in France. The charges were easily documented. Shariati spent some eighteen months in prison under particularly debilitating conditions. He was released in 1965.

Thanks to his French doctorate from the Sorbonne, Shariati was able soon after his release to secure a teaching and research post at the University of Mashhad. The university appointment gave him the opportunity to present his ideas on Islam to Iran's youth. As a credentialed sociologist, he sought to explain how sociology, in the light of Islamic principles, could illuminate a progressive path forward for Islamic societies. From the first, students were entranced by the complexities and contradictions of Shariati's intellectual explorations. Very soon, he gained an unprecedented hold on the city's university students. Before long, Shariati's impact in Mashhad extended beyond the university lecture halls. His unconventional ideas on Islam made him a force in the city beyond.

Unnerved by the response Shariati was evoking outside university gates, the regime pressured the university administration to void his appointment. The administrative decision was made to transfer the troubling intellectual from Mashhad to Teheran. It was apparently reasoned that in the capital Shariati would not have the same deep personal roots that he had in Mashhad. This disciplinary transfer to the capital proved to be a serious regime miscalculation. In Teheran, Shariati lectured at Houssein-e-Ershad Religious Institute. Before long, his classes and lecture series on Islam were attracting thousands. Crowds of students and ordinary citizens, far larger than those in Mashhad, overflowed into the streets surrounding the Institute. Young and old were fascinated by Shariati's provocative analyses of Islam not only in its spiritual dimensions, but also as a social force for change. The number of his followers increased steadily and soon reached dramatic proportions. Shariati's writings proved as attractive as his oratory. Sixty thousand copies of a first important book sold out almost immediately.

Alarmed by Shariati's immense popularity, the authorities acted. Police and security forces surrounded the Institute. Shariati and a large number of his followers were arrested. Shariati spent eighteen more months of brutal mistreatment in prison. Once again, the difficult conditions took a severe toll on his fragile health.

It became clear that Ali Shariati could not endure further imprisonment. Under international and mass domestic pressure, the regime lifted his sentence. However, on his release Shariati discovered that his "freedom" came with strict constraints. He was prevented by Iranian security from teaching, lecturing, or publishing. Severe restrictions effectively ended both his scholarly and broader social activities. "Freedom" under these conditions was not freedom at all. Shariati found it impossible to meet with students, other intellectuals, or the general public. He could neither publish his thoughts nor interact directly with his students, colleagues, or followers.

Given such stifling conditions, Shariati sought permission to leave Iran. It was granted by a regime eager to exile this critical intellectual with so large a following. Shariati left for England. However, the easing of pressures on his frail health came too late. Shortly after arriving in London, Shariati died at the age of forty-three. It may well be that death resulted from his history of poor health, exacerbated by the trials of regime persecutions and imprisonments. However, to this day, Shariati's most passionate followers insist that the ubiquitous Savak, the shah's security force, martyred their mentor.

182   JUSTICE IN ISLAM

Shariati died *a believing revolutionary*. This sobriquet sums up his greatest intellectual legacy. As an Islamic intellectual, Shariati succeeded in two seemingly contradictory projects. Both had sweeping implications. On the one hand, Shariati explicitly identified the pattern of complicity of official Islam in the tyranny and corruption of the repressive dictatorships that dominated in the Islamic world. At the same time, he dramatically reasserted Islam's progressive message, symbolized by the Prophet's companion Abu Dharr al Ghifari. Shariati's theoretical work guides his followers through this challenge of simultaneously keeping two contradictory visions of Islam in view. The first is the corrupt and complicitous Islam of despots. The second is the Islam of those like Abu Dharr who find in Islam a righteous force for change. Writing in the shadow of the shah's tyranny, Shariati often was forced to express his ideas indirectly in metaphoric and poetic language. He succeeded, nevertheless, in explaining how over the centuries a reactionary clerical caste gained control of the faith. Encased within elaborate invented traditions and distorted values, an official Islam was put at the service of the rich and powerful. Islam's revolutionary message appeared to be lost.

Shariati was not alone among intellectuals in a time of Islamic Awakening to seek to retrieve and reassert Islam's core message of resistance in the name of justice. He does stand out, however, for his success in advancing that message as preparation for revolution. Shariati came to this critical project as a believer in the spirit of Mashhad. He had deep roots in Shi'i Islam. The overlay of his Paris experience did deepen Shariati's conviction of the imperative of revolution. Shariati brought to his mature scholarship a sophisticated understanding of Marxist and Third World revolutionary theory. In the most general terms, Shariati looked to socialism rather than liberal democracy and the market economy to inform his efforts to elaborate a contemporary version of a just Islamic society.

Advanced education in Paris became an undeniable part of his intellectual identity. It was the critical dimensions of Shariati's thinking that attracted Iranian youth. Paris mattered. Yet, Shariati consistently mounted his critical analyses from the perspective of a believing Shi'i Muslim. Mashhad mattered more. Ultimately, the deepest roots of Shariati's ideas were set in the formative years of his connection to Iran's holy city. The Western secular intellectuals he came to know in Paris did lend breadth to Shariati's embrace of revolution. However, the fundamental idea of the necessity of overthrowing the existing order was already a constituent part of the thinking of the youthful Iranian activist. Shariati came to Paris with an impressive résumé of leadership of street demonstrations. He brought with him the steeling experiences of harsh imprisonments. Moreover, Shariati did not travel alone to the West's intellectual capital. His writings from the early years abroad make it clear that Abu Dharr traveled with him and shaped the fundamental character of his message.

To Iran's youth, Shariati conveyed the critical insight that they could be both believers and revolutionaries. They need not, as Third World theorist Franz Fanon (1925–1961) had judged, set aside their faith to support revolution. To the contrary, Shariati believed that Islam in general, and Shi'i Islam, in particular, had its own vibrant and distinctive revolutionary tradition that dated back to Islam's earliest years and to figures like Abu Dharr. Shariati named that venerable tradition "Red Shi'ism." At the same time, he recognized the contrary notion of a Shi'i Islam that was complicit in the corruption and tyranny that plagued Iranian leadership. He understood that Iranian youth were in revolt against that Islam. He labeled that form of Islam as "Black Shi'ism."

In the eyes of many, it was Black Shi'ism that defined Islam. Not so for Shariati. His sweeping intellectual project can be summarized as an effort to revive Red Shi'ism and make it the dominant face of Islam. Seen in the framing of Red Shi'ism, the earliest years of the faith provide a model for radical change. The radical monotheism that defined Islam emerged as a message that explicitly and vigorously challenged the multi-theism of Bedouin culture. Islam, Shariati insisted, had thus originated as a force for social transformation. The faith was from the first faced by powerful external enemies that represented authoritarian and retrograde social systems. Moreover, Islam faced internal barriers to advance as well.

Shariati made it clear that there would be no easy walk to Islamic utopia. Alongside the promising liberation promised by Red Shi'ism, there remained in the shadows the pressures of Black Shi'ism that fostered complicity with domestic corruption and tyranny. Black Shi'ism worked inexorably from within to obstruct and slow any forward advance. In Shariati's view, the historic struggle between Red and Black Shi'ism infuses great challenges into the work of *istikhlaf*. God's charge to humanity to found just communities is a call to righteous struggle. In Islam, humanity is defined by this mission and the inevitable trials and victories for justice it provokes.

Shariati re-envisioned the major figures of Shi'i history to bring their characterizations in line with the dichotomous template of the Red and the Black that he elaborated. Imams Ali and Hussein are envisioned by Shariati

184   JUSTICE IN ISLAM

as social revolutionaries who defended the oppressed classes in the name of Islamic justice. In more sweeping, but only loosely defined terms, Shariati projected a classless society as Islam's vision of the just community. Pointedly, he called for transcendence of the institution of private property. Shariati argued that it was private property that ultimately fostered a class society. His Islamic view of socialism looked to a society suffused with *rahmah* (compassion), rather than ruthless market competition and class struggle.

In Shariati's commentary, the otherworldly speculation and abstract theological squabbles of the Shi'i seminarians completely lose their prominence. Shariati did, however, preserve the venerable Shi'i emphasis on martyrdom. In his thinking, that tradition of willful self-sacrifice strengthened his interpretation of Red Shi'ism as the source of uncompromising commitment to action for radical change. By Shariati's reading, Red Shi'ism defined itself as activist resistance to tyranny, rather than in abstract theological disputations or otherworldly mysticism. The contrast to Black Shi'ism is dramatic. Shariati declared that Black Shi'ism was a debilitating deviation from the pure Red Shi'ism that he identified with Imam Ali.[6]

Shariati's sweeping critique had both political and theological dimensions. Politically, Shariati charged that the Shi'i clerical establishment had developed narrow class interests. Drawn into the pervasive corruption of the shah's rule, they had lowered their gaze. They failed to act to oppose the shah's despotism. Their strongest ties were to the privileged classes. Forgotten was the commitment to social justice. Compromised clerics lent their support to the shah's repression. They failed to speak for justice. They were the heirs of the Caliph Osman against whom Abu Dharr first spoke out. Osman, Abu Dharr concluded, did not believe that religion should interfere with the poverty of the majority and the opulence of the minority.[7]

In Shariati's stinging words, the clerics of the regime were locked in "eternal coalescence with dominant powers and ruling classes."[8] They were little more than apologists for a corrupt regime that responded only to the needs of the wealthy classes. In religious terms, Shariati excoriated the clergy of Black Shi'ism for their exaggerated emphasis on pious ritual and abstract mysticism. He charged that both were simply diversionary from Islam's higher purposes. They had little connection to Iranian realities. In Shariati's view, Red Shi'ism's activist commitment to social justice was lost in the meaningless haze that their speculative mysticism too often generated.

The duality of Shariati's view of Islam's historical legacy allowed him, on the one hand, to highlight revolutionary Red Shi'ism, while on the other hand not losing sight of the repressive potential of reactionary Black Shi'ism. This complexity of Shariati's understanding of Islam in history explains apparent contradictions in his thinking. Shariati never embraced Western democracy. He argued that true democracy appeared only in the time of Imam Ali during the golden age of Shi'i Islam.[9] At same time, Shariati never advocated clerical rule. Shariati did recognize and support the Ayatollah Khomeini's critical role in bringing revolution to Iran under an Islamic banner. He did not, however, envision direct rule by clerics in the wake of revolution.

On the contrary, Shariati authored a prescient and utterly devastating critique of the dangers of clerical rule. He was clear that "a religious regime is one in which, instead of the political figures, religious figures take up political and governmental positions." He was blunt about the implications of such a system of governance. He warned that "one natural consequence of such a regime is dictatorship. The cleric naturally sees himself as God's representative who carries out His orders on earth. People have no right to express their opinion nor criticize and oppose him." The religious ruler does not owe his ascendency to any expression of the will of the people over whom he governs, by votes or otherwise. He therefore feels no responsibility to them. The results, Shariati concluded, are devastating. The religious ruler is encouraged to view himself as the "the shadow and representative of God." He comes to believe he has absolute jurisdiction over people's belongings and their very lives. He tolerates no resistance to his rule, no matter its character. God's approval is believed to find expression in all his actions. No independent rights are recognized for any opposition or the followers of any other religion, not even the right to live. If they experience suffering, it is because they are the rightful target of God's wrath. Shariati explains that, for the religious ruler, these enemies are considered "deviated from the true path, unclean, and an enemy of religion's path; he views their oppression as God's justice."[10]

Sharply critical writings such as these explain why those who travel to Iran today to experience firsthand the outcomes of Iran's "earthquake" should not expect monuments to the revolution's most important theorist. They will find only a single street named after him that runs from the north to the south of Tehran. Along that route, one will not locate imposing statues dedicated of Ali Shariati in the capital's large public squares. Iran's most influential revolutionary theorist enjoys little favor with those who have inherited the mantle of the revolution.

The negative assessments of Shariati's work by the post-revolutionary clerical leadership came fast and furious. The reaction to his thinking was swift

186 JUSTICE IN ISLAM

and harsh. The Ayatollah Khomeini joined the chorus of attacks. Critics of Shariati opened with condemnation of the temerity of an intellectual with no theological training to dare assess the grand sweep of Iran's Shi'i legacy. Hostile clerics ridiculed Shariati's lack of credentials in the Islamic sciences. Many concluded that Shariati's writings and lectures represented a Trojan horse that aimed to infect Iranian society with the deadly virus of Western ideas under the cover of reflections on Islam. Others focused more directly on the pointed attacks made by Shariati on the Shi'i clerical class. They denounced Shariati as a "closet Sunni" whose writings represented a disguised and dangerous sectarian attack on Shi'ism. Others went even further. Right-wing figures such as Ayatollah Mohammad Tag Mesbah Yazdi (b. 1934) branded Shariati a heretic. Yazdi later achieved political prominence as spiritual advisor of former president Amadinejad (b. 1956). The tenure of Amadinejad from 2005 to 2013 was itself marked by corruption and abuses of power. Disparaging assessments from such compromised figures rank among the highest accolades that Iran's revolutionary theorist has received.

In the end, the harsh and multifaceted attacks had little very impact on Shariati's appeal to educated Iranian youth. His view of Shi'i history as dominated by warriors and martyrs in struggles against the powerful and unjust took hold. Shariati set out to restore the true Shi'ism of Imam Ali. He concluded that the collusion of the existing regime with imperial powers meant that Iranians must overthrow the shah's illegitimate rule in order to liberate Iranians from the evils of despotism and Western imperialism. The duality of Shariati's understanding of historic Islam allowed youth to acknowledge the reactionary character of official Iranian Islam while retaining their faith as Muslims.

Shariati's harsh judgment of what had become of Iranian Islam never dimmed his faith. In his view, the Islam of justice and compassion could be restored. Ali Shariati preserved his faith through a commitment to an impressive rethinking of the fundamentals of Shi'i Islam. Shariati spelled out the main outlines of his radical reasoning in his essay *Red Shi'ism, Black Shi'ism*. This influential work makes clear that his rethinking of Shi'ism aimed for nothing less than an interpretation of Islam as a revolutionary ideology that was at once Islamic and radical. Such an ideology would be the vehicle not only for revolution in Iran, but for the sweeping transformation of Islamic societies everywhere.[11]

There can be no doubt about Ali Shariati's overall importance to the Iranian revolution. It was Shariati who retrieved Islam's revolutionary potential for

Iran's youthful radicals. Shariati's reliance on Abu Dharr al Ghifari to recapture Islam's revolutionary spirit is explicit. It is incontestable. The absolute clarity of that influence contrasts to the many other mysteries that obscure important aspects of the life and work of Iran's great revolutionary intellectual. Nagging questions about the circumstances of Ali Shariati's death persist. There is no final judgment on the cause of his death. Many of his followers believe to this day that this vocal critic of tyranny was assassinated by the shah's henchmen while traveling abroad. It is also quite possible that Shariati's history of poor health, exacerbated by grim imprisonments, ended his life prematurely with a heart attack. Conclusive judgement has thus far not been possible.

In parallel fashion, no settled assessment has emerged on his character and status as an intellectual. Shariati was clearly not an Islamic scholar in the traditional mold. He simply did not have the requisite training in the most advanced Islamic sciences to produce the comprehensive scholarship characteristic of the most accomplished Shi'i scholars like Muhammad Hussein Fadlallah of Lebanon (Chapter 6.) or Muhammad Baqir al Sadra of Iraq (Chapter 7.). However, many scholars who have studied Shariati's work of Qur'anic interpretation have concluded that the brilliance of the fragments he left compensates for the lack of an overarching classic framing. I consider myself one of their number.

The distinctive character of Shariati's thinking has nevertheless meant that the relationship of his scholarly work to the various currents of contemporary Islamic thought remains unclear. Many consider Shariati to be essentially a Westernizer who, whatever his ultimate commitments, brought progressive secular thinkers of stature to the attention of the Iranian intellectual class. In his writings and lectures, he clarified the relevance of their thinking to Iran. Those influences most notably included Jean Paul Sartre (1905–1980), Franz Fanon (1925–1961), and Jacques Berque (1910–1995). On the other hand, others make a strong case that Shariati's primary importance resides in unearthing Islamic roots for ideas that only appear to be Western. The striking seventh-century progressivism of Abu Dharr is the most important case in point here. My own reading of Shariati aligns best with this second camp.

With characteristic flair, Shariati pronounced Abu Dharr "the world's first socialist." He turned to the Prophet's companion, rather than Western thinkers, to provide the reservoir of radical ideas to inspire revolution in Iran. For all the unresolved questions about Shariati, on one matter there is

188 JUSTICE IN ISLAM

absolute clarity: *Ali Shariati positioned himself explicitly and consistently as an unqualified disciple of the Prophet Muhammad's beloved companion, Abu Dharr al Ghifari.*

Understanding the force of that determinate Islamic influence does not require denial of the secondary impact of Western progressive intellectuals on Shariati's intellectual formation. Shariati readily acknowledged these secular influences. He insisted, however, that they did not define the essentials of his position. Shariati assessed his own radicalism that contributed so greatly to the revolution as ultimately inspired by Islamic thought and practice of the classical period.

The Iranian Earthquake

The Iranian Revolution of 1979 stands as the centerpiece of the contemporary Islamic Awakening. Iranian youth and the radical Islam that inspired them made the Awakening a world-class phenomenon. Guided in making their revolution by Ali Shariati, Iran's youthful revolutionaries projected their revolution as *Islamic*, rather than simply Iranian or Shi'i. The more inclusive designation had significant implications. By this move, they sought to position Iran's revolution as a global phenomenon with wide-ranging effects. It is not a bridge too far to say that the Iranian success made possible the surprising victory of Shi'i Hizbullah as an Islamically inspired movement of national resistance in Lebanon. In just the same way, the Iranian example of Islam in revolt lent support to Sunni Hamas in its struggles as an Islamic movement of resistance against a tenacious and aggressive settler colonialism in occupied Palestine.

At the heart of Iran's Islamic revolution resides the inclusive Qur'anic vision of human community. The Islamic idea of revolution is more than a political concept. The community celebrated is for Muslims one of divine inspiration. It aims to make possible a life lived in justice and compassion. Those core values are understood to be God-given. They are elaborated fully in all of God's wisdom in the Qur'an. They are exemplified in the words and actions of the Prophet Muhammad. The Iranian Revolution reaffirmed Islam's character as a revolutionary force.

Islamic intellectuals do not make the mistake so common in the West of equating revolution with violence. Revolution in midstream Islamic discourse means change at the most fundamental level of the values and institutions that define and structure a society. Such change may be realized with a variety of means. Violence is but one path to revolution in this sense. The political arena is but one of the domains in which it can be enacted. The idea of the *radical* in midstream Islamic discourse directs attention to the roots of the most fundamental elements of any social order. With such an understanding, the social and the personal are as salient as the political and economic dimensions as sites of radical transformation.

In this sense, Islam in seventh-century Arabia appeared as a revolutionary alternative to tribalism and idol worship. Islam appeared as a universalist message in a world of conflicting tribal loyalties. In that Bedouin world, a plethora of idols arrayed themselves on all sides to sanctify the tribal divisions that defined the social order. Yet, the impact of Islam's radicalism reached even further. The example of the Prophet Muhammad made manifest the ways the transformative reach of the faith extended seamlessly to social and personal domains that appeared to be beyond the reach of deep change. The Prophet in his person expressed new ways of being and acting in the world. They too were revolutionary.

The striking innovations the Prophet Muhammad exemplified were previously unavailable to the Bedouin society into which he was born. The Prophet comes into view as one of those men who actively seek out and love the company of women. Such figures are unabashed in making this personal characteristic an integral part of their public persona. By his doing so, the Prophet challenged the prevailing conception of masculinity in his community. Female infanticide in seventh-century Arabia represented a particularly horrific expression of the prevailing valuation of the male over the female. The Qur'an explicitly condemns that practice in several verses.[12] The *hadiths* of the Prophet make clear his high regard for the women in his personal life. Khadija, the Prophet's wife, was respected as a successful businesswoman. Her social status was higher than that of the orphaned Prophet. Aisha, the Prophet's youngest wife, emerges as a greatly loved and respected life partner. After the passing of the Prophet, she is also represented as playing an important social and political role as well.

The Prophet stands forth in the general imagination as the founder and defender of the first Islamic community. Muslims steeped in the *Sunnah* (the record of all the deeds and words of the Prophet) also know a more personal dimension of their Prophet as a gentle and caring soul. He was quick to shed unashamed tears for the suffering of others. Those others were as often girls and women as boys and men. For the early converts, the greatest and

190 JUSTICE IN ISLAM

most wrenching struggles their commitment to Islam imposed were personal battles within. The Prophet's example challenged the very basic idea
of what it meant to be a man. He did so with modest ideas and actions that
reverberated in forceful ways. For example, the Prophet rejected the idea that
manliness prevented men from expressing emotions. A well-known *hadith*
tells the story of a figure in the Prophet's circle whose sense of masculinity
prevented him from kissing his children. The Prophet is reported to have
objected strongly that such behavior was un-Islamic.

On the individual level, converts came to understand that wrenching
shifts were required not only in social values, but also in personal emotions
and feelings. Assertive individualism and competitive manly pride characterized prevailing male cultural norms in seventh-century Arabia. Islam
tamed both. In Arabic the very word "Islam" connotes submission. Passivity
is perhaps the last thing a culture of proud Bedouins could entertain. The
challenge is usually cast as placing commitment to the faith above family
and clan. In fact, it went far deeper. The most basic cultural concepts were
challenged. Islam, modeled by the Prophet, made girls a valued part of the
family. A man who could not show affection for his own children, including
his daughters, fell short as a Muslim.

To cry, the Prophet pronounced, is human. Stories of the Prophet include
treasured legends of the tears he shed for the brutalities inflicted on girls and
women. One such story recounts that a figure close to the Prophet had daughters in greater numbers than the sons he valued more. The man brought his
youngest daughter to the edge of a well. He urged her to look into the well.
When the child did, her father pushed her into the depth. The story reports
that the child cried out for help from her "daddy" as she plunged to her death.
When the Prophet first heard this story, he is reported to have wept openly.
His tears expressed his grief for the innocent child, but also his deep sorrow
for the inhumanity of her father. The Message, the Prophet made clear, was
sent to end such horrors.[13]

The Islamic community of Qur'anic inspiration was to be value-based. The
core Islamic values, as examples of the behavior of the Prophet made clear,
had revolutionary impact on all spheres of life. With their value-based vision, Islamic intellectuals explained that ruling power was to be prevented
from excesses by the restraint that justice inspires, freedom makes possible,
and compassion demands. In the Qur'anic vision of human community, the
rough edges of market competition, power struggles, and individual moral
failings were to be smoothed by the compassion on which the Qur'an insists.

ALI SHARIATI 191

A damaging challenge to this Islam of justice and compassion has come from the distorted Islam of the small and damaged minds of Islamic extremists. Their diminished Islam is cruel and unfeeling. It is incapable of grasping the Islamic value of inclusive justice and its corollaries. The presence of the Qur'an on earth does assure, however, that the Islam of higher purposes always remains within reach. The realization of that vision relies on the response of humanity to the Message. Periodically, this Islam of the Qur'an and *Sunnah* has asserted itself through the work of scholars and activists, inspired by the Qur'anic message. At times, movements of renewal and revitalization have swept across Islamic lands for exactly this purpose. The Islamic Awakening of our time, in which Ali Shariati played so important a role, is the fourth such movement in the modern era.

For many, like Ali Shariati, the contemporary Islamic Awakening without Abu Dharr is almost inconceivable. The Islam of Abu Dharr confronts the tyranny of wealth and power with its brave call for freedom and justice. At the same time, it reaffirms the Islam of compassion that the Prophet and his companion modeled. In sharp contrast, the Islam of Orientalist scholarship, in which I was initially trained at Harvard, is backward looking and inevitably retrograde in its social dimension. It is an Islam that is all rigidities and brutalities. Shariati acknowledged the historical reality of such an Islam. It was a rigid (*mugamid*) Islam that he excoriated as Black Shi'ism. He judged it to be the Islam of the morally flawed, the criminal, and the despotic. To such a retrograde interpretation of the faith Shariati juxtaposed Islam *haraki*, an Islam of activist values in the service of a revolutionary spirit. Such, he pronounced, was Red Shi'ism, the Islam of Abu Dharr al Ghifari.

Shariati's admiration for Abu Dharr rested in the first instance on the recognition by the Prophet's companion of the great dangers that tyranny and corruption represented. Abu Dharr understood that Islam itself could be entrapped in tyranny's web. The Prophet's companion stood as critical witness when the first compromising steps were taken that ultimately defined the majority Sunni accommodation to dynastic rule. He sounded the alarm. He warned against the resurgence of the old ties of blood and affection to family and tribe that revolutionary Islam sought to supersede. Ultimately, however, the pact with dynastic power was sealed. The majority Sunni community accepted the compromise. Rulership was left in the hands of the sultan. In return, *'ulama* (Islamic scholars) accepted the compromise that meant the shepherding of the faith would remain their prerogative.

192 JUSTICE IN ISLAM

Shi'i intellectuals have consistently evinced a much greater suspicion of this Ummayad compromise with power and the ways it can be misused than their Sunni counterparts. Similar sentiments of disapprobation, however, do find expression on the margins of the majority Sunni community. Such, for example, was the message of Sayyid Qutb. He condemned the Sunni accommodation to ruling power as perhaps the gravest mistake in Islamic history. In this one critical dimension, useful parallels can be drawn between the Islam of Shariati and of Sayyid Qutb. For both men, their radicalism had little to do with the plotting of a secretive vanguard party. What really made Qutb radical as an Islamic thinker was his frontal attack on the accommodation with ruling power of his own majority Sunni community. Shariati's Red Shi'ism evinces the same resolute refusal of compromise with governing power.

Shariati's engagement with Western ideologies was from the first mediated by his Islamic cultural formation. Islam understood as an uncompromised revolutionary force dominated. To label Abu Dharr as *the world's first socialist*, as Shariati himself did, risked misinterpretation in an age when secular ideologies are so ascendant. The expression could be taken as an effort to legitimate Abu Dharr's radicalism by seeing him as a precursor of nineteenth-century Western socialism. Shariati's intent was most likely quite different. He believed that core socialist ideas were Islamic in origin. Socialism, in his view, was an Islamic concept that first acquired form in the earliest years of Islam. In his asceticism, rejection of the structuring of society by classes, and concern for the poor, the Abu Dharr of Shariati's description does have a reasonable claim as the world's first socialist.

Shariati himself is often mistakenly seen as the proponent of the radical thinking of figures like John Paul Sartre and Frantz Fanon. Shariati did knowingly inject the radical Western thought of such progressive secular figures into the Iranian revolutionary context. He understood how the move would appeal to leftist Iranian youth who had been drawn to Marxism. However, Shariati took the measure of Western radical theory by the standards of classical Islamic thought, rather than the reverse. Shariati was fully aware that the West had appropriated the concept of socialism and identified it exclusively with the nineteenth-century movements of "scientific socialism." Shariati refused that appropriation. He aimed to reclaim a value-centered socialism as an original part of the legacy of Islam.

Shariati took Abu Dharr as a classical advocate for a faith-based rather than science-grounded socialist order. Shariati insisted that Abu Dharr's progressivism anchored itself in Islamic values rather than the purported laws and regularities of economics and politics. These regularities, Shariati explained, lack moral grounding. The circumscribed morality of this Western vision comes with the alleged regularities of economics and politics. Ultimately, it relies on mystical notions like the purported alchemy of the market that mysteriously transforms individual greed into influences to advance the common good. Shariati believed such views to be irrational. In contrast, the Islamic notion of a value-based economy is explicitly grounded in the values of the Qur'an. Justice and compassion are identified as the guideposts for the economic system. They are God-given gifts to humanity. The original Islamic concept of socialism is a clearly value-centered. John Paul Sartre signaled that he understood this critical value marker when he made the otherwise enigmatic statement that, should he ever turn to religion, he would embrace the Islam of Ali Shariati.

To move with awareness into the orbit of the most influential intellectual of the Iranian revolution instills appreciation of the importance of the Prophet's beloved companion. The Islamic socialism of Abu Dharr modeled the moral imperative of justice for all the major Islamic thinkers of the Awakening who move through the chapters of this book. They are all *du'a* (Callers to Islam). They are all advocates for Islam's core value of justice and its associated values of freedom and compassion. They are all visionaries who follow Abu Dharr al Ghifari in embracing a morally grounded vision of the just society. The life and work of Ali Shariati brings this profound influence into sharpest focus.

The Qur'an defines the Islamic concept of justice. Justice in the Qur'an is inextricably linked to freedom and compassion. The struggle for justice is inherently and inevitably a political struggle. It is inconceivable without freedom. Freedom as an Islamic value is anchored in the Qur'anic pronouncement that humanity has freedom in the most fundamental of choices, whether to believe in divinity or not.[14] Battles for freedom and justice, the Qur'an insists, must be waged with compassion. The value triad of justice, freedom, and compassion is juxtaposed by Islamic thinkers to the amoral market competition and power struggles built into Western notions of the regularities of the market and international relations. In Islam, Qur'anic values provide the most powerful drivers for humane social progress.

The deep roots of the Islamic radicalism of the Prophet's companion are nourished by Islam's uncompromising monotheism. It is no mere accident of biography that Abu Dharr was a monotheist before there was Islam. Monotheism did have a presence in Christian and Jewish tribes of the

194 JUSTICE IN ISLAM

Arabian peninsula before the Prophet received the Message. However, multi-theism defined the prevailing cultural context of seventh-century Bedouin Arabia. Before the Prophet Muhammad, the very idea of turning one's back on the idols of tradition was unthinkable.

Islam's radical monotheism shattered those constraints. With *tawhid* (the Islamic belief in the oneness of God), all manner of revolutionary possibilities appeared on the expanded horizons. The Qur'an mapped possible pathways from this theological starting point to its economic, social, and political implications. Those pathways find their exemplification in the *Sunnah* of the Prophet.

There was a political economy wrapped around the sanctuary in Mecca and the over 350 idols that inhabited that sacred space. The Message of the Prophet had significant political economy implications. The worship of one God would replace a myriad of tribal gods. All the tribes were represented by their idols. Idol worship was not simply a question of personal belief. The idols played an implicit political representational role. They also had an economic function. The presence of the idols inspired pilgrimages. The expenditures of the pilgrims, in turn, generated a reliable revenue flow.

Both the theology and political economy that arose around the pilgrimages were undermined by the appearance of revolutionary Islam. The unification of the tribes under the leadership of the Quraish depended on the prestige associated with the control of the sanctuary and the economic benefits that flowed from it. With the entire tribal order under threat, rage mounted against the Prophet Muhammad and those like Abu Dharr who embraced Islam's monotheistic Message.

Shariati believed that the beloved companion provided a compelling affirmation that Islam's Message was revolutionary as both theology and worldly project. From the outset, Abu Dharr refused all circumstances that impeded expression of his Islamic monotheism. As one of the very earliest converts, Abu Dharr had made himself a monotheist even before the Prophet had revealed the Message to the tribal peoples of 7th century Arabia. Once Abu Dharr heard the radical message of Islam and its refusal of tribal attachments, not even the Prophet could dissuade him from the public declaration of his faith.

Abu Dharr's impatient temperament positioned him on the most activist end of the spectrum of responses to Islam's call for change. At times, he found it hard to follow the example of the Prophet's characteristic caution and inclination to seek the middle ground. Moderate centrism came to characterize the Islamic midstream. The life and record of the Prophet's beloved companion left a venerable record from within Islamic tradition of the ways the sacred texts could be read in more activist ways. The radical implications of the Qur'anic message were undeniable. Abu Dharr simply brought them to the fore. Rejection of the idols of inherited Bedouin tradition was compounded by Islam's demand that even attachments to family and tribe be subordinated to the faith. To be a Muslim demanded redefinition of self and community. The embrace of Islam challenged all inherited and sacred traditions. The loss of family and tribal connections meant the stripping away of those attachments that defined one's humanity.

Abu Dharr understood those risks. He nevertheless moved into that space. He did so with a boldness that many through the centuries have found jarring. Abu Dharr refused any compromise in expressing this refusal of all that had been most sacred. His robust embrace of Islam's radical break with the past defined Abu Dharr. It set him apart. The costs were high. Abu Dharr showed no hesitation in accepting them. His consistent pattern of impatient activism meant that the Prophet's companion would never define the Islamic mainstream. Midstream Islam was more circumscribed and more inclined to accommodation. These qualities in many ways reflected the characteristic stance of the Prophet himself. Abu Dharr's restive radicalism, in contrast, cut a parallel and complementary channel through which flowed a more assertive interpretation of the faith. Through the long centuries, Abu Dharr's documented closeness to the Prophet has guaranteed that his more activist interpretation of Islam's message remained available. Periodically, springs from those subterranean waters have erupted to herald moments of radical reform in the name of justice. The contemporary Islamic Awakening has been one such moment. Abu Dharr has found his central place in the more radical expressions of the Awakening. Iran at mid-century was brought to revolution by the US-backed tyranny of the shah. Ali Shariati, the most revolutionary of the intellectuals who responded, very explicitly turned for inspiration to the Prophet's beloved companion.

Abu Dharr's lasting impact owes a great deal to his status as an Islamic historical figure who comes before Islam's most damaging split into a Sunni majority and a Shi'i minority. Compromise with worldly power came to define Sunni Islam. Shi'i communities proved somewhat less inclined to adopt that stance. Abu Dharr, however, has a place in the traditions of both sects. His presence has loomed larger among the Shi'i. That greater salience in Shi'i communal memory owes most to Abu Dharr's closeness to Ali. In particular,

196 JUSTICE IN ISLAM

Abu Dharr's early and persistent support for Ali's candidacy to the caliphate etched itself into Shi'i communal memory. Abu Dharr came to be regarded as one of the four founding figures of Shi'ism.

Shariati came to his commitment to the centrist Islam of Qur'an and *Sunnah* through the experience of the Iranian Shi'i community. That experience clarified for Shariati the nature of tyranny and the complicity of official Islam in sustaining it. It pointed as well to an alternative reading of the legacy. Shariati spoke for that alternative. He did so with awareness of the threat of losing radical Iranian youth to Marxism. During his last years in Paris, Shariati thought through a theoretical approach rooted in Islam but framed in a way responsive to the insights and appeal of Western radical thinking, notably Marxism and existentialism. That distinctive blend of influences brought Shariati's work within the reach of radical Iranian youth. He succeeded in preserving the relevance of Islam to Iran's revolutionary moment. He galvanized Iranian revolutionary youth with the conviction that the changes they would bring to Iran would represent a model for revolutionary transformation across Middle Eastern societies. On the level of praxis, Shariati's interpretive work was critical to turning Iranian youth from Marxist ideologies to the Islamic banner of Ayatollah Khomeini. Whatever his intentions, he succeeded in diluting the moral and intellectual appeal of leftist Western ideologies. He provided an Islamic formulation of the most appealing revolutionary values that have proved to be his most enduring intellectual contributions.

Shariati explicitly built his own distinctive understanding of a revolutionary Islamic socialism on the ground that Abu Dharr had prepared. The faltering of the global left and the resurgence of populist nationalisms, notably in the United States, Russia, and China, has only enhanced the imperative of more humane visions of the human future, including those rooted in humankind's inherited religious traditions. Shariati, with Abu Dharr at his side, has renewed relevance.

Shariati's revolutionary instincts were sound. The example of Abu Dharr, as interpreted by Ali Shariati, did play a pivotal role in convincing Iran's radical youth that Islam, with its distinctive value-based concept of socialism, could serve as a Shi'i revolutionary ideology. "Revolutionary," as noted, should not be taken to mean violent. Both violence and nonviolence could function as means to revolutionary ends. It is too often willfully forgotten in the West that Iran's 1979 revolution had an overwhelmingly nonviolent character in its inaugural stages. There has been an opportunistic demonization of Iran that obscures this history. It is now often forgotten that, initially, the most potent weapon in the hands of Khomeini followers were the cassette tapes of the sermons of their charismatic Imam.

The terrible repressiveness of the Khomeini clerical regime came later. It was not inevitable. It was not Islamic. That violence, it should be noted, was opposed on Islamic ground by Iranian Islamic scholars. These critics from within included Shi'i scholars senior to Khomeini in the Shi'i hierarchy. They contested as vigorously as possible the violent and tyrannical direction Khomeini and his allies in the Iranian military and security forces gave the revolution. Major Islamic non-Iranian Shi'i scholars, like the Grand Ayatollah Fadlallah, based in Lebanon, celebrated the energy and confidence the success of the revolution gave to Islamic activists across Islamic lands. Nevertheless, such supporters of the 1979 mass uprising very early identified the most serious flaw in the Iranian experience to be the egregious failure to enforce limitations on the power of the ruler. In doing so, they stood quite explicitly with Abu Dharr al Ghafari. The Prophet's companion had seen clearly how power without proper constraints threatened the most essential Islamic values.

In the Iranian power struggle in post-revolutionary Iran, Khomeini's Islamic critics lost. Khomeini, greatly assisted by American hostility and the prolonged hostage crisis, managed to assert total control over the Revolution and subject Iranians to clerical dictatorship. To do so, he relied on the military and various security forces. By that alliance, the fate of the Iranian Revolution as a theocratic military dictatorship was sealed. It bears emphasizing that neither its theocratic nor military dimensions defined the regime as *Islamic*. Dictatorship and military rule are often falsely identified with the Islamic heritage. The military dictatorships that litter the Islamic world are more accurately understood as part of the legacy of authoritarian colonial rule, rather than intrinsic to Islamic rule.

Conclusion: To Be a Revolutionary

Ali Shariati was not the most systematic of thinkers. Much of his work has a fragmentary and discontinuous character. His thinking is an eclectic blend, anchored in Islamic thought but shaded by Western revolutionary theory. Shariati, without contradiction, was at the same time the most influential intellectual to emerge out of the Iranian Revolution of 1979. In the actual

198 JUSTICE IN ISLAM

making of the revolution, he does not compete with the Ayatollah Khomeini. However, as a theorist of the Iranian Revolution and its global importance, he is more important than the Ayatollah. Shariati's lasting legacy rests on his ideas on the revitalization of Islam and on his critical contributions to Islamic revolutionary theory. Shariati clarified, as no other, the simple fact that Islam has an inherently revolutionary character. Shariati left no doubt as to the importance of a neglected classical figure to the origins of this Islam. The major figures of the contemporary Islamic Awakening, whether Arab, Turkish, or Iranian, endlessly made reference to the Prophet's companion Abu Dharr al Ghifari. All framed those remembrances of Abu Dharr around his status as a venerable symbol of the core Islamic value of justice. Shariati went further. He stated simply and directly that his own Islam was the Islam of Abu Dharr. For Shariati, the essence of Islam was the struggle for justice and resistance to tyranny. Abu Dharr, more than any other figure of the classical period, represented that struggle for Shariati. He did all he could to make Abu Dharr a presence for Iranians. To that end, Shariati translated the Egyptian author Abd al-Hamid Jowdat al-Sahar's book on Abu Dharr. Abu Dharr held a special place in Shariati's heart. Some Iranian commentators have gone so far as to suggest that Shariati's admiration for Abu Dharr was even greater than his fondness for the Prophet and Ali.[15]

As a Shi'i Muslim, Shariati made that judgment the basis for nothing less than a rewriting of the history of Shi'ism. As faith and historical project, Shi'i Islam, in his view, aimed for the just social order that only a classless society could make possible. Key theological concepts were reinterpreted. *Tawhid* became unity in that grand purpose, while *jihad* enlisted believers in battles for justice without end. The Iranian intellectual who translated key writings of Frantz Fanon and Che Guevara into Persian re-envisioned the beloved Shi'i Imams Ali and Hussein as warriors who fought for revolution in the name of *the wretched of the earth*.

Ali Shariati's soaring Islamic rhetoric captured and amplified the revolutionary mood of Iranians, particularly the activist youth, in the late 1970s. He created a bridge that allowed those who had made their way to Marxism to return to their Islamic cultural roots. They brought with them the transcendent goal of a classless society. They did so, guided by the spirit of Abu Dharr al Ghifari. Revolution in Iran could come, in Shariati's formulation, as a *return to ourselves*. Shariati's Red Shi'ism elaborated the ways that the *return*, inspired by the world's first socialist, could come with a radical difference that was at once Islamic and revolutionary. Shariati did no less than create a school for revolution that prepared Iranian youth for their critical role in the "earthquake" of 1979. Disappointments and deviations would come later. Shariati did not live to see the triumphs he inspired. Nor did he live to experience the betrayals and profound disappointments that the post-revolutionary regime would bring. The abuse Shariati suffered and his early death on June 18, 1977, did not alter the fact that his contributions as an Islamic and revolutionary intellectual in the mold of Abu Dharr al Ghifari assured that a progressive and hopeful interpretation of Islam would have a place in the Islamic Awakening of our time.

9

Muhammad Ali

Global *Caller* to Islam

Muhammad Ali did not get the part. The role of Bilal was perfect for Ali. In 1956, Mustafa Akkad, a Syrian-American filmmaker, announced plans for a film to present Islam's core message of piety and justice. The film would be called *The Message*. It was to be set in seventh-century Arabia, the time and place of the revelation. Akkad knew firsthand the veil of ignorance and hostility that clouded understanding of Islam in the West. He hoped to offer a film that would capture Islam's core truths in the least distorted and most accessible way.

As a Muslim, Akkad knew that the Prophet himself could not be represented in his film. However, those around the Prophet could appear on screen. One such secondary role interested Muhammad Ali (1942–2016). Bilal Ibn Rabah (580–640), a freed African slave and Muslim convert, was a companion of the Prophet. The Prophet appointed Bilal as Islam's first *muezzin* ("caller" to the Friday communal prayer). As himself a black man and convert, Muhammad Ali felt a strong connection to Bilal's story. He let it be known that he wanted that part.

The story of Bilal's close relationship to Abu Dharr al Ghifari (d. 652), another of the Prophet's companions, is one of the most frequently retold. The Prophet had conferred on Bilal an important role. Bilal had standing in the community. In a heated discussion with Bilal, the excitable Abu Dharr forgot himself. He referred to Bilal disparagingly as "you son of a black woman." The description was accurate. It was also intolerable. Islam's message is addressed to *al nas*, all humanity. The use of race to disparage another was anathema to all the Prophet taught.

Hearing of the incident, the Prophet counseled Abu Dharr that racism and other such distortions of *jahilliyya*, the pre-Islamic age of ignorance, still clung to him. He had not yet fully become a Muslim. Abu Dharr immediately realized the egregious nature of his comment. He went to extraordinary lengths to secure Bilal's forgiveness.[1] Legend has it that Abu Dharr dropped

Justice in Islam. Raymond William Baker, Oxford University Press. © Oxford University Press 2022.
DOI: 10.1093/oso/9780197624975.003.0009

to his knees before Bilal. He put his head on the ground and implored Bilal to walk on him. The gentle Bilal refused. However, he was so deeply moved by Abu Dharr's gesture that he immediately gave him his unqualified forgiveness. Henceforth, Bilal and Abu Dharr were forever linked. The story of this racist lapse by Abu Dharr, and the many details surrounding the incident, has for centuries been used to instruct Muslim children in Islam's absolute refusal of racism.

The director reportedly did seriously consider Muhammad Ali for the Bilal role. As cinema, *The Message* is a respectable Islamic counterpart of such biblical "epics" as *The Ten Commandments*. Ultimately, however, Akkad turned that prospect away. He feared, most likely rightly, that the appearance of Muhammad Ali on screen would overwhelm the film. Ali was simply too famous and too imposing a figure to stay tucked into a secondary role in a modest film.[2]

There are several wonderful scenes in *The Message* that in artful ways do capture a great deal about Islam. Muslims do not represent their Prophet. In the Islamic tradition, any such representation would inevitably diminish the Prophet's incomparable stature as final Messenger of God and seal of the Prophets. The director was challenged to make his film without the Prophet's appearance on screen. Akkad found a creative solution. He transformed the camera itself into a character who could not be filmed. Responsive movements of the camera let viewers feel the unseen presence of the revered Prophet when he is indispensable to the meaning of a scene. The camera assures the Prophet a presence without actual representation. This indirection respects Muslim sensibilities.

The Message opens with mounted messengers bringing the Word to lands beyond Arabia. God is a presence in the stunning desert backdrop for their journeys. The riders carry no weapons. They bear only parchments with verses from the revelation. As emissaries from the Prophet, they go to the citadels of the powerful armed only with the Word. They go as *callers* to Islam.

One very brief scene captures the film's essential message. Bilal is seen climbing to the top of the highest communal building. He has been charged by the Prophet to summon believers to prayer. Bilal does not carry the ram's horn of the Jews. There are no bells at hand to ring, as Christian tradition provides. Bilal's unadorned voice, the voice of a freed black slave, is to sound Islam's call to prayer. For that scene alone, there is no blaming Muhammad Ali for wanting the part.

202 JUSTICE IN ISLAM

From Bilal to Abu Dharr: Prototypes of
the Islamic *Da'i* (*Caller*)

To evoke Bilal Ibn Rabah is always to invite Abu Dharr al Ghifari into the narrative. Bilal and Abu Dharr, bound by legend, each brought distinctive features into the privileged circle of the companions of the Prophet. Bilal was the original *da'i* (caller to Islam), designated by the Prophet to summon the community to the communal prayer. Abu Dharr represented the caller as *zahid* (ascetic), who acted as guardian of the memory of the simple and pious life the Prophet modeled in Islam's first years.

The Prophet Muhammad's death on June 8, 632 AD, meant the emergence of a series of successors to lead the community. The third in that line, Osman ibn Arfan (c. 579–July 17, 656), proved deeply flawed in Abu Dharr's eyes. Osman amassed great wealth. He appointed relatives and friends to important and lucrative administrative positions. Abu Dharr protested such behaviors. He judged that they contradicted the example of the Prophet. He did so peacefully. Abu Dharr organized no opposition movement to Caliph Osman. He supported no conspiracies against the ruler. Abu Dharr did no more than go to the mosque to read Qur'anic verses aloud. The verses warned against abuses of power and wealth. They were offered as prayers. They were also his call to justice.

By criticizing the behavior of the powerful caliph in this way, Abu Dharr created a template for nonviolent resistance in Islam. Abu Dharr knew there would be punishment. There was. He understood there would be enticements. There were. Unmoved, Abu Dharr chose simply to accept the consequences of his peaceful protest. He died in poverty in an exile ordered by the caliph.

Abu Dharr had honored Islam's "straight path." Embodying the *da'i* as ascetic, Abu Dharr created a venerable model of nonviolent resistance at the very center of the Islamic tradition. Centuries later, the convert Muhammad Ali followed exactly in those footsteps. It is doubtful that Ali knew exactly who had first laid that pathway. But he did know it was Islam's preferred way.

Courageous *du'a* (callers to Islam) have regularly emerged in the most diverse and often unlikely forms in Islam's storied history. In their often improbable representations, such *du'a* to Islam all walk in the shoes of Bilal and Abu Dharr. Their overlapping stories have defined the prototype for the ages. The general idea of the *da'i* is grounded ultimately in the call to prayer. The call expresses the Islamic character of a place. Cairo, where I have had an apartment for some forty years, is known as the city of 1,000 minarets. When the call to prayer is sounded, it ripples through the city's minarets as testimony to lives lived in Islam.

Muslims are called to prayer five times a day. Each prayer is performed at a particular time of day. Each is enacted in a prescribed way. Each is given a name. In this way, the calls to prayer structure daily life. The Friday prayer is collective. The community comes together to pray. They listen to the *khutbah* (sermon) of the shaikh of their mosque. In Arabic, the word for mosque connotes simply a place of assembly for Muslims. There is an unspoken asceticism built into the very notion of proper prayer. I am reminded of this character almost daily when I encounter Egyptians of modest means praying in the streets of their cities on a cardboard sheet or newspapers. Muslims around the world have created splendid mosques, as have Egyptian Muslims. But they are not necessary to Islam. All the earth is potentially a mosque.[3] Newspaper spread on the ground functions just fine as a prayer rug. The earth and the sky define a sacred place.

Muhammad Ali's international fame cost him the role of Bilal in Akkad's film. However, a far more expansive role as *Global Caller* to Islam was reserved for him. As a celebrity known around the world, Ali won access to a stage with an audience of millions. He rose to that stature despite acknowledged shortcomings of behavior and character. Regretful missteps in his life trajectory did not block his way forward. The flaws coexisted with accomplishments of the highest order. Ali is recognized by many as a figure in many ways as important to black civil rights in America as Martin Luther King, Jr. Ali is also often credited with bringing more black Americans to Islam than any other figure. Yet, it is just as true that Muhammad Ali over the course of his life held racist views on whites, notably including Jews, expressed sexist views on women, and at one point argued for a ban on miscegenation.[4]

Muhammad Ali's shortcomings would not have phased Abu Dharr. Abu Dharr's own origins were compromised. He came from a tribe of brigands. The men of his tribe lived by raiding caravans that passed through their territories to the north of Mecca on the trade route from Syria to Yemen. From his unpromising beginnings, Abu Dharr succeeded in making himself a symbol of Islamic justice. Callers to Islam need not be perfect. Shortcomings can be overcome. Lapses can be redeemed. The lessons of Abu Dharr's life story taught Muslims through the centuries that there was a place of redemption in Islam for the compromised among them. What is required of the

204 JUSTICE IN ISLAM

caller, as Shaikh Muhammad al Ghazalli often explained, is simply a deep love for Islam and the ability to convey the meaning of that love to others.[56] Abu Dharr had both essential qualities. They coexisted with very human flaws. Together, they defined the realistic and accessible pathway of the *caller* to Islam.

Muhammad Ali, as all the world knows, had made his way to the spiritual enlightenment of Islam from the murky world of American professional boxing. Organized crime infiltrated the high-stakes business that grew up around American professional boxing. In the eyes of critics, the sport itself celebrated brutality. Islamic intellectuals shared these harsh views. They were inclined to generalize them. Sayyid Qutb (1906–1966) typifies the pattern. Qutb was an important literary critic and Qur'anic scholar, although he is best known for his ideas on political Islam that are judged radical. Less well known is Qutb's commentary on his several years of study in the United States. He authored a small book on his experiences. Qutb describes in detail just how captivated he found Americans to be with violence and its effects. They gravitate in huge numbers to the violent spectacle of such combative sports as boxing, wrestling, and football. Qutb argued that such enthrallment with violence was by no means limited to the sports arena. He judged that it was pervasive in American culture.[7]

Muhammad Ali emerged as a public figure from the shadowy world of American boxing. Such questionable roots represented but one of the contradictions in the story of Ali's trajectory. His path to midstream Sunni Islam passed as well through membership in a violence-tinged Islamic sect. The Nation of Islam was led by a false prophet. Elijah Muhammad (1897–1975) taught racial hatred as an essential tenet of the profoundly distorted Islam he preached. Not all of the teachings of the Nation were as damaging as its black racism. The Nation also taught young black men respect for their bodies, personal dignity, and military style discipline. They were encouraged to eschew alcohol, drugs, and exploitive sex. It is not hard to see how Muhammad Ali was drawn to these features. At the same time, the aberrant sect was also rife with hate. In his young manhood, Muhammad Ali drank from this poisonous well. The effects were devastating. Ali made the racist perspective of the Nation his own. It is painful to read Ali's remarks from those years when he advocated for the religiously sanctioned separation of the races. He also embraced the Nation's view that men were to dominate women by divine design.

Eventually, in the mid-1970s, Muhammad Ali left the Nation, but only after the death of the founder Elijah Muhammad (1897–1975). In 1975 he joined midstream Sunni Islam, following a path that Malcolm X had chartered. After his experience with the Nation, Ali would never again allow others to define him. As his fame grew, he took utmost care to exercise the decisive hand in shaping the public persona that captured the attention of the world. Along the way, others periodically claimed that role. They included Ali's father. Ali turned away all such claimants. With characteristic expressiveness, he pronounced, "who made me is me."[8] The public figure who captured center stage in the global media as a black man and a Muslim was a new, self-made man with a new name. Simply and directly, Ali explained that "Cassius Clay is a slave name, I didn't choose it and I don't want it. I am Muhammad Ali, a free name—it means 'beloved of God.'"[9]

Deep Structures and the Making of Muhammad Ali

Muhammad Ali was far more successful than most in exercising control over the creation of his public persona. The conditions under which the making of Ali's public persona took place were another matter. There were factors beyond his sway. The stage on which Ali emerged was shaped by three powerful global forces outside his control. Muhammad Ali was very much a product of the Cold War era. He received his initial boost to fame in a competitive Cold War context. The rivalries of the Cold War assured that an American champion would be promoted worldwide. In the wake of World War II, the United States stood as the global hegemon with a solid foundation of hard power. America enjoyed unprecedented economic wealth, political stability, and military supremacy. Such commanding hard power strengths translated seamlessly into a parallel dominance in the soft power domains of language, the arts, entertainment, and sports. At the heart of American soft power was the global media. Its unprecedented reach was indispensable to Ali's rising international profile.

The media recognized a star in Ali. It was Ali's American origins and his unique sports celebrity that first made him a figure known around the world. His record as a boxer was dazzling. A three-time world champion, Ali's final ledger reads 56-5-0 (37 KOs). Over his twenty-one-year career, he faced and defeated a murderers' row of heavyweights, including Sonny

206   JUSTICE IN ISLAM

Liston, Floyd Patterson, Oscar Bonavena, Ernie Terrell, George Chuvalo, Joe Frazier, Ken Norton, Jerry Quarry, Ron Lyle, and George Foreman. He fought frequently and ducked no one. Throughout his boxing career, Ali won a total of 56 fights. He lost only five. Of the total of 56 wins, 37 of them were knockouts. Throughout his entire legendary career, Ali himself only lost one fight by knockout. Estimates of his lifetime earnings range from a path-breaking 60–80 million dollars.[10] Few athletic accolades eluded Ali. In 1999 Ali was crowned "Sportsman of the Century" by *Sports Illustrated*. He won the World Heavyweight Boxing championship three times and won the North American Boxing Federation championship, as well as an Olympic gold medal.

There was from the start, however, more to Ali than this Cold War identity as an American sports hero. Most surprising to Ali himself was the adoration showered on him by Third World peoples. The wave of Third Worldism first swept across the world in the 1960s. It added immeasurably to Muhammad Ali's later global following. As a man of color, Ali emerged as an accessible hero whom ordinary brown and black Muslims from underdeveloped lands claimed with great fervor as their own.

Third World radicalism, however, was not the most powerful of such global forces. Muhammad Ali had no way of knowing that his conversion to Islam came at a time that thrust him into the fast-moving currents of a worldwide Islamic Awakening. Ali had shed the narrow sectarian identity of the Nation of Islam in the mid-1970s. He stepped forward before a global audience to embrace midstream Islam. A transnational movement of centrist reform and renewal of Islam gathered subterranean power in precisely those years. Successive waves of Islamic renewal asserted themselves with great force. The Islamic Awakening fostered a longing for an Islamic civilizational hero. For many around the world, Muhammad Ali as a celebrated convert became that Muslim hero.

Recognition of the power of such structural forces does not in any way diminish Ali's creativity. What could not have been predicted by such determinants was Ali's sheer genius in shaping his media presence within these structural determinants. Islam's foundational notion of human accountability means that whatever the force of the deep structures that shape human destinies, there is always a margin for human freedom. Ali understood that his faith would hold him accountable for what he did with the opportunities available to him.

The Islam of the Awakening assumed a character as practical as it was spiritual. Such a pragmatic Islam spoke in powerful ways to Muhammad Ali. The Awakening promised a program of realistic Islamic reform and renewal. The scholars who took the lead in sounding that call for Islam's revitalization took great care to ground their efforts in the rich resources of the Islamic legacy.

Spirituality, Islam's Jesus, and the Islamic Awakening

The example of the Prophet Muhammad loomed large in the visualizations of the way forward of leading Islamic scholars. Less expected were the ways that the special closeness of the Prophet to the Muslim Jesus brought the spirit of Jesus into the most important writings of the scholars who guided the Awakening. The Qur'an clarifies a general understanding that all the Prophets of Islam are ranked the same. However, within that equal framing, the Prophet Muhammad himself acknowledged in a strong trusted *hadith* his special closeness to the Prophet Jesus.[11] Alongside the guidance of the Prophet Muhammad, the spirit of the Muslim Jesus is pervasive in the most important writings of the scholars of the Awakening.

Jesus in Islam is a prophetic rather than a divine figure. The prophetic identification of the fully human Muslim Jesus contrasts sharply to the otherworldly character of the divine Jesus of Christianity. The mission of the Christ of Christianity is atonement for the sins of all humanity. The core elements of the story of the divine Jesus of Christianity are the high spiritual dramas of crucifixion and resurrection. Neither has a place in Islam. Rather, Jesus the Muslim Prophet has the worldly but inspirational role of guiding humanity's struggles for justice. This Jesus, Islam's Jesus, spoke directly to Muhammad Ali.

The spirit of the Muslim Jesus permeates the scholarship of the Awakening. It is surprising, therefore, that direct references to the prophet Jesus are relatively infrequent. However, to study that literature is to notice that there are, instead, frequent evocations of Abu Dharr al Ghifari. As we have seen, in Islamic tradition, Abu Dharr is an important figure as a companion of the Prophet Muhammad. He has standing as well as a venerable symbol of Islamic justice. In the literature of the Islamic Awakening, Abu Dharr is further recognized as sharing the crucial qualities of humility, piety, and compassion for the poor that characterized the Islamic Prophet Jesus. In those

208 JUSTICE IN ISLAM

major writings of the contemporary Awakening, references to Abu Dharr consistently evoke the spirit of Islam's Jesus. The spirit of Jesus, whether directly or indirectly brought into consciousness, provides inspiration for the righteous actions for which the Islamic Awakening called.

Exemplifying the Activist Scholar: *The Lawyer of the Poor*

Islamic intellectuals from across the Islamic world advanced the work of the Awakening. Muhammad Ali entered their ranks. For all the self-confidence he projected, Ali had doubts about his possible status as a caller to Islam. He was fully aware of the limitations of his formal education. He knew all too well that he lacked the schooling to speak the middle-class English of the media, let alone to compile the dossier of published writings of an Islamic scholar.

The inclusive Islamic tradition came to Ali's rescue. Islam made available to Muhammad Ali an alternative conception of the intellectual. Alongside the mold of the traditional scholar, Islam offered an activist alternative. It was perfectly suited to Ali's talents and sensibilities.

The model of the activist as Islamic scholar found a very early exemplar in none other than Abu Dharr al Ghifari, the Prophet Muhammad's companion. Abu Dharr established himself as a scholar by recording some three hundred *hadiths*. The great significance of his contribution in preserving the record of the thoughts and actions of Prophet Muhammad in the earliest years of the *ummah* (Islamic community) was universally acknowledged. The Qur'an repeatedly makes clear that in Islam, social actions, rather than abstract theology or rarified beliefs, matter most.[12] A portfolio of texts composed in the refined language of Islamic scholars was beyond Muhammad Ali's capabilities. However, he could offer an impressive public record of righteous actions.

The venerable Abu Dharr had shaped the mold of the activist Islamic intellectual as one who fought for social justice. The Prophet's beloved companion was known in seventh-century Arabia for his struggles on behalf of the poor. The history and legends of Abu Dharr all center on his battles for the most vulnerable. Abu Dharr waged those struggles for justice with actions that showed him fearless and uncompromising in confronting the abuses of the rich and powerful. That activism was complemented by his expressions of love, respect, and compassion for the poor. Abu Dharr was more than inspiration. His example demonstrated the pronounced advantages of a life record inscribed in a format of righteous actions. A social text written in such a way escapes from the confines of any particular language, place, or time. The record of *actions* on behalf of righteousness can be read across the world and through the centuries.

The emphasis in Islam on righteous actions has facilitated its development as a global faith. Midstream Islamic intellectuals who speak authoritatively for the faith have always done so in a myriad of dialects and very distinct languages. They have created libraries of scholarly works in countless languages. Yet despite the richness of their scholarship, whether their language is Arabic, Turkish, Farsi, or American English, among endless others, Islamic scholars in the modern era have only very rarely commanded the place on the Western-dominated international stage that their intellectual work and social activism merited.

Muhammad Ali achieved exactly that elusive position. Ali enjoyed unprecedented success in projecting his narrative of conversion to Islam worldwide. He spoke to the world in a new and succinct language punctuated by actions, rather than scholarly references. By doing so, he was able to break through religious, national, ethnic, and language barriers. What made the difference is that Ali took the stage, with the spotlight fixed on a sports hero known around the world. Once in that spotlight, he transformed himself into a *da'i* to Islam. His story was guaranteed a hearing. Prominent intellectuals across the Islamic world, including those who themselves made the greatest contributions to the scholarship of the Islamic Awakening, recognized and celebrated Ali's status in the global media.

Muhammad Ali himself looked beyond his athletic triumphs to define the significance of his life. Ali wanted something more for the public self he was crafting. Ali had things to say, only a small part of which had much to do with athletics. In his reflective moments, he made it clear that he fully appreciated all that the boxing arena had given him in resources to overcome the racism he confronted and the opportunity to speak his truth to the world. Yet, Muhammad Ali wanted a larger meaning for his own life. Ali was intent on waging his struggles *for* something. In time, Ali reported that he found that something in Islam. Ali's embrace of Islam was central to his struggles to free himself and his dreams from the efforts of a racist society to define him. In the end, Ali turned his renown as the most powerful man in the world into the role of a Muslim convert who advocated tirelessly for universalist Islam and its promise of justice.

210 JUSTICE IN ISLAM

Like the venerable Abu Dharr, Muhammad Ali came to see himself as an instrument to advance core Islamic values. It was their shared love of justice that bound the two figures from such different times and places. Both men, for all that differentiated them, were made more credible in their role as advocates for justice for the least among us precisely because of their compromised beginnings. Both emerged from damaged pasts. Neither figure was without flaws. Yet, their love and devotion to Islam and ability to express that love brought both Abu Dharr and Muhammad Ali to spiritual heights that their compromised origins made unimaginable.

In 1961 Muhammad Ali had announced his conversion from Christianity to Islam. It was a time a time of great hostility to Islam, comparable to what Muslims have experienced in the United States in recent years. The gifts that Ali brought to Islam went beyond the breathtaking grace and power of his athleticism. As important were his courage, creativity, and inventive intelligence. Ali drew on those qualities to express his adopted faith and its core message of the quest for justice. As importantly, he also used those talents to tame a hostile corporate media. Muhammad Ali had no rivals in his success in bending the international media to Islam's purposes.

As a celebrity, Ali commanded boundless media coverage. What he did with that attention continually stunned the world. Muhammad Ali had things to say. When he took the stage, he had messages to convey. They were the messages of Islam, as Ali understood them. Muhammad Ali's thoughts and expressions of his feelings and understandings were original and powerful. He spoke for Islam with a unique combination of passion and inventive playfulness.

For the most part, the depth of the religious dimension of Ali's message has been little understood outside the Islamic world. Muhammad Ali exuded an intense, childlike love for the inclusive midstream Islam of piety and peace. He expressed that commitment with no hint of defensiveness and even less deference for the red lines that normally defined allowable discourse. Neither Russian leaders nor Palestinians were beyond the reach of Muhammad Ali.

One small incident perfectly captures the nature of Muhammad Ali's uncomplicated and confident faith. Ali learned that Soviet general secretary Mikhail Gorbachev was to visit the White House in 1990. He requested a very brief meeting with the Russian leader. His mission was simple: Ali welcomed Gorbachev to the United States with the gift of a Qur'an. He then in all sincerity invited the Russian leader of the *godless communists* to convert, as he himself had done. Images of that remarkable moment flashed across the globe.

Islam on Two Legs

Muslims around the world came to believe that Muhammad Ali represented the best of Islamic teachings. They embraced Ali as a figure very much entitled to speak in Islam's name. For millions of Muslims, he was, as an Egyptian scholar noted, "Islam on two legs."[13] Islamic scholars, featured in these chapters, seek to provide guidance to millions in Islamic lands who wish to live their lives in ways they believe God and their Prophet Muhammad intended for them. These intellectuals offer models of how sound religious beliefs can be lived, whatever the time and place. Such figures emerge out of a rich cultural landscape, though one largely invisible to those beyond the borders of the Islamic world. They inhabit complex scholarly and activist networks that bring their words and actions to the attention of intellectuals and ordinary Muslims across the Islamic lands. Such networks are, for the most part, unseen elements of the Islamic cultural continent.

Muhammad Ali was not born into that world. Yet, he succeeded in making himself a part of it. Ali's passport was his transparent love of Islam and readiness to express that love in righteous actions. Muhammad Ali exuded an intense love for the inclusive Islam of piety and peace. He expressed that commitment in the most inventive ways. As a celebrity, Ali commanded boundless media coverage. What he did in Islam's name with that attention stunned the world.

Muhammad Ali had things to say. He had messages to convey. Ali's thoughts and expressions of feeling were as original and unconstrained as his boxing style. He took unthinkable moral and political risks. He did so directly and without hesitation. Ali's Islamic commitments refused all arbitrary restrictions. He crossed the red lines that limited freedom of expression, including those drawn in the United States. His support for the Palestinian people was a case in point. Muhammad Ali spoke out against the Israeli illegal colonization of Palestinian lands in the West Bank and Gaza. The "complications" of the Middle East that inhibited such candor dissolved with his willingness to speak plainly of the overarching historical injustice suffered by the Palestinian people.

212 JUSTICE IN ISLAM

Muhammad Ali took seriously the Islamic injunction to love the oppressed and to act on that love. Ali launched innumerable social projects in Asia and Africa to alleviate poverty. He made himself a tireless advocate for the needy, irrespective of their religion, ethnicity. or race. Muhammad Ali, probably the most famous man on the planet in the 1970s, transformed the athletic celebrity into a significant humanitarian actor in relief and development efforts in the Global South. Photos of Ali hand-delivering food and medical supplies to hospitals, orphanages, and street children in Africa and Asia flashed across television screens around the world.[14] Those images touched the hearts of millions.

Everywhere Muhammad Ali went in poor Islamic lands, ordinary Muslims rushed in droves to greet him. The children were always in the vanguard. Scenes were often overwhelming. The images from one such moment in Bangladesh in 1978 left me with an indelible impression that has stayed with me for a lifetime.[15] The poorest of the poor in that impoverished Muslim nation rushed, thousands strong, many barefooted, to welcome "their" hero. Pictures documenting this unforgettable moment were projected around the world. I found them the most moving of all the thousands and thousands of photographs of Muhammad Ali.

Those images convinced me that, for all that has been written about him, Western publics had not yet really heard the story of the mature Muhammad Ali. Only an Islamic framing could bring Muhammad Ali fully into view. It was only in the mirror of the believing Muslim masses of the Global South, rushing to greet him, that Ali achieved his full stature. It was only in those experiences that Ali himself came to see and understand what he had become.

Islam privileges action for higher purposes above all else. As always, the Qur'an defines the standard. Ali's example brought to mind the innumerable verses that call on the faithful to *act* for the faith.[16] The history of the Islamic world is remembered as the record of successive waves of activist reform and attempted renewal. Historians with an Islamic orientation, like the distinguished Egyptian scholar Tareq al Bishri, clarify that the Islamic Awakening was the fourth such wave to surge through Islamic lands in the modern era.[17]

In the United States, Muhammad Ali had made his presence known as a sports hero who was, almost from the start, a great deal more. His commitments were diverse. Ali touched all the major social movements of his time. He registered as an anti-racism, anti-war, and anti-poverty figure. He did not give himself exclusively to any one of those causes. His commitments were always multiple. Moreover, there was always a surplus of meaning to Muhammad Ali that took him through and beyond such movement engagements. That surplus was always Islam. Undoubtedly, Ali was a social and political actor of importance in the American context and far beyond. However, at his deepest core, he was also a global actor in the contemporary Islamic Awakening. Muhammad Ali had made himself a figure who belonged ultimately to Islam.

The Scholarship of Muhammad Abdou

Muhammad Ali took the center stage globally against a changing Islamic intellectual and moral horizon. The major contemporary effort to rethink Islam was already well underway when Ali stepped forward. The serious intellectual groundwork for the Islamic Awakening had been prepared by Muhammad Abdou (1849–1905), the great nineteenth-century Egyptian thinker. Abdou placed the challenge of fresh interpretation of Islam's sacred texts squarely before the major Shi'i and Sunni Islamic intellectuals of the mid-twentieth century. Abdou's work put forward the imperative of reimagining Islam. Abdou taught that the Jews had done precisely that with Judaism. His call for the centrality of interpretation was advanced in the service of a practical vision of reform in the name of justice. Such a vision inevitably brought Abu Dharr al Ghifari into view as a venerable symbol of struggles for justice.

Abdou's penetrating message took aim at what he saw as the atrophy of spirit plaguing Islam. He exposed the dangers, in particular, of mindless literalism that threatened to rob Islamic law of its vitality and relevance. Above all, Abdou deplored the influence of what he described as a dangerous class of religious "clerics." He judged that they exploited their monopoly over hardened traditions to advance their own narrow caste interests.

Muhammad Ali joined scholars and activists across the Islamic world in accepting the grand interpretive challenge that Muhammad Abdou posed for the revitalization of Islam. He did so in distinctive ways and without the scholarly background typical for Islamic thinkers. It is instructive that intellectuals across Islamic lands nevertheless accepted Muhammad Ali as one of their own. The most distinguished Islamic intellectuals welcomed him everywhere he traveled in the Islamic world. There was a prized importance to be seen in conversation with Muhammad Ali.

214   JUSTICE IN ISLAM

Ali's own dossier as an Islamic intellectual opened with simple stories from the small southwestern American town of his birth. Ali reports, for example, going to a modest local restaurant to have lunch. The owner confronted him with the exclusionary pride of a man in full charge of his "white" world. He defined that world as one with no place for a black man. The owner told Ali that his restaurant did not serve Ni###r food. Without raising his voice, Ali responded: "That's fine. All I want is a hamburger." He then quietly left.[18]

All the elements of the mature Ali style were already in evidence in that brief encounter. There was courage. There was directness. There was also a refusal of provocation. Without himself knowing it, Muhammad Ali moved in exactly the way of Abu Dharr al Grifari. In public encounters, Muhammad Ali was most often restrained in his words and actions. For the ring, Muhammad Ali perfected a playful and purposefully undisciplined patter. Muhammad Ali could entertain. Yet, Muhammad Ali also had depth. Very early, he developed a quite different public voice that he consistently ran parallel to the playful chatter developed for the ring. As a public Islamic intellectual, Ali spoke in a low voice, accented with a gentle southern drawl. "All I want is a hamburger." His mostly single-syllable words were at once conversational and strong. It was impossible not to hear in his dialogue with the restaurant owner echoes of Abu Dharr, who calmly told the indentured servant from the caliph that he would lose his freedom if he accepted the gold coins sent by the caliph. Those coins, Abu Dharr added in a message to the caliph, were better given to the poor whose conditions had worsened under his rule. Muhammad Ali studded his short and pointed sentences with easily accessible and always improbable metaphors. His distinctive public voice, cultivated over a lifetime, proved indispensable for the higher purposes that ultimately defined Ali. With that voice, Ali built a worldwide following. He reached millions in Islam's name.

Vietnam: Muhammad Ali Takes the World Stage

It was Ali's very vocal opposition to the US involvement in Vietnam that transformed Muhammad Ali from a sports hero with an activist social conscience to an international anti-war hero. In March 1966, Ali made headlines globally when he refused to serve in the US military to fight in the Vietnam War. It is now often forgotten that Ali did so by explicitly invoking his constitutional right of conscientious objection *as a Muslim*. At that time, an overwhelming majority of Americans supported the war. Ali's refusal to serve created a huge controversy. He initially won little popular support and a great deal of opprobrium. Politicians attacked him as a traitor and coward.

Faced with these attacks, Ali's voice did not fail him. His initial response was brief. It was all the more telling for that. "I ain't got nothing against them Vietcong," pronounced Ali. "How can I shoot those poor people? Just take me to jail." Ali's genius for expressing complex conclusions in language that everyday people could understand did not fail him as the implications of his refusal of the draft played out. For Ali, and for great souls across the globe, the matter was simple. Why, asked Ali, would a black man travel thousands of miles to kill brown men who had done him no harm? As a Muslim, Ali went on to explain: "I pray five times each day for peace. How then can I go to war to kill people who have done me no harm? Does that make any sense?"[19]

The question could not have been more pointed. With time, it registered. Here we see Muhammad Ali addressing one of the great moral and political issues of his day with striking clarity. He did so explicitly as a black man and as a Muslim. By this time, these two dimensions of his public character appeared fixed and permanent. They had a steel-like quality that reflected the power and strength of a man with a claim to be not only one of, but *the* greatest athlete the world had ever seen. But Ali was more than that. In the United States, Muhammad Ali appeared as a courageous truth teller and moral conscience for his age.

Race and religion did define essential dimensions of Muhammad Ali as a public figure. Those core categories, however, did not exhaust the complexities of Ali's persona. Rather, their fixedness created the perfect backdrop for the highly flexible elements of his complex character. Muhammad Ali had an intuitive grasp of the alchemy at work in his crafted public person. His hand was critical in projecting the most manifest and unchanging aspects of the "greatest" as a black man and a Muslim. Without contradiction, Ali played the same role in determining how sub-rosa dimensions of his life experience would be screened.

As a public figure, Muhammad Ali was not without flaws. The serious shortcomings caused less damage than one might imagine. Islam did not demand perfection. The legends of the irascible Abu Dharr reflected that truth with particular clarity. The Qur'an addressed humanity with understanding and acceptance of human frailty. In Islam, the burdens of his flaws would not inevitably overwhelm. The Qur'an states clearly that "on no soul doth God place a burden greater than it can bear."[20] An Islamic framing brings

216 JUSTICE IN ISLAM

Muhammad Ali into focus as a flawed yet enormously talented convert who found in Islam "all that I was looking for." Ali's Islamic faith became the organizing and enabling center that added balance to his strength.

Muhammad Ali's improbable religious journey had taken him through the bruising white racism of his youth and the reactive black racism of his early manhood. He did not emerge unscathed from these trials. Yet, at the height of his fame, Ali fulfilled his spiritual quest and came to rest in the embrace of the inclusive Islamic midstream. Such was the interpretation of Islam that dominated the Islamic Awakening. It was the multifaceted Islam of justice for which Abu Dharr al Ghifari had acted so memorably in the first years of the *ummah*. It was the Islam permeated by the spirit of the Muslim Jesus. Ordinary Muslims around the world celebrated in Muhammad Ali a representative of this venerable interpretation of the faith that they embraced as a mirror of their own.

Muhammad Ali as Islamic Intellectual

Islamic intellectuals achieve their standing in important part by the body of scholarly work they produce. The corpus of that scholarship is brought before the community of Muslims from which they emerge. The reception of that community matters greatly. Islam is a practical and communal faith. Islamic scholarship reflects these qualities. Wisdom locked in personal godliness or intricate speculative theological formulations should be set aside. Elaboration of the meaning of the faith should be socially engaged. It should be relevant to the lives of *al nas.*

Righteous actions achieve precisely that. The clarity of Qur'anic verses on the primacy of righteousness expressed in behavior leave no room for doubt. Islam offers no counterpart to the Christian notion of salvation by faith alone. Believers are advised by the sacred texts that their faith should find expression in their actions. For the final reckoning, Muslims are made to understand that they will be judged by the record of what they have *done* for justice over the course of their lives. When the day of judgment comes, the record of their righteous *actions* over a lifetime will matter most.[21]

From Muhammad Abdou, the activist scholars of the Awakening learned that such righteous engagement with the world necessarily relied on reason. Deep exploration of the intimate relationship in Islam between reason and revelation runs like a bright thread through all of Abdou's writings. That same connection is made by the intellectuals and activists of the Islamic Awakening. From Abdou, scholars of the Awakening understood that faith without the interpretation and adaptations to particular times and places that reason makes possible would be still-born. From Abdou, they understood as well that reason in itself, for all its importance, would never alone be sufficient. Abdou taught that reason could enhance revelation, particularly by clarifying the meaning of general precepts for one's own circumstances. Reason, however, could not ever displace revelation.

Reformation demanded a program that relied on reason *and* revelation. Islamic intellectuals at the forefront of the Awakening understood the need for spiritual inspiration. Their writings make it clear that Abu Dharr al Ghifari, with his close links to the Muslim Jesus, provided such a pathway. In the prophet Jesus, scholars identified a fully human but exemplary figure whose worldly example would motivate activists spiritually as they undertook their practical work of the Awakening. They looked to Jesus to imbue their scholarly and social works of renewal with a diffuse and uplifting spirituality. To this end, the spirit of Muslim prophet Jesus is a pervasive influence on the Islamic Awakening.

Abdou did not shrink from the bold conclusion that an activist and justice-centered program of reform would be needed to rescue Islam. Theologically, this conclusion invited the spirit of the Muslim Jesus into the reform effort. Jesus in Islam occupies the place of a revered prophet. The political circumstances of Abdou's day, however, did complicate the relevance of such a model. The invocation of a Jesus-centered program of reform at a time when Islamic lands were under assault from the Christian West could well be problematic for some.

At just this point, Abu Dharr came to the rescue. On the one hand, as we have seen, Abu Dharr was understood to share the most important qualities of the Prophet Jesus. He was like Jesus in his asceticism, modesty, and commitment to the welfare of the poor. At the same time, he occupied an unassailable position in Islam as one of the earliest converts to the faith and as a close companion of the Prophet. He was also known to Muslims as a venerable symbol of the core Islamic value of justice. The example of Abu Dharr could be invoked without raising any possible Islamic civilizational sensibilities.

The Muslim Jesus, like all prophets in Islam, is understood to be a fully human figure. However, he did have qualities that set him apart. Jesus in the Islamic tradition is an exceptional human being. Most importantly, Jesus is

218 JUSTICE IN ISLAM

recognized in the Qur'an as the son of the *virgin* Mary. For Christians, Jesus's miraculous conception and birth confirmed their belief that Jesus had a divine character as the son of God. For Christians, Jesus has primary importance for his atonement. The gentle Jesus suffered the torments of the Passion to win forgiveness from God, the father, for the sins of all humanity.

The Muslim Jesus, in contrast, was a figure to be revered but not worshipped. The Qur'an explicitly warned against any inclination to worship either his mother, the Virgin Mary, or her son.[22] Unlike the divine Jesus of Christianity, the prophetic Jesus of Islam had primarily a worldly role. Islam's Jesus was linked above all to justice as a practical value in human affairs. His close connection to worldly justice regularly brought Abu Dharr into view when speaking of the Muslim Jesus.

In the literature of the Awakening, Jesus and Abu Dharr at times appeared almost indistinguishable. In fact, one could reasonably conclude that references by many Islamic scholars to Abu Dharr often function as coded references to the prophetic Jesus. The reasons for the indirection are clear enough. They are practical. They reflect the realism of Islamic intellectuals. At a time when the "Christian" West was assaulting and occupying Islamic lands, a Jesus-centered program of reform of an Islam under attack from Christian powers might well raise Islamic "civilizational" sensibilities, however misplaced. While scholars would understand the reference, a great deal of that theology might well be lost on ordinary Muslims.

Beyond Politics: The Complexities of Muhammad Ali

Muhammad Ali fought for the absolute right to define himself as a Muslim engaged in the major battles for justice of his time. For these struggles, Ali understood that he needed complete control over the most fundamental elements of his public persona as a black man and a Muslim.

However, Muhammad Ali's self-awareness extended further to the most intimate dimensions of his being. Those elements included, most importantly, the language he spoke in the public arena. Ali's unique way of expressing himself, more than any other single attribute, defined his public presence. There was nothing accidental or "natural" about Ali's signature use of language. Ali's gift for language was not inherited. It was not a product of his environment. Ali understood that he could not communicate successfully in the middle-class language of the mainstream media. His formal education was far too limited. Moreover, the English that Ali naturally spoke was coded by birth in a very different way from the media in the region, class, and race it invoked. Ali came to see that there was in fact no language available to express the aspirations of a black man of talent and vision but with only limited education and modest social standing. He faced two options. Ali could either remain silent or embrace imitation of the established media language. Neither choice was acceptable.

Muhammad Ali's solution was breathtaking. Ali invented his own variation of English. He then used his celebrity status and command of the media as a global sports celebrity to impose that unique way of speaking on the world. Muhammad Ali consistently spoke in simple but original ways. His language was unbridled by middle-class grammar. It was studded with fanciful and unexpected metaphors. Yet, his gifts made that speech always understandable and accessible. Framed in this way, Ali's entertaining word play can be understood to have some of the characteristics of poetry. The modernist poet Marianne Moore, with whom Ali developed a relationship, suggested that much. I am not fully convinced by Moore's judgement. However, I do not believe that Ali's word play was either childish or simply doggerel, as so many have concluded. Rather, to my mind, Muhammad Ali anticipated the linguistic creativity of later rap musicians, whether his patter is understood as playful prose or poetry.

From the first, I was personally subject to the magic in Ali's pre-match chatter. Muhammad Ali emerged as a public figure before the eruption of rap music by at least a decade. Rap musicians themselves have signaled their debt to Muhammad Ali's verbal experimentations. They make explicit references to his rhythms and phrasing in their work. Black rap musicians embraced Muhammad Ali as a pioneer who facilitated their later efforts to bring the provocative "trash talk" of the street culture of black urban youth to the mainstream. More particularly, Ali's outsized ego foreshadowed the boastful vanity of a Kanye West and so many others. Ali's Afrocentric consciousness and fearless honesty about race in America anticipated as well figures like Rakim, Nas, Jay-Z, and Kendrick Lamar.[23]

For a child of the sixties, there was much to admire in Muhammad Ali's political courage. At the same time, it should not be forgotten that some of the most important contests of that decade of liberating promise for America were waged on the personal rather than the political plane. Activists of the sixties made the personal political. So did Muhammad Ali. He undoubtedly broke through political and race barriers. It is less frequently noted that he

220 JUSTICE IN ISLAM

also acted in ways that weakened the force of restrictive gender and sexual orientation stereotypes.

The Personal Complexities of Muhammad Ali

Most analysts take his brave political stands for justice as the marker of Muhammad Ali's courage. Equally remarkable is his boldness in the personal realm. In addition to language, Muhammad Ali exerted control over the gender definitions he projected. Social theorists who address gender identification or sexual orientation very often do so abstractly. In contrast, when Ali raised these issues, he was always clearly drawing on his own experience. Muhammad Ali made fluidity of gender and even more subtle nuance in orientation part of his own crafted and deliberately provocative persona.

Muhammad Ali took direct personal ownership of these transgressive projections with little hint of sensitivity. Ali provided more clarity and documentation than one has a right to expect for his treatments of such personal matters. Muhammad Ali regularly flaunted his own feminine dimension. Movement black power activists would tell the world that "Black is Beautiful." Muhammad Ali had made the same case by pointing out how "pretty" he was. In case one thought the more pointedly feminine phrase was a slip of the tongue, Ali kept at hand a frequently recounted story from his mother. She told her son that he was such a beautiful baby that people regularly thought he must be a girl. While most boys and men would have found ways to bury such a story, Muhammad Ali heard only the pride in his mother's description. Ali kept front and center this memory of that beautiful baby boy who was regularly mistaken for a baby girl. On some level, Ali had embraced a gender ambiguity that had been his forever.

Exceptional physical attractiveness, as enjoyed by Muhammad Ali, often itself has a transgressive quality. Beautiful people very often exert appeal across gender and sexual orientation demarcations. For many, such attentions can be a source of distress. For Ali, these sentiments were rather something to be projected and celebrated. Muhammad Ali's striking good looks and the charisma that came with them suggested that Ali must have understood same-sex attraction. His own fundamental orientation appears to have been heterosexual. However, whatever his personal reality, it was always clear that the way American culture disciplined such matters mattered little to Muhammad Ali. The "Greatest" quite deliberately suggested subversive alternatives.

Enter Gorgeous George

These very personal dimensions of Muhammad Ali's experience undoubtedly prepared him for his momentous encounter with the wrestler "Gorgeous George." George Wagner (1915–1963) was a very flamboyant and extremely successful wrestler. Meeting George, Ali appears to have understood immediately that there were important lessons to be learned from the way the wrestler presented himself.

The encounter with Gorgeous George had an impact that is hard to exaggerate. Ali figured out that this unlikely figure held the keys to the successful marketing of his own persona in the global media.[24] As an athlete, George Wagner was in no way in the same class as Muhammad Ali. Yet, the limits of a wrestler of very average abilities mattered little to George's success. George understood the basic rule for marketing a sports figure. Athletics in a consumer society is a commodity. Ticket sales matter most. People pay to see a performance. Athletes who established themselves as "stars," as George did with great success, are first and foremost star *performers*. George, to be sure, represented an extreme. Yet, his exaggerated posturing drove home the critical lesson. Performers could be outsized, even outrageously transgressive, and still be highly successful, often for those very reasons.

From Gorgeous George, Muhammad Ali adopted an unabashed self-promotion that had all these qualities. Ali also learned from Gorgeous George just how powerful gender transgressions could be. George's "stage" title, his platinum blond curls, and the dramatic lace and fur-lined cloaks he wore to enter the ring all had a deliberately provocative and unmistakably feminine character. They were especially attention-grabbing in the hyper-masculine setting of a professional wrestling arena. For Gorgeous George, the aim was to be noticed. Mixed gender projections worked with great effect to that end.

Muhammad Ali took these lessons to heart. He did so with creative adaptations to make George's insights work for his own distinctive character. Muhammad Ali, by virtue of his three-time title of heavyweight champion of the world, had an unchallengeable status as a figure of unquestioned masculinity. From that position of gender and apparent orientation clarity, Muhammad Ali did something quite unexpected. Ali dared to suggest a more fluid persona that put gender in play. Inevitably, if inconclusively, he went further by hinting very subtly at sexual orientation nuance as well.

Boxing boasts a venerable tradition of eroticized and transgressive commentary that Aeschylus launched some eighteen hundred years earlier in

222   JUSTICE IN ISLAM

"noisy haunters of gymnasiums." Boxing writers literally swooned over Ali: George Plimpton wrote that Ali had "great good looks." Pete Hamill remarked that Ali had "beautiful legs." Norman Mailer unabashedly commented that the first round of the Ali-Frazier rematch was the "equivalent to the first kiss in a love affair." He continued that "later the fighters moved like somnambulists slowly working and rubbing one another, almost embracing, . . . locked in the slow moves of lovers after the act."[25]

What is clear is that Muhammad Ali himself feminized his public persona in the most subtle ways. He scripted a professional biography that include hints of gender and orientation ambiguity. Ali was a man who had devoted the best years of his life to the intense training required of a world-class athlete. Yet, he was nevertheless able to understand from Gorgeous George that a provocative stage presence mattered as much or, for some purposes, even more in defining what "winning" meant.

Muhammad Ali learned quickly that the rules were different for an entertainer. They were the rules of the market and of the media that fed it. Those in actual attendance at a sporting event should be entertained. Yet, above all, it was critical to play to the media beyond any particular venue. It was there that the massive numbers and the real profitability were to be found. The primary aim was always to attract and sustain attention. Behavior that in personal life might be scandalous could be just right as media performance. At the heart of Ali's performances was always an inviting and memorable public persona. Muhammad Ali came to understand that the aim was not to depict a likable or even admirable personality. The over-riding objective was to create an unforgettable one.

To that end, messaging had to be kept simple, direct, and as provocative as possible. The media thrive on stories. Therefore, messages were most effective when given narrative form. The stories could be repeated. The repetitions, however, should always come with enough variation to sustain interest. Stories should never be allowed to grow stale.

Muhammad Ali displayed sheer genius for keeping his own narrative as world heavyweight champion fresh and uniquely his own. He gave the reporters who swarmed around him engaging stories in endless iterations. Muhammad Ali made himself the very definition of a perpetual marketing phenomenon. The story of Ali's knockouts to preserve his title was not allowed to grow old. Ali added new twists in a variety of ways. He at times might predict the exact round in which a particular challenger would go down. He might anticipate the particular strategy that would bring a formidable opponent to his knees. Given his athletic prowess, Muhammad Ali knew he could deliver on such things in ways others could not. When they originated with Ali, such predictions were both believable and yet improbable enough to make interest in his matches surge. Time after time, Ali provided the media the engaging story they craved.

Muhammad Ali's inclination to break the mold went further. He brought recitations of poetry into the boxing experience. To take Ali's poetry with even a modicum of seriousness is to notice that Ali's most unforgettable poetic lines and metaphors are laced with a feminine sensibility. It was that provocative sensibility that made them memorable. It would be reasonable to expect a heavyweight champion of the world to move like a tank and strike like a sledgehammer. Yet, today the whole world remembers that Muhammad Ali "floated like a butterfly and stung like a bee." The fanciful metaphors are more than playful. They convey improbable but truthful meanings. Ali brought speed, grace, and beauty to a heavy and plodding sport. He did so with a remarkable intelligence and lightness of touch. They also evoked the feminine. It is hard to imagine a creature at once as fragile yet beautiful as a butterfly. Bees, too, are small, vulnerable, and apparently helpless animals. Except that they are not. Anyone who has felt their sudden sting will attest to that. Butterflies and bees have no place at all in a boxing ring. They have no place, that is, until they are introduced by Muhammad Ali. Ali transformed boxing. That transformation made butterflies and bees relevant and easily understood metaphors that hinted at transgression.[26]

The Imperfection of the Muslim Muhammad Ali

Muhammad Ali never claimed to be perfect. However, he did boast endlessly of his greatness. Ali's public persona was marked not only by transgressions but also by weaknesses and imperfections. These complex attributes coexisted with impressive talents to make him "the greatest."

Islam as a moral and ethical tradition does not demand freedom from shortcomings in believers, including Islam's prophets. It is sometimes difficult for Muslims to acknowledge that their beloved Prophet Muhammad, however exemplary, was himself not perfect. However, like all the prophets of Islam, the Prophet Muhammad was fully human. He was subject to error. The Qur'an makes that truth, uncomfortable at times for some, perfectly clear. Islam's Holy Book records times when the Prophet of Islam faltered in

224   JUSTICE IN ISLAM

very human ways.[27] The best known is the story of a blind man who sought to engage the Prophet. Deep in conversation with prominent tribal figures, the Prophet chose to ignore him. Surrounded by companions who were attentive to his every word and action, such lapses did not go unnoticed.

Muhammad Ali, in a very different time and under very different circumstances, also lived much of his life before the public. A human life, subject to such unending witness, no matter its accomplishments, inevitably yields a record of shortcomings. Muhammad Ali was no exception. Most importantly, there were instances of unnecessary cruelty. There were betrayals. They could not be hidden. The world took notice. In the end, Muhammad Ali himself acknowledged them all. They did not overwhelm him.

The most damning spectacle of unnecessarily cruel actions came in February 1967 in the match between Ali and Ernie Terrell. Terrell held the world heavyweight title, after the boxing association stripped it from Muhammad Ali for his refusal to fight in Vietnam. Terrell knew Ali as Cassius Clay. In the publicity for their match, Terrell insisted on using that name. He also knew that Ali had assumed and insisted on use of his Muslim name of Muhammad Ali. Once the fight was underway, Ali taunted Terrell with the question: "What's my name?" Ali, who had the upper hand from the start, is accused, with justification, of prolonging the match in order to punish Terrell.

The personal betrayals were less public. Ultimately, they proved far more damaging. Muhammad Ali betrayed the two great loves of his life. The first was his first wife Sonje. The second was his friend and mentor Malcolm X. Both betrayals came while Ali was under the influence of Elijah Muhammad, the Nation of Islam's false prophet. The Nation opposed Ali's marriage to Sonje. The Nation's leader believed her background as a waitress in night clubs raised questions about her character. Under pressure from the Nation, Ali divorced Sonje. He was fearful that disobedience would bring down on him the violence Elijah Muhammad commanded.

On March 8, 1964, Malcolm X broke very publicly with the Nation of Islam. Like Malcolm, Muhammad Ali knew from his membership in the Nation that there would be retribution. He also understood that it could well be violent. Yet, Ali did nothing to protect his friend. On February 21, 1965, Malcolm X was assassinated. All indications point to the fact that Malcolm X paid with his life for leaving the Nation. It goes too far to say that Muhammad Ali was an accomplice in Malcolm's murder. Yet, it is true that Ali knew the dangers Malcolm faced. Still, he failed to act in any way to save the man who had twice paved his way to Islam. It was Malcolm's brilliance as orator and independent thinker that occasioned Ali's initial enthrallment with the Nation of Islam. It was also Malcolm who charted the way out of the Nation to universal Islam.

Ali loved Malcolm but his courage failed him. It took a decade, but eventually Ali did recognize and acknowledge to himself and then the world how egregious his betrayal of Malcolm was. Toward the end of his life, Ali said simply that failing Malcolm was the single thing he most regretted.

The White Dogs of Racism

Racism of all colors is deadly. In the America of the 1950s, the social worlds through which Muhammad Ali moved inevitably bore the overt markings of white racism. Ali had no illusions about the viciousness of American racism. He was all his life haunted by the battered face of Emmett Till. The impact on Muhammad Ali of the handsome fourteen-year-old boy's disfigurement, torture, and lynching in 1955 never faded. Till was visiting Mississippi from the North. A white woman accused the teen of flirting and touching her. We now know the charges were false. The fourteen-year-old was kidnapped three days after the alleged incident. He was so savagely beaten and mutilated by the woman's husband and half-brother that the boy was unrecognizable in death.

When his mother, Mamie Till, received her son's battered body in Chicago, she insisted on a public funeral and an open casket so the world could see what they had done to her son. Over the course of a five full days, the boy's mutilated body and horribly disfigured face could be viewed at the Roberts Temple Church of God in Chicago. Jesse Jackson reported that "more than 100,000 people saw his body lying in that casket here in Chicago. That must have been at that time the largest single civil rights demonstration in American history."[28] Till's assailants were subsequently acquitted. They later admitted that they had in fact tortured and killed the boy. The unbearable image of Emmett Till's battered face motivated generations of civil rights activists. Overcome with inconsolable grief, Mamie Till had made sure her son's terrible death had meaning. In the years that followed, Mamie Till transformed herself into a prominent civil rights activist. Her son's murder became a galvanizing event in what would become the civil rights movement. Recently, the killing of George Floyd and the Black Lives Matter protests it

226 JUSTICE IN ISLAM

inspired has been compared to Till's killing. For both murders, an unbearable visual record heightened the savagery of the deaths and amplified their impact.[29]

In Till's brutal murder, Ali always saw forebodings of his own fate. Ali said, "I realized that this could just as easily been a story about me or my brother."[30] All his life, Muhammad Ali was tormented by the image of what Till had suffered. Ali could never quite overcome his fears that the dogs of white racism would be unleashed on him. Muhammad Ali lived all the rest of his life in the shadow of those fears. There was always a pronounced restraint about Muhammad Ali, even at the height of his fame and his powers. Muhammad Ali's psyche carried the deep scars that fear imparted. He was a boxer. Unlike his mentor Malcolm X, he was never a street fighter. Ali's conversion to Islam opened him to a tradition with a finely balanced view of violence. In Islam, only defensive violence is sanctioned. Aggressive violence is deplored. On this question, Islam's sacred texts are clear. The historical record of Muslims is, of course, another mater.

The restraint of the Islamic view, as declaimed in the Qur'an, suited Muhammad Ali. Haunted by the memory of Emmett Till, Ali all his life rejected the path of aggressive violence in all its forms. At the same time, despite his Protestant background, the Christian stance of turning the other cheek when struck proved alien to Ali's nature. The divine Jesus of Christianity did not provide the model he sought. Ali embraced instead Islam's worldly prophetic Jesus. In the Islamic tradition, the aversion to violence and embrace of nonviolence was conjoined with an activist and assertive stance. Muslims were called to defend themselves and their community when attacked. The Qur'an could not be clearer in recognizing the right of self-defense "for those who have been expelled from their homes, in defiance of right. . . ."[31] As we have seen, the Prophet's companion and symbol of justice, Abu Dharr al Ghifari, represented this careful balance. He resisted the tyranny of power and wealth. He did so nonviolently.

Ali's interventions on the national and international levels did require that the volume be turned up. Ali brought to that more expansive arena the same directness of expression. Yet, he carefully framed his verbal assertiveness with physical restraint. The tone and attitude were instantly recognized. It could only be the voice and demeanor of Muhammad Ali. Ali's actions on the national stage spoke to an entire generation of Islamic activists around the world. His verbal assertiveness became his trademark, though his physical restraint was always equally important. Muhammad Ali clarified the

MUHAMMAD ALI 227

responsibilities of nonviolent civil disobedience. His cultivated restraint meant that Ali always presented himself for the consequences of his actions.

The unjust price Ali paid for challenging the American draft to fight in Vietnam was particularly steep. He was convicted of draft evasion. He was sentenced to the maximum of five years in prison and a $10,000 fine. Ali submitted himself for judgment, though he immediately appealed the conviction. He escaped imprisonment. His popularity declined sharply, however. The president of the United States denigrated him as a "draft dodger." Banned from boxing for three plus years at the height of his powers, Ali used that time out of the ring to speak out against racism in America and the Vietnam War on college campuses across the country.

In April 1967, Ali gave one of his most memorable speeches. The particulars of Ali's invitation to Howard University, the nation's preeminent black university, defined an act of militant student defiance. Days prior to the speech saw a campus in uproar. Scores of students marched in Black Power rallies against a Howard administration that had failed to respond to the upsurge of black pride.

It was the activist students who extended the invitation to Muhammad Ali. The university administration denied a venue for Ali's appearance. Ali would not disappoint the students. He went ahead with his visit. He spoke outside on the steps of the Frederick Douglass Memorial Hall. The Hall was a national landmark designed by early twentieth-century African-American architect Albert Cassell. An estimated thousand or more students attended.

Ali addressed the issue of black identity raised by the students head on. *"All you need to do,"* Ali advised, *"is know yourself to set yourself free. We don't know who we are. We call ourselves negroes, but have you ever heard of a place called Negroland?"* Ali blamed a sense of inferiority among African Americans on white domination. Whites sought to erase them and their accomplishments, as if they did not exist. His words were stinging:

> *See, we have been brainwashed. Everything good and of authority was made white. We look at Jesus, we see a white with blond hair and blue eyes. We look at all the angels, we see white with blond hair and blue eyes. Now, I'm sure if there's a heaven in the sky and the colored folks die and go to heaven, where are the colored angels? They must be in the kitchen preparing the milk and honey. We look at Miss America, we see white. We look at Miss World, we see white. We look at Miss Universe, we see white. Even Tarzan, the king of the jungle in black Africa, he's white!*[32]

228   JUSTICE IN ISLAM

Ali validated the black power agenda of the radicalized students with that unfailing voice.

It was his athletic prowess that first catapulted Muhammad Ali to fame and fortune. But it is what he did with that fame that ultimately defined his legacy. A place for Ali in history, it seemed clear, would be secured by his record as a world class boxer. Then, everything changed. The United States entered the Vietnam War in 1965. America was at war. The draft was in place. The best-known American in the world refused induction. Muhammad Ali announced that he would not serve. Ali's refusal commanded worldwide attention. Ali was transformed from a sports hero to a global political icon.

Ali placed Islam at the very center of his conscientious objection. The general American populace had not yet turned against the war. In the full glare of a hostile American media, Ali's gift for words and memorable expressions did not fail him. "No Vietcong ever called me a N***" he explained to an attentive world. Muhammad Ali appealed the criminal judgment against him. He defied the most powerful nation on the planet. In the end, he won. Ali's conviction was overturned in 1971 by the Supreme Court of the United States. It was a victory more consequential than any he won in the ring.

Having won the opportunity in the courts to return to the ring, Muhammad Ali fought his way back to the championship title. The cost had been high. The ban from the ring for some three plus years was devastating. Nevertheless, Ali's successful defiance of the American government taught the lesson that Muhammad Ali was not only successful. He was right.

Like Abu Dharr, Ali had turned to words not weapons. His words of resistance, like those of Abu Dharr, called for justice. Ali wondered aloud: "Poor Americans killing poor Vietnamese; dark skinned Americans fighting dark skinned Vietnamese who had caused them no harm. What sense did that make?" Ali gave his refusal an Islamic framing in the most personal terms. He cast his conscientious objection to serving in Vietnam explicitly on the basis that Islam of the Qur'an was a religion of justice and peace. The West paid no attention to that aspect of his refusal.

Muslims across the globe took note. In the Islamic world, Muhammad Ali was seen as a hero in an entirely new dimension. Ali himself never fully understood the love and affection that was showered on him by common people in Islamic lands. Ordinary Muslims, or so it seems, saw in Muhammad Ali an expression of core Islamic values that allowed him to triumph. Simply put, Ali had spoken and acted for an Islam they could recognize as their own.

Conclusion

For Americans of his generation, Vietnam loomed largest. For younger Americans, it would be the assault on Iraq that would define issues of war and peace. Once again, Muhammad Ali fearlessly stepped forward. Saddam Hussein held a special place in the American imagination as the tyrant of distinction. Ali's encounter with Saddam came with a dramatic gesture in 1990 to rescue hostages held in Iraq just before the start of the Gulf War.[33] There were some fifteen American hostages in Iraq as an American attack loomed. Ali went to Iraq in Islam's name. He went to Iraq to free American civilians. To do so, he defied White House displeasure with an announcement that he would meet with Saddam Hussein. At the height of war fever in America, under a right-wing president, the imperturbable Muhammad Ali in 1990 traveled to Iraq with Ramsey Clark, former attorney general and an icon of the left.

At this point, Ali was six years into his battle with Parkinson's. The disease had taken its toll. Iraqis did not notice. They swarmed to meet their world-famous Muslim hero. Ali took time to interact with ordinary Iraqis, including, as always, the crowds of children. For no clear reason, Saddam delayed their meeting. By the time Saddam agreed to meet him, Ali could barely move. He couldn't talk at all. Finally, foreign doctors in Iraq came to Ali's rescue by providing medications to restore his mobility and speech. Once the treatment took effect, Ali met Saddam. He completed his mission with as little attention to his debilitating disease as possible. Saddam Hussein commented: "I'm not going to let Muhammad Ali return to the US without having a number of the American citizens accompanying him."[34] Muhammad Ali had registered an improbable success. Government officials accused Ali of a publicity stunt. He refused to let the charge stand without retort. "I do need publicity—but not for what I do for good!" Ali was quoted as saying by the *New York Post*. "I need publicity for my book, I need publicity for my fights, I need publicity for my movie—but not for helping people. Then it's no longer sincere."

Abu Dharr had set the general pattern for the activist Islamic intellectual in the way he confronted the deviations of the Caliph Osman. Ali, like Abu Dharr, did not elaborate moral and ethical teachings theoretically. Rather, he embodied them in his actions. There would be no further such grand gestures. In the wake of the 9/11 slaughter of innocents by Islamic extremists, a greatly weakened Muhammad Ali could no longer act in his characteristically bold way. His body was failing him. His voice, however, remained

230   JUSTICE IN ISLAM

strong. Ali summoned the strength to make a final public statement. It was heard around the world. As ever, Muhammad Ali spoke as no other. The personal inflections captivated. The Islamic resonance of the message lent depth and reach. The core truths of one of humanity's great monotheisms had reached Muhammad Ali. He conveyed what he had learned with direct and compelling phrasing. Reacting to the Islamic extremist attacks on 9/11, Muhammad Ali explained how "that really hurt me, because Islam is peace and is not violent. The few that do these things that make the religion as a whole look bad." Ali continued that "rivers, ponds, lakes, and streams— they all have different names but they all contain water. So religions all have different names, but they all contain the same truths."[35] Those who heard Muhammad Ali articulate those inclusive truths did not always understand fully the intuitive redefinitions they were absorbing from the "greatest." But absorb them they did.

When Muhammad Ali embraced Islam, he had only a minimal idea of what that embrace meant. Enlightenment came over a lifetime of struggle in thought and action to bring himself closer to Islam. There is nothing unusual in such a trajectory for a Muslim. The journey to Islam always entails both a moral and an intellectual dimension. Islam celebrates the divine gifts of both faith and reason. Islam's sacred texts have proven so durable through the centuries precisely because Muslims must interpret and adapt their meaning for their own time and situation. The texts themselves do not change. The way they are understood does.

Islam sets the bar for entry at the most accommodating level. Then a lifetime of study and practice is the expected pathway to realize oneself more fully as a Muslim. Reason and revelation always go hand in hand in that process. What made Muhammad Ali distinct was the fact that he waged these moral and intellectual struggles for self-realization as a Muslim on a global stage. He had a worldwide audience of millions. Alongside his advances, there were inevitable missteps and shortfalls. By making his voyage to Islam so public, Ali allowed others to see what the embrace of Islam could mean. By doing so, he made himself one of the most influential "callers" to Islam in our time. In the end, he secured the role he had sought in that film *The Message*. Muhammad Ali had made himself the Bilal of our global age.

10

Conclusion

The Companion, the Prophets, and the Unseen

They have hearts
with which they do not understand,
They have eyes with which they do not see,
They have ears with which they do not hear.

Qur'an 7:179

The Prophet Muhammad walks hand in hand with the Muslim Jesus through the pages of this book. The Qur'an instructs that all the prophets of Islam, from Adam to Muhammad, have the same stature.[1] Without contradiction, Islamic tradition also recognizes a particularly close personal relationship between the Prophet Muhammad and the Islamic prophet Jesus. A celebrated hadith records that the Prophet Muhammad advised those who would know Jesus to look to his beloved companion, Abu Dharr al Ghifari. Viewed in this complex way, Islam's Jesus models not only humility, kindness, and piety, but also the passion for justice he shared with Abu Dharr.

The Islamic scholars who made major contributions to the literature of the Awakening regularly bring Abu Dharr al Ghifari into the company of the Prophets Muhammad and Jesus. The substantive chapters of this book chronicle their struggles for justice across the Islamic strategic triangle of Turkey, Egypt, Iran, and beyond. Commonalities in the record of those struggles lend coherence to the contemporary Islamic Awakening. They define a value-centered program of reform and renewal of Islam. In the face of Islamic extremist and secular distortions of Islam's message, the broad project of the Awakening aims for a reassertion of the midstream Islam of Qur'an and *Sunnah*.

The literature of the Awakening registers the compassionate guidance of the Prophet Muhammad, the centrality of justice symbolized by Abu Dharr

Justice in Islam. Raymond William Baker, Oxford University Press. © Oxford University Press 2022.
DOI: 10.1093/oso/9780197624975.003.0010

232 JUSTICE IN ISLAM

al Ghifari, and, perhaps less anticipated, the loving spirit of the Muslim Jesus. Islam's prophetic Jesus is revered by Muslims as the miraculously conceived son of the *virgin* Mary. However, for Muslims, that extraordinary conception did not make Jesus the son of God, as it did for Christians. In the Qur'an, Jesus is embraced rather as a prophet of Islam. Jesus is known to Muslims simply as "the son of Mary." Jesus is not to be worshipped, as the Qur'an cautions.[2] He is, however, to be revered as an exemplary figure. The prophet Jesus models not only asceticism and deep piety, but also a profound love of justice. Following the Prophet Muhammad, the quest for justice inspires struggles to create societies where the tyrannies of wealth and power are held in check. Such communities will make it possible for believers to live in accordance with the higher purposes of their faith.

Vigorously engaged struggles for justice energize and sanctify the Islamic Awakening of our time. As Shams al-Din al Sarkhasi, a noted classical Islamic jurist, explains, "to render justice ranks as the most noble of acts of devotion next to belief in God. It is the greatest of all the duties entrusted to the prophets . . . and it is the strongest justification for man's stewardship of earth."[3]

Each of the previous chapters has focused on the major intellectuals who have provided leadership for these contests. They have been the mind and heart of the very human and therefore inevitably flawed efforts to advance the cause of justice. The intellectuals featured are all understood as "Callers" to Islam. In their narratives, the guidance of the Prophet Muhammad, an emphasis on Qur'anic values, and the pervasive spirituality of the prophet Jesus are all manifest.

For all their distinctive features and whatever the balance of achievements and shortcomings, each story presents itself as part of the Islamic quest for justice. References to Abu Dharr are more frequent in these narratives than one might expect. At play is the companion's unquestioned identification with the Muslim Jesus. The presence of the spirit of the Muslim Jesus is understood to enhance the worldly quest for justice so central to Islam's message. While Jesus is a figure viewed differently by Christians and Muslims, Abu Dharr has a clear and uncomplicated Islamic identity as a beloved companion of the Prophet Muhammad and one of the very first to enter Islam. He provides the perfect complement to the Muslim Jesus.

Walking with Abu Dharr alongside these contemporary Islamic intellectuals through local struggles for justice in the Islamic strategic triangle of Turkey, Egypt, and Iran offers a rare opportunity to take note of

CONCLUSION   233

the unseen things their interactions take for granted. The unseen remains unnamed. It is never argued. It is simply there for "those with eyes to see."[4] However, interactions in very diverse struggles for justice are shaped by the presence of these critical unseen factors. Without them, interactions would be very different. They might be entirely impossible. When they are held in common, the magic of generative synergy takes place. Old values are affirmed. "Truths we already know," in Qur'anic phrasing, are refreshed.[5] Nuanced new meanings for new times are created for those unchanging truths. Bonds are forged that defy what would otherwise be insurmountable barriers of space and time. In the process, the spirit of Islam's Prophetic Jesus is itself renewed for successive generations of Muslims.

Only with insight into the critical importance of the unseen can the strenuous efforts be mounted to learn the new ways of seeing that bring the unseen into view. The correction takes place against the background of the landscapes to be explored. Most important is prior attention to the lenses and the blinders that observers bring with them from their own contexts. Islam's Jesus can help with the correction.

Each of the previous chapters of this book tells the story of an Islamic intellectual and of the inspirational role of the direction of the Prophet Muhammad, the spirit of the Muslim Jesus, and the lodestar of justice. The ways their intellectual and activist work have contributed to contemporary efforts to reform and renew Islam are documented. The narratives at their core are all elaborations of refreshed ideas of Islamic justice. In all cases, local circumstances define distinctive dimensions of the battles waged and the outcomes achieved. In each case, as we have seen, struggles for justice inevitably take on a very different character.

The key figures in each chapter are all *Islamic* intellectuals, whatever national, ethnic, or sectarian attachments they may also have. All are guided by the wisdom of the Prophet Muhammad. All reflect the influence of the spirit of the Muslim prophet Jesus. All find inspiration in the transcendent idea of Islamic justice that Abu Dharr has symbolized for centuries. They all take certain things for granted. They all see and react to things of which their Western secular counterparts may not even be aware.

The unseen in the interactions of contemporary Islamic intellectuals, inspired by the quest for justice, are as simple as they are powerful. Walking with these figures through their very different settings provides the opportunity to develop awareness of three particularly important, though most often unrecognized dimensions of the Islamic cultural landscape. They are

234   JUSTICE IN ISLAM

all taken for granted by the Islamic intellectuals and activists featured in each chapter.

First in importance is the very idea of a unitary Islamic world. These realistic and pragmatic figures are all intimately familiar with the rifts and fragmentations that plague Islamic lands. They are painfully aware, in particular, of the Shi'i-Sunni divide. They stand on both sides of that schism. They do not fail to note the divisions that ethnic nationalism imposes. Yet, with the Prophet Muhammad, the Muslim Jesus, and Abu Dharr at their side, they see beyond all these fractures. These Islamic intellectuals feel and understand the underlying unities that constitute the Islamic world. The unitary Islamic world is real. It has distinctive and durable features that Islamic intellectuals take for granted. In this Islamic world, one always finds the Qur'an and the *Sunnah* as defining references.

The *second* dimension complements awareness of the underlying connectedness of the Islamic world with a sense of the extraordinarily varied cultural and historical elements that make up Islamic civilization. Elements are shared, though not homogenized. The Islamic world through which the intellectuals featured in each chapter move has a recognizable yet polychromatic social and cultural character. This world is a world of deep faith, ideas, emotions, and values. For all the variety encountered, there are always believers present who look to the Message and the example of the Prophet Muhammad for guidance on how to live as Muslims in the world they confront as they prepare for the world to come. As we have seen, it matters not at all whether prayers are expressed in Arabic, Turkish, Farsi, or American English.

The *third* dimension of immanent experience of the Islamic world brings clarification that the Islamic challenge to the West is not really political, as so many Western scholars assume. Political resistance does define a great deal of the dynamic of interactions. However, in its essence, the Islamic contestation goes deeper. Civilizational Islam questions the most fundamental settled conclusions of Western secularism. Moreover, Islam has the capacity to generate genuine, compelling, and variegated civilizational alternatives.

Delusional Western strategic thinking assumes that the mass of ordinary Muslims are secularists at heart. If given the opportunity, it is believed, they will opt for secular social and cultural systems. Everyday Muslims are presumed to have no interest in societies built on Islamic foundations.

No matter how many times events expose the falseness of these illusions, they persist. Not even the earth-shattering debacle of Iraq could extirpate

CONCLUSION 235

this irrational thinking that is at the root of what passes for Western strategy for dealing with the Islamic world. Invading Americans expected that ordinary Iraqis would embrace their vision of an Iraq rebuilt on secular foundations. The fantasies went deeper. It was believed that Iraq rebuilt in this way would stand as the model for the remaking of the entire Islamic world along Western ideas of progress. Iran, it is important to remember, was next in the cross hairs. "Anyone can go to Baghdad," the war planners boasted on the eve of the American assault on Iraq, "real men go to Teheran."[6] The embrace never came. "Real men" found themselves holed up in the Green Zone. Iran emerged as the major winner from the ill-conceived onslaught on Iraq. Ordinary Iraqi citizens and the incomparable cultural treasures that Iraqis had given the world were the major losers.

A cardinal and distinctive lesson emerges from the study of Islamic history. It is for the most part systematically ignored. Islam, like all the great monotheisms, has had its share of extremisms throughout its fourteen centuries as a force in world history. The general pattern has been for extremist movements to experience an initial vitality that allows them to wreak havoc at the margins. With time, that destructive energy subsides. Islam's heart belongs to the center, as the Qur'an makes clear:

> Thus have made of you
> An Ummah justly balanced that
> Ye might be witnesses over the nations. . . .[7]

The extremists and their movements are eventually reabsorbed into the Islamic midstream. Their distortions of the faith are corrected over time. Over and over again through the centuries, Islam has demonstrated this striking capacity to re-center itself.

Instructive exceptions to this pattern have come when the extremists are supported by outside forces. Outsiders may convince themselves that extremist movements can be wielded as a weapon to advance their own interests. American strategists have been particularly prone to these illusions. Assistance to the extremists takes both direct and indirect forms. Ronald Reagan judged the violent jihadists drawn to Afghanistan to be *freedom fighters*. He broadcast his belief that they would contribute to the defeat of the Soviet Union in Afghanistan. He boasted of arming and training fighters who had assembled under the banner of Islamic extremism. The emergence of transnational networks of violent jihadists owes more than is usually

236 JUSTICE IN ISLAM

acknowledged to the icon of American conservatism. Reagan both armed and legitimated these transnational movements.

George W. Bush, for his part, announced that the American assault on Iraq to rid the country of nonexistent weapons of mass destruction would topple the dictator and open the way for American-style democracy in Iraq and beyond. The misinformation that Saddam Hussein supported the violent groups lent credence to what was understood to be an indirect blow against the extremists. Calculations of oil and strategic advantage were shrouded in this misty rhetoric of loftier aims. In the event, successfully "ending the Iraqi state" created a space of chaos and unparalleled destruction in the heart of the Arab world.[8] The most violent of extremist movements were gifted with the perfect setting for incubation and proliferation. There are, of course, local roots as well of the chaos today in great swaths of the Middle East. No reasonable analyst, however, should ignore the contribution of what is now given the anodyne label of "the Iraq factor."

America has won none of its recent wars in Islamic lands. Everywhere, conditions have worsened in the wake of invasions and interventions. Everywhere long-term American interests have suffered. The pain of losing wars is salved for Western elites and the mega-institutions they control by a reality only rarely acknowledged. There is black magic at work. Losing wars can be as enormously profitable as winning them. *Merchants of death* continue to thrive in conditions of ineffectual American twenty-first-century war-making.[9] Even lost wars can provide astronomical profits for the large corporations and related institutions that arm and supply "our warriors." The profits are there, whatever the outcomes on the fields of destruction. As disconcerting is the consistency with which the military commanders who consistently lose these wars are rewarded and celebrated. The mediocrity of American military commanders is screened from view by the sheen of the medals they are awarded and the status of the promotions they are given. It is the ordinary soldiers recruited from the common people who join the citizens of Islamic countries to bear the terrible costs of the string of lost wars. Meanwhile, generals are promoted. Political careers are launched. Rich and powerful others reap the profits.

The persistent fantasy of rebuilding the Islamic world on Western secular foundations rationalizes the endless failed wars that have been the hallmark of Western policies in Islamic lands. A pivotal assumption, for which there is absolutely no empirical support, sustains this fantasy. At work is the persistent idea that ordinary citizens in the Islamic world are, at the deepest levels, free market democrats. In their hearts, they are believed to have accepted the idea that democracy and the market economy define their desired future.

Americans are especially prone to this messianic thinking. *Manifest destiny* worked to bring the United States "from sea to sea." Today that same ideological formulation provides the affirmative rationale for global dominance by *the indispensable nation*. America now bears the heavy, self-imposed burden of Westernizing the entire world. Even if this project were a plausible and worthy one—which it is not—the blunt truth is that America simply does not have the necessary intellectual resources and moral authority to carry it out successfully. The idea of substituting military power for understanding simply has not worked. Nor has the addition of massive corruption. American power and wealth can overwhelm and destroy. It can corrupt. It can even mobilize extremists to do the dirty work of terrorizing civilian populations into submission. However, America does not now, nor will it ever, have the means to accomplish that unworthy goal. America simply cannot rebuild. It does not know how.[10]

There is an unacknowledged and utterly improbable void at the heart of these American imaginings. They are in their essence political and theological. Religious dimensions are masked. Projections of American power are nevertheless accepted as ordained. Relentless expansion of American power requires an empty space into which it can extend its civilizational model, unimpeded. The violence of the process is often misleadingly characterized as *creative destruction*. It is rather divinely sanctioned cultural cleansing. Rhetoric aside, it does not aim for rebuilding. There were plans to protect the Interior and Oil Ministries in Baghdad. There were no plans to put a shattered Iraq back together. Thought was given only to the ways that America's destructive role could be masked. The failings were all Iraqi. Iraqis were judged incapable themselves of dislodging the dictator. Unable to rise above debilitating sectarian divisions, Iraqis had plunged their nation into the chaos of civil war.

At just this point, Islam takes to the stage as the very heart of Iraqi incapacity. Islam's message of remembrance is the absolute antithesis of a grand Western project of cleansing and building anew. Few have characterized Islam as "challenger civilization" to greater effect than my Harvard mentor, the late Samuel Huntington. His endlessly cited and now rarely read classic, *The Clash of Civilizations and the Remaking of the World Order*, radiates an intense and uninformed hostility to all things Islamic. For the little he knew of Islam, Huntington relied uncritically on Orientalist scholarship. That

238   JUSTICE IN ISLAM

tradition was represented for him by Bernard Lewis and, to a lesser degree, by Fuad Ajami. Huntington borrowed his core notion of the "clash" and the title of his most famous book from Lewis. From Ajami, Huntington took his firm convictions of the fundamental irrelevance of Islam to all "hard" efforts at economic and political development. Islam, in this still influential view, was all about the "soft" dimensions of faith, identity, and culture.

Huntington's representations of Islam offer little of value for the historian or student of Islamic culture. However, out of the over-heated antipathy of Huntington's still influential approach, two clear insights do emerge. Islam, in Huntington's view, was both disorganized and indigestible. These formulations are inevitably cast by Huntington in negative terms. They are no less insightful for that. Tilting the valence of these hostile but accurate observations from the negative to the positive is easy enough. Disorganized becomes de-centered. Indigestible becomes resilient. Islam's Jesus and the contemporary intellectuals he has inspired would have no problem with either characterization.

Neither the market nor state power orders the Islamic world through which the intellectual heirs of Abu Dharr al Ghifari move. To the degree there is order, it emerges from a moral vision and is loosely structured by values, notably justice and its corollaries of freedom and compassion. Islam, like justice, is one. It is also, without contradiction in the astute Sufi formulation, many. For the secular West, such an ordering cannot possibly hold. It is unrealistic. It is, if truth be told, unthinkable.

Yet, the Islamic formula has worked for some fourteen centuries. Abu Dharr al Ghifari, a figure who steps out of Islam's classic period, to symbolize the core Islamic value of justice, has survived into the twenty-first century. At times, his image is strong. At others, it fades. Through the changes, he nevertheless endures as a venerable symbol of Islamic justice. The years from the end of the sixties to the first decade of the twenty-first century were years of Islamic Awakening. Abu Dharr left a defining mark on the Awakening. The Awakening in turn rescued the Prophet's companion from the fading of his influence among the world's Muslims. The legacy of Abu Dharr was renewed and revitalized during these critical years by leading Islamic scholars and the movements they inspired across Islamic lands.

To bring Abu Dharr to life, as all of these scholars did, was to remind Muslims of the lessons their holy book teaches. These lessons are reinforced by the example of the prophets of Islam. Muslims revere their Prophet Muhammad as *the seal of the Prophets*. However, that does not mean that

CONCLUSION   239

they deny or even downplay the role of earlier prophets. Muslims know that all the prophets have contributed to the collective wisdom through which the *ummah* (the Islamic community) has restored and renewed itself through the centuries. In the Islamic tradition, as we have seen, the prophets are not ranked. Yet, it is nevertheless true that special attention is given to Jesus as the prophet who worked his effects in a time and place closest to the Prophet Muhammad. In communities of Muslims across the globe, young Muslims all grow up with rudimentary knowledge of "the story of the son of Maryam." It is not uncommon for baby boys to be called "Isa," the Arabic version of "Jesus." Even more common is the fact that their mother and sisters carry some variant of the name of Jesus's revered mother, Mary.

The Islamic vision of community explicitly rejects ideas of community based on blood and soil. It does have a place for markets. It does not, however, share the Western secular view that the market should be *the* organizing principle for *all of society*. Islamic tradition judges that competition is an unworthy substitute for compassion. Islamic intellectuals find strange and untenable the mystical notion of an *invisible hand* to reconcile unfettered individual competition and greed with the collective good.

In sharp contrast, Islam of the Qur'an looks explicitly and forcefully to values and a moral code to achieve that balance. Justice is the core Islamic value. Islam asserts no exclusive ownership of this most fundamental value. Muslims are taught that justice is a value Islam shares with others, including but not limited to the world's other great monotheisms, Judaism and Christianity. Pluralism in the Islamic tradition is not only possible but embraced. Midstream Islamic scholars judge that pluralism should be counted an Islamic invention, as Shaikh Muhammad al Ghazzali frequently argued.

Ultimately, the Islamic vision of community rests not on blood, territory, or the all-pervasive market. Islam rejects the idea of governance based on the mysterious workings of an amoral market. Protection of the common good cannot be achieved by the workings of a morally indifferent market. The Islamic vision of the moral community is anchored in the value of justice. Muslims are taught that this foundational idea is not in any way new or distinctive. Simply put, it is a reminder of the core message sent innumerable times by God to humanity. It is a compelling *message of remembrance* shared by all the great monotheisms.[11]

The Islam of the contemporary Awakening radiates this spirit of justice. There is great power in its extreme simplicity, as pronounced by the major

240 JUSTICE IN ISLAM

Islamic intellectuals who have moved through the pages of this book. Their collective message gives coherence to the Awakening. These *callers* to the faith *all* affirm a core message: *Only by anchoring relationships within and between communities in justice can a diverse humanity live in righteousness and peace.*

Notes

Chapter 1

1. Shariati's account of the prophetic description can be found in *And Once Again Abu-Dhar, Part 6* (http://shariati.com/english/abudhar/abudhar7.html; accessed September 4, 2010).
2. See Qur'an 2:136; and 2:253; 2:285; 4:150–152. For these Qur'anic citations and all others in this book I have relied on Abdullah Yusuf Ali, *The Holy Quran: Text, Translation and Commentary*, revised edition (Al Khobar, Saudia Arabia: Al Subayie Printing Press, 1989).
3. Hadith: Abu Hurairah, Muslim, *Sahih Muslim*, 2365.
4. The following authors have contributed influential works to this critical literature: Fuad Ajami, Daniel Pipes, and Samuel Huntington.
5. These broad themes are developed in Samuel Huntington, *The Clash of Civilizations and the Remaking of World Order* (New York: Simon & Schuster, 1996).
6. For a balanced assessment of the massacre, see Kareem Fahim and Mayy El Sheikh, "Memory of a Mass Killing Becomes Another Casualty of Egyptian Protests," *New York Times*, November 13, 2013.
7. The very idea of an Islamic Awakening. it should be noted, has not gone unchallenged. The weightiest argument has come from the Egyptian philosopher and social critic Fouad Zakaria (1927–2010) in his book *The Illusions of Islamic Awakening*. Zakaria argues that what is happening is merely a reflection, not an independent and self-generated reaction, to what is taking place happening globally (foreign exploitation of religion), regionally (enhanced rich oil conservative monarchies), and locally (Anwar Sadat's sharp turn to the right). This is a serious argument but one I have not found ultimately persuasive, particularly when developments across the Islamic world and not just in Arab lands are considered.
8. See Qur'an 21:107; 2:136; 3:45; 3:59; 5:46
9. See Raymond William Baker, *One Islam, Many Worlds of Muslims: Spirituality, Identity, and Resistance Across Islamic Lands* (New York: Oxford University Press, 2015).

Chapter 2

1. Shams al-Din Sarkhasi, *al-Mabsut'*, vol. 14, 59–60; cited in https://www.islamreligion.com/articles/376/justice-in-islam/; accessed September 15, 2017.
2. Qur'an 2:177.

242 NOTES

3. For elaborations of the concept of *istikhlaf*, see Qur'an 2:29; 24:55; 11:56; 6:134, 165; 57:7; and 7:129.
4. For an insightful discussion, see Karen Armstrong, *Islam: A Short History* (London: Phoenix Press, 2001), 13–14.
5. Qur'an 34–35.
6. Hadith, *Sahih Al-Bukhari*, volume 7, book 64, number 265.
7. For variations on the Qur'anic idea of the Message of Remembrance, see Qur'an 30:11; 39:21; and 11:120.
8. Armstrong elaborates on this important point. See Armstrong, *Islam: A Short History*, 7.
9. Alija Izetbegovic, president of the nation of Bosnia and Herzegovina from 1990 to 2000, made this notion of balance the central theme of his influential interpretation of Islam. See his *Islam between East and West* (Indianapolis: American Trust Publications, 1984).
10. Qur'an 2:286.
11. See, for one example among of many such verses, Qur'an 59:7.
12. *Istikhlaf* is the Qur'anic term for this responsibility. It defines a mission for humanity at once sacred and historical. For elaborations of the concept, see Qur'an 2:29; 24:55; 11:56; 6:134, 165; 57:7; 7:129.
13. Qur'an 112:1–4.
14. The Qur'an warns repeatedly against concentrations of wealth and power in verses such as Qur'an 59:7.
15. This guidance is offered in numerous Qur'anic verses, including Qur'an 6:56; 9:31; 16:51.
16. The reference is to Marshall G. S. Hudgson's classic history of Islam, *The Venture of Islam: Conscience and History in a World Civilization* (Chicago: University of Chicago Press, 1974).
17. See Raymond William Baker, *Islam Without Fear: Egypt the New Islamists* (Cambridge, MA: Harvard University Press, 2004) and Baker, *One Islam, Many Worlds of Muslims: Spirituality, Identity, and Resistance across Islamic Lands* (New York: Oxford University Press, 2015).
18. This characteristic Islamic fusion of belief and action bears comparison between midstream Islamic thought and American pragmatism. The Bosnian Islamic thinker Alija Izetbegovic explicitly draws this parallel as a major theme in his *Islam between East and West*.
19. Qur'an 18:29.
20. Tarif Khalidi, *The Muslim Jesus: Sayings and Stories in Islamic Literature* (Cambridge, MA: Harvard University Press, 2001), 31–36.
21. Ibn al 'Arabi, *Bezels of Wisdom* (New York: Paulist Press, 1980).
22. The findings of that project are reported in Baker, *One Islam, Many Worlds of Muslims*.
23. For a brief biography of this distinguished educator and scholar, see https://www.nyti mes.com/1991/05/25/obituaries/ilse-lichtenstadter-89-middle-east-authority.html.
24. Ibn al 'Arabi, *Bezels of Wisdom*.

NOTES   243

25. Mass Islamic movements, it should also be noted, have with the same consistency invoked classical figures like Ibn Taimiyyah (1250–1328), understood in conservative ways, as well as contemporary intellectuals like Abul Ala Maududi (1903–1979), whose complex thought is cast in the most reductionist ways.

26. For those with this particular interest, the classic study of A. J. Cameron remains helpful. See A. J. Cameron, *Abu Dharr al Ghifari: An Examination of His Image in the Hagiography of Islam* (New Delhi: Adam, 2006).

27. For an authoritative examination of the role of the Islamic *Caller*, see Muhammad al Ghazalli, *Studies in Du'a* (Dar al Nahdit Masr, 2005), 16.

28. In an explanation that Ghazalli frequently offered, the *Caller* must have one eye on the unchanging texts, but the other on the shifting reality in all its complexities that those sacred texts address for each generation of Muslims.

29. Ghazalli himself explains that he joined the Brotherhood when barely out of his teens and for some seventeen years took an active part in Brotherhood activities. Over time, he rose to the highest leadership ranks until a dispute with the Brotherhood leader (*murshid*) led to the termination of his membership.

30. Ghazalli frequently expressed his gratitude for the foundational role the Brotherhood played in his own formation as an Islamic intellectual. Ghazalli's comments on the Brotherhood were characteristically balanced. He explained that he never saw the Brotherhood in totally black or negative terms. On the other hand, he understood just as clearly that the Brotherhood was certainly not without mistakes and shortcomings. He aimed for fairness. Consistently, Ghazalli had a more dangerous fear. Ghazalli's major concern was that criticisms of the Muslim Brothers not be turned to denigrations of Islam itself. See Ghazalli, *The Bombshell of the Truth* (Damascus and Beirut: Dar al Qalam, 1991), 81. (Arabic).

31. See Ghazalli, *Studies in Du'a*, 16.

Chapter 3

1. *Al Ahaly, al Wafd,* and *Rose al Yusuf* published a flood of such condemnatory articles in 1993. The thrust of their case was to read Ghazalli's testimony as exculpatory and then ask, if this is the position of a leading moderate, are there really any differences between moderates and extremists?

2. Some half dozen Islamic parties made their appearance in the wake of the 2011 Egyptian Revolution.

3. "Jimmy Carter: 'Egyptian elections have been fair and there is an international consensus on recognizing their results,'" *Middle East Monitor* [online]. Rev. January 13, 2012. Available: https://www.middleeastmonitor.com/news/middle-east/3273-jimmy-carter-egyptian-elections-have-been-fair-and-there-is-an-international-consensus-on-recognizing-their-results; accessed October 23, 2014.

4. https://www.hrw.org/news/2013/08/19/egypt-security-forces-used-excessive-lethal-force; accessed December 26, 2015.

244 NOTES

5. http://www.theguardian.com/world/2013/sep/23/muslim-brotherhood-egyptian-court; accessed December 6, 2015.

6. Muhammad al Ghazalli, *Culture among the Muslims* (Cairo: Dar al Sharuq, 2010), 223 (Arabic).

7. Cited in Richard Mitchell, *The Society of the Muslim Brothers*, 2nd edition (Oxford: Oxford University Press, 1993), 30.

8. See, for example, Hassan al Banna, "Tract of the Fifth Conference," *Collected Tracts of the Imam Martyr Hasan al-Banna*, Cairo: Dar al-Shihab, n.n.a., 169; cited by Roel Meijer, "The Muslim Brotherhood and the Political: An Exercise in Ambiguity," www.clingendael.org/sites/default/files/pdfs/20120000_14_meijer_muslim_brother-hood_in_europe.pdf; accessed August 21, 2020.

9. Cited in Ammar Ali Hassan, "Rising to the Occasion," *al Ahram Weekly*, December 19, 2012.

10. Sayyid Qutb, *Milestones* (Damascus: Dar al Ilm, n.a.).

11. Tareq al Bishri provided a nuanced view of Qutb as a serious Islamic intellectual who made important contributions. At the same time, he contrasted Qutb's attitude of withdrawing from and condemning society unfavorably to Banna's work to connect with and strengthen society. See Tareq al Bishri, *The General Features of Contemporary Islamic Political Thought* (Cairo: Dar al Sharuq, 1996), 31–33 and 40–41.

12. Qutb's sweeping speculative formulation was not subject to proof, and it was rejected by the majority of Sunni Islamic intellectuals. For an incisive discussion of Qutb's thinking and its radical implications, see Alastaire Crooke, *Resistance: The Essence of the Islamist Revolution* (New York: Pluto Press, 2009), 106–107.

13. An appreciation for the necessity of force and "physical power" to build the Islamic society runs through Qutb's later work. See especially Qutb, *Milestones*, 55, 63, 96, and 80.

14. A General Guide of the Muslim Brotherhood is given as the author of a book intended to discredit the thinking of Sayyid Qutb, though the book is clearly a collective effort. See Hassan al Hudeibi, *Callers Not Judges* (Cairo: Dar al Tauzir wa al Nashr al Islammiyya, 1977) (Arabic).

15. Qutb, *Milestones*, 11–12.

16. On opposition to theocracy, see Qutb, *Milestones*, 58, 85; on servitude to man-made systems, 45.

17. Cited in Paul Berman, *Terror and Liberalism* (New York: W. W. Norton, 2003), 75.

18. Sayyid Qutb, *In the Shade of the Quran* (Leicestershire, UK: Kube Publishing Ltd for Islamic Foundation, 2007), vol. 3, 282.

19. Rachid al-Ghannouchi, "How Credible is the Claim of the Failure of Political Islam?" *Current Trends in Islamist Ideology* 16 (2014): 48ff.; accessed August 17, 2020.

20. For an ongoing critique from a leading Islamic intellectual of the Brothers in power and their subsequent removal by the military, see the weekly Fahmi Huwaidi columns in *al Sharuq*. Rashid al-Ghannouchi has also offered a valuable critical commentary from an Islamic perspective, most notably in "How Credible is the Claim of the Failure of Political Islam?"

NOTES 245

21. See the Press Release of Amnesty International, January 28, 2013, http://www.amne sty.org/en/for-media/press-releases/egypt-uprising-commemoration-unleashes-death-and-destruction-2013-01-28; accessed August 1, 2014.

22. The movement was financed and supported by wealthy business figures, such as Naguib Suwiris, as well as the elements in the military that overthrew the regime. Details remain cloudy, but the general outlines of the manipulated demonstrations and inflation of the number of participants have become clear. For a start, see Max Blumenthal, "People Power or Propaganda: Unraveling the Egyptian Opposition," July 19, 2013. http://m.aljazeera.com/story/2013717115756410917; accessed October 12, 2014.

23. Human Rights Watch, "Egypt: Security Forces Used Excessive Lethal Force," www. hrw.org, August 19, 2013; accessed July 11, 2014.

24. See, among others, Carrie Rosefsky Wickham, *The Muslim Brotherhood: Evolution of an Islamist Movement* (Princeton, NJ: Princeton University Press, 2013), 247–288; and Abdullah al-Arian, *Answering the Call: Popular Islamic Activism in Sadat's Egypt* (Oxford: Oxford University Press, 2014), 215–240.

Chapter 4

1. Muhammad al Ghazalli provides a very personal account of one such arrest in *Islam and Political Tyranny* (Cairo: Nahdit Masr, 1961).

2. The Qaradawi description, on which the following account is based, can be found in his Introduction to Ghazalli, *Islam and Political Tyranny*, 6th edition (Cairo: Nahdit Masr, 2005) (Arabic).

3. Qur'an 2:143.

4. Qur'an 7:31; 25:67.

5. Both the theory and record of practice of the "intellectual school" are documented and assessed in Raymond William Baker, *Islam Without Fear: Egypt the New Islamists* (Cambridge, MA: Harvard University Press, 2004).

6. Kamal Abul Magd, *A Contemporary Islamic Vision: Declaration of Principles* (Cairo: Dar al Sharuq, 1991) (Arabic).

7. Muhammad Selim al 'Awa, *al Sha'ab*, July 21, 1995.

8. Fahmi Huwaidi, *The Right Word That Is Due* (Cairo: Dar Al Sharuq, 1994), 15.

9. Huwaidi, *The Right Word*, 15.

10. Fahmi Huwaidi, *The Censured Articles*, 3rd edition (Cairo: Dar al Sharuq, 2003).

11. Huwaidi, *Censured Articles*.

12. The testimony was published in *al Sha'ab*, June 25, 1993.

13. See the transcript of the testimony, *al Sha'ab*, June 25, 1993.

14. For a brief but reliable review of these incendiary attacks, see Ibrahim 'Issa, *Rose Al Yusuf*, June 28, 1993.

15. *Al Ahaly, al Wafd*, and *Rose al Yusuf*, among others, published a flood of such condemnatory articles in 1993. The thrust of their case was to read Ghazalli's testimony

246 NOTES

as exculpatory and then ask, rhetorically, "if this is the position of a leading moderate, are there really any differences between moderates and extremists?"

Chapter 5

1. http://www.au.af.mil/au/afri/aspj/apjinternational/aspj_f/digital/pdf/articles/2015_2/alvi_e.pdf.
2. Sükran Vahide, *Islam in Modern Turkey: An Intellectual Biography of Bediuzzaman Said Nursi*. Albany: State University of New York Press, 2005, chapter 8.
3. For a discussion of this incident, see Ibrahim M Abu-Rabi, editor, *Theodicy and Justice in Modern Islamic Thought: The Case of Said Nursi* (New York: Routledge, 2010).
4. See Ediz Sozuer, *Beiuzzaman Said Nursi vi Risale-i Nur* (Ankara, 1974), 57.
5. Cited in http://risaleinur.com/articles/2290-bediuzzaman-said-nursi-and-manevi-jihad.html; accessed September 7, 2020; Ataturk's statements on Islam are also cited in Jonathan Matusitz's *Symbolism in Terrorism* (Lanham, MD: Rowman and Littlefield, 2014). 58.
6. See Galal Amin, *The Age of Slandering the Arabs and Muslims* (Cairo: Dar al Sharuq, 2004) (Arabic).
7. For examples, see Qur'an 25:52 and 29:6 .
8. Cited in https://en.wikipedia.org/wiki/Said_Nurs%C3%AE.
9. For the original citation, see http://risaleinur.com/risale-i-nur-collection/64-al-mathnawi-al-nuri/2976-00g-said-nursis-concept-of-science.html.
10. https://eddai.org/2014/a-contemporary-perspective-on-islamic-jihad-from-said-nursi.
11. See, in particular, historian Tareq al Bishri on Nursi's importance as a caller:*The General Features of Contemporary Islamic Political Thought* (Cairo: Dar al Sharuq, 1996), 26–29 (Arabic). The important Egyptian Islamic journalist Fahmi Huwaidi provides a highly informative overview of this work in his articles, widely read in the Arabic-speaking world. See in particular *Sharuq*, October 9, 2011.
12. For a sober assessment of the terrible costs of Atatürk's homogenization strategy as central to the founding of the Turkish republic, see Alastaire Crooke, *Resistance: The Essence of the Islamist Revolution* (New York: Pluto Press, 2009), 47–54.
13. For a highly critical yet compelling portrait of Atatürk, see Crooke, *Resistance*, 2009, 56–58.
14. For all the complexities of Islam in Turkey today, the situation can be summarized as a power struggle between Gülen, the head of a faith-based movement, and Erdogan, the strongman president and earlier prime minister of Turkey. The Gülen movement was initially aligned with Erdogan but is now denounced, without persuasive proof, as a terrorist organization. In reality, the two men and their respective followers represent two variants of centrist Islam. Both were profoundly influenced by the work of Sa'id Nursi. See the most reliable commentary on this contemporary conflict between two variants of centrist Turkish Islam by Grahame Fuller, author of the influential *A*

NOTES 247

World Without Islam (New York: Little, Brown,) Fuller is an astute political analyst who has kept his analyses fresh with periodic updated articles, such as "I am lucky not to be living in Turkey now," online at https://stockholmcf.org/graham-fuller-i-am-lucky-not-to-be-living-in-turkey-now/; accessed August 25, 2020.

15. Hadith: *Sahih Muslim* Abu Dharr. 520.
16. For a discussion of Nursi's views on the second coming of Jesus, see David R. Law, "The Prophethood of Jesus and Religious Inclusivism in Nursi's Risale-i Nur," *Australian Journal of Islamic Studies* 2, no. 2 (2017): 96–111.
17. Qur'an 4:157–158.
18. Qur'an 43:61.
19. Qur'an 3:45–48; 3:55; 4:157–159.
20. Qur'an 4:75.
21. Qur'an 3:52.
22. Qur'an 65:11.
23. Qur'an 18:29.

Chapter 6

1. https://www.nytimes.com/2010/07/05/world/middleeast/05fadlallah.html; accessed November 17, 2019.
2. This characterization of Fadlallah's portrayal of Abu Dharr relies heavily on Fadlallah's succinct biographical essay of the Prophet's companion. For all Fadlallah articles and books, see http://www.shoaraa.com/section-35940.html; accessed August 26, 2020.
3. See http://www.shoaraa.com/section-35940.html; accessed August 26, 2020.
4. http://english. Bayyanat.org.lb.
5. This translation is from the official Fadlallah English site. http://english. Bayyanat. org.lb.
6. Selim al 'Awa, *Insan Allah* (Beirut: Markaz al Islami al Saqqafi Lebani, 2012), 57.
7. The text is available on the official Fadlallah site: http://www.shoaraa.com/section-35940.html; accessed August 26, 2020.
8. Ahron Bregman, *Israel's Wars: A History since 1947* (London: Routledge, 2002).
9. https://en.wikipedia.org/wiki/Operation_Grapes_of_Wrath; accessed August 26, 2020.
10. https://smallwarsjournal.com/jrnl/art/the-lebanon-israel-war-of-2006-global-effe cts-and-its-aftermath.
11. al 'Awa, *Insan Allah*, 56–60.
12. The text is available on the official Fadlallah site: http://www.shoaraa.com/section-35940.htmll; accessed August 26, 2020.
13. https://www.al-islam.org/abu-dharr-al-ghifari-kamal-al-sayyid/abu-dharr-al-ghif ari#sunrise; accessed August 26, 2020.
14. His love for the poor was so deep that he used to pray: "O Allah, keep me poor in my life and at my death and raise me at resurrection among those who are poor." *Nasai.*

See https://muslimvillage.com/2017/10/10/28626/prophet-muhammads-love-of-the-poor/.

15. Islamic *Shari'ah* protects lawfully acquired wealth. However, in Islam the possessor of wealth is regarded as a trustee who holds his wealth as a trust on behalf of God and the community. For a concise characterization of this notion of wealth in Islam, see https://www.islamreligion.com/articles/295/work-and-wealth#:~:text=While%20Islam%20considers%20lawfully%20acquired%20wealth%20as%20subject,the%20forfeiture%20of%20his%20right%20to%20his%20wealth.

16. See "Obituary for an Anti-Semite," https://cst.org.uk/news/blog/2010/07/07/ayatollah-fadlallah-obituary-of-an-antisemite; accessed August 26, 2020.

17. As a graduate student at Harvard, I received an authoritative articulation of this view from my mentor Naday Safran. Safran, deeply committed to Israel, did more than most to establish this mythic view of Israel. See Safran's *Israel: The Embattled Ally* for his enduring statement of this characterization of the Israeli state. https://www.amazon.com/s?k=Israel-the+Embattled+AllySafran/dp/0674468821.

18. The references are to Thomas Friedman's *The Lexus and the Olive Tree*, Francis Fukayam's *The End of History*, and Marshal McLuhan's concept of *the global village*.

19. Harvard's Stephen Walt, among other realist strategists, comes instantly to mind. For a particularly incisive sample of his thinking on realism, see his "Is Barack Obama More of a Realist than I Am?" (https://foreignpolicy.com/2014/08/19/is-barack-obama-more-of-a-realist-than-i-am/).

20. The concept of *istikhlaf* is elaborated in numerous Qur'anic verses. See, for example, Qur'an 2:29; 24:55; 11:56; 6:134, 165; 57:7; 7:129.

21. Qur'an 9:71.

22. Qur'an 9:71.

23. For a rare, brief, and accurate Western mainstream coverage of Fadlallah's positions on women's issues, see Jim Muir, "Mixed Legacy of Ayatollah Fadlallah" (BBC News Beirut, https://www.bbc.com/news/10504175); accessed September 5, 2020. Muir reports, "Some of the fatwas (religious edicts) he issued were against female circumcision and 'honour' killings, and he ruled that women had the right to hit back if beaten by their husbands. He also opined that abortion could be permitted in cases where a woman's health was at risk." Fadlallah himself sums his most controversial positions, including those on women's right, in a particularly revealing interview: bayynat.org.lb/Archive_news/Interview_20022009.htm; accessed September 7, 2020.

24. https://www.nytimes.com/2010/07/05/world/middleeast/05fadlallah.html; accessed November 17, 2019.

25. https://en.wikiquote.org/wiki/Mohammad_Mosaddegh. https://www.nytimes.com/2010/07/05/world/middleeast/05fadlallah.html.

26. By 2019, the "Battle of the Ayatollahs" was a headline story in the *Economist*. https://www.economist.com/middle-east-and-africa/2019/05/02/why-shia-clerics-are-turning-on-irans-theocracy.

27. *The Economist*, May 2, 2019. https://www.economist.com/middle-east-and-africa/2019/05/02/why-shia-clerics-are-turning-on-irans-theocracy.

NOTES 249

28. The Masada site is promoted as one of Israel's most popular tourist destinations. The story of the mass suicides is treated as a celebrated element of the nationalist mythology.

29. Qur'an 5:32.

30. Restrictions on excesses is anchored in the clear verse Qur'an 2:190 that states: "And fight in the way of Allah with those who fight with you, and do not transgress the limits, surely God loveth not transgressors."

31. The revolutionary theorist Franz Fanon makes such an argument in its most influential form in his classic, *The Wretched of the Earth*.

32. See Stephen Walt's understated article, "Why They Hate Us (II): How Many Muslims Has the U.S. Killed in the Past 30 Years?" https://foreignpolicy.com/2009/11/30/why-they-hate-us-ii-how-many-muslims-has-the-u-s-killed-in-the-past-30-years/.

33. Robert Fisk is a plain-spoken, unsentimental, and uniquely well-informed British journalist. Fisk spoke frequently and uncharacteristically of the "epic kindness" of the Ayatollah. For his words on learning of the death of the Ayatollah, see https://www.independent.co.uk/voices/commentators/fisk/robert-fisk-cnn-was-wrong-about-ayatollah-fadlallah-2023179.html.

Chapter 7

1. Haifa Zangana, Iraqi artist, author, and opposition activist, describes the scene in her essays. See, for Zangan's understanding of her role as creative and witness, "Solitude and Dream: Literature Post-9/11," *Open Democracy*, available online at https://www.opendemocracy.net/en/solitude-and-dream-literature-post-911/; accessed August 28, 2020.

2. Here, as throughout this book, I have relied on the Qur'anic interpretation of Abdullah Yusuf Ali, *The Holy Quran: Text, Translation and Commentary*, revised edition (Al Khobar, Saudia Arabia: Al Subayie Printing Press, 1989).

3. Qur'an 4:29.

4. Qur'an 9:34.

5. Qur'an 9:34.

6. Qur'an 49:10.

7. Qur'an 64:11.

8. See the story of Abu Dharr's timely appearance in my neighborhood in Alexandria, Egypt, that opens the book's Introduction (Chapter 1).

9. Qur'an 59:7 explicitly warns that the circulation of wealth should not be limited to the richest strata: "So wealth should not become confined only to the richest amongst you."

10. For the classic elaboration of these themes, see Samuel Huntington, *The Clash of Civilizations and the Remaking of World Order* (New York: Simon & Schuster, 1996).

11. Qur'an 57:25.

250 NOTES

Chapter 8

1. See Ali Shariati's biography of the companion, *And Once Again Abu-Dhar, Part 2*, http://shariati.com/english/abudhar/abudhar2.html.
2. The complete text is available in English translation on the official Shariati site, http://www.shariati.com/kotob.html.
3. Hadith: Ibrahim Hagri 1604.
4. For a sense of the beauty and massive size of the shrine, see "The Journey of Love to the Kind Imam," https://www.youtube.com/watch?v=xjtImRNmoXg.
5. The title of the most widely read of the books of the radical Martinique theorist Franz Fanon, whose work Shariati admired.
6. For a parallel reading, see https://institute.global/insight/co-existence/who-was-ali-shariati.
7. See Ali Shariati, *And Once Again Abu-Dhar, Part 1*, shariati.com/english/abudhar/abudhar1.html.
8. https://institute.global/policy/who-was-ali-shariati.
9. https://historica.fandom.com/wiki/Ali_Shariati.
10. See https://www.pbs.org/wgbh/pages/frontline/tehranbureau/2009/08/shariati-on-religious-government.html.
11. For a broadly similar assessment, see Ali Rahnema, *An Islamic Utopian: A Political Biography of Ali Shariati* (London and New York: I. B. Tauris, 2000), 128.
12. Qur'an 6:151 and 60:12. https://www.pbs.org/wgbh/pages/frontline/tehranbureau/2011/10/ali-shariati-and-the-ideologization-of-religion.html.
13. Qur'an 17:130; 81:8, 9.
14. Qur'an 18:29.
15. Abdolkarim Soroush, distinguished Iranian philosopher and scholar, argues that for Shariati, "Abu Zarr was the most important and lofty personage of Islam.... Shariati's fondness of Abu Zarr was even greater than his fondness for the Prophet and Ali." See Rahnema, *An Islamic Utopian*, 57–61.

Chapter 9

1. Quoted in https://www.voanews.com/usa/muhammad-ali-american-muslim.
2. For a discussion of the rumors surrounding this incident, see Joumane Chahine, "Keeping the Faith," Film Comment, May–June 2014; https://www.filmcomment.com/article/moustapha-akkad/; accessed September 9, 2017.
3. *Hadith*: Bukhari no: 745 Narrated / Authority of: Abu Said Al-Khudri "The Messenger of Allah (saw) said: 'All the earth is a masjid (mosque), except for graveyards and Hammam.'"
4. *Hadith*: Abu Dharr reported: I said: Messenger of Allaah, which mosque was set up first on the earth? He said: Al-Masjid al-Haram (the sacred). I (again) said: Then which next? He said: It was the Masjid Aqsa. I (again) said: How long the space of time

(between their setting up)? He (the Prophet) said: It was forty years. And whenever the time comes for prayer, pray there, for that is a mosque; and in the *hadith* transmitted by Abu Kamil (the words are): "Whenever time comes for prayer, pray, for that is a mosque (for you)," Sahih Muslim. 1056.

5. On requirements for an effective Islamic *Caller*, see Shaikh Muhammad al Ghazalli, *Studies in Du'a* (Dar al Nahdit Masr, 2005 edition), 16.

6. Qur'an 7:179.

7. Qutb loathed the violence of American sports and considered it pervasive in American culture. His condemnation is sweeping: "This primitiveness can be seen in the spectacle of the fans as they follow a game of football . . . or watch boxing matches or bloody, monstrous wrestling matches. . . . This spectacle leaves no room for doubt as to the primitiveness of the feelings of those who are enamored with muscular strength and desire it." Cited from "Sayyid Qutb's America," https://www.npr.org/templates/story/story.php?storyId=1253796; accessed September 7, 2020.

8. Thomas Hauser, *Muhammad Ali: His Life and Times*, https://www.goodreads.com/work/quotes/669759-muhammad-ali-his-life-and-times; accessed February 28, 2020.

9. www.voanews.com/usa/muhammad-ali-american-muslim.

10. https://www.google.com/search?q=How+much+did+Muhammad+Ali+make+in+his+career%3F&sa=X&ved=2ahUKEwj165OgsZjjAhUIGhQKHUzEBScQzmd6BAgOEBM&biw=1259&bih=574.

11. *Hadith*, Abu Ruwai. *Shahih Muslim*, 236.

12. Qur'an 2:25, 62, 82, 110, 149.

13. *Twitter*, Egyptian historian Muhammad al Gawadi, June 2016.

14. See https://mashable.com/2016/06/04/muhammad-ali-charity-legacy/#FIEHXvCOQkq9.

15. Fahmy Huwaidi included the picture with his article on the event. See *Sharuq*, June 2016.

16. See, for example, Qur'an 2:25, 62, 82, 110, 149.

17. Tareq al Bishri, *The General Features of Contemporary Islamic Political Thought* (Cairo: D'ar al Sharuq, 1996). 52–61 (Arabic).

18. Ali recounted this and similar incidents many times. See, for example, https://www.theguardian.com/lifeandstyle/2009/aug/23/muhammad-ali-words.

19. https://www.rollingstone.com/culture/culture-sports/muhammad-ali-4-ways-he-changed-america-155463/https://www.rollingstone.com/culture/culture-sports/muhammad-ali-4-ways-he-changed-america-155463/.

20. Qur'an 2:286.

21. See, for examples of this emphasis, Qur'an 2:25, 62, 82, 110, 149.

22. Qur'an 5:17.

23. https://www.rollingstone.com/feature/muhammad-ali-4-ways-he-changed-america-155463/

24. https://www.youtube.com/watch?v=Ed-3HxoMdKg.

25. https://electricliterature.com/feasting-with-panthers-the-curious-connection-between-boxing-and-gay-rights/.

252 NOTES

26. There were those who noticed. Former President Bill Clinton awarded Ali the Presidential Citizens Medal at a White House ceremony. At Ali's passing, President Clinton and presidential candidate Hilary Clinton issued an incisive statement that Ali expressed "a blend of beauty and grace, speed and strength that may never be matched again."
27. Qur'an 66:1–2; 80:1–6; 8:68–69; 9:43; 18:23–24; 5:89; 33:37–39.
28. https://www.biography.com/crime-figure/emmett-till.
29. See the account by Cary Clack in the *San Antonio Express News*, June 12, 2020. Available online: expressnews.com/opinion/columnists/cary_clack/article/Clack-This-generation-s-Emmett-Till-moment-15336352.php.
30. Quoted in Clack, expressnews.com/opinion/columnists/cary_clack/article/Clack-This-generation-s-Emmett-Till-moment-15336352.php.
31. Qur'an 22:40.
32. https://blogs.weta.org/boundarystones/2014/04/14/muhammad-alis-speech-howard-university-1967.
33. https://scribol.com/anthropology-and-history/muhammad-ali-save-lives-hostages-iraq-president-blasted-methods-saddam-hussein/.
34. https://face2faceafrica.com/article/how-muhammad-ali-convinced-saddam-hussein-to-free-15-u-s-hostages-in-1990.
35. https://mashable.com/2016/06/04/muhammad-ali-charity-legacy/#FIEHXvCOQkq9.

Chapter 10

1. "And the Prophets From their Lord We make no distinctions between one and another among them." Qur'an 3:84.
2. Qur'an 5:17–18.
3. Shams al-Din Sarkhasi, 'al-Mabsut,' vol. 14, pp. 59–60.
4. Qur'an 7:179.
5. On remembrance of "truths already known," see Qur'an 30:11; 39:21; and 11:120.
6. A senior Bush official in May 2003, quoted in *Counterpunch*, January 17, 2006.
7. Qur'an 2:143.
8. For an elaboration of the war aim of "ending the Iraqi state," see Raymond W. Baker, Shereen T. Ismael, and Tareq Y. Ismael, eds., *Cultural Cleansing in Iraq: Why Museums Were Looted, Libraries Burned, and Academics Murdered* (London: Pluto Press, 2009), 3–49.
9. "Merchants of death" was an epithet used in the United States in the 1930s to attack industries and banks that supplied and funded World War I. The phrase originated as the title of a 1934 book by H. C. Engelbrecht and F. C. Hanighen.
10. See https://www.google.com/search?q=Peter+Van+Buren%2C+%E2%80%9CWhy+the+Invasion+of+Iraq+Was+the+Single+Worst+Foreign+Policy+Decision+in+American+History%2C%E2%80%9D+Foreign+Policy%2C+March+

7%2C+2013&rlz=1C1PASC_enEG956EG956&oq=Peter+Van+Buren%2C+
%E2%80%9CWhy+the+Invasion+of+Iraq&aqs=chrome.1.69i59l2.3984j0j7&sourc
eid=chrome&ie=UTF-8

11. For elaborations of the idea of remembrance of "truths already known," see Qur'an 30:11; 39:21; and 11:120.

Bibliography

'Abduh, Muhammad. *The Theology of Unity* (London: George Allen & Unwin, 1966).

Abrahami, Ervand. *Radical Islam: The Iranian Mojahedin* (New York: I. B. Tauris, 1989).

Ahmad, Eqbal. *The Selected Writings of Eqbal Ahmad* (New York: Columbia University Press, 2006).

Amin, Galal. *The Age of Slandering the Arabs and Muslims* (Cairo: Dar al Sharuq, 2004). (Arabic)

Amin, Hussein Ahmed. *Islam in a Changing World and Other Essays* (Cairo: Madbouli, 1988). (Arabic)

'Arabi, Ibn al. *The Bezels of Wisdom* (New York: Paulist Press, 1980).

Arian, Abdullah al-. *Answering the Call: Popular Islamic Activism in Sadat's Egypt* (New York: Oxford University Press, 2014).

Armstrong, Karen. *Islam: A Short History* (London: Phoenix Press, 4th impression, 2002).

'Awa, Muhammad Selim al. *Copts and Islam* (Cairo: Dar al Sharuq, 1987). (Arabic)

'Awa, Muhammad Selim al, *Insan Allah* (Beirut: Markaz al Islami al Saqqafi Lebani, 2012).

'Awa, Muhammad Selim al. *Islamic Fiqh on the Road to Renewal*, 2nd edition (Beirut: al Maktab al Islami, 1998). (Arabic)

'Awa. Muhammad Selim al. *The Political and Constitutional Crisis in Egypt* (Cairo: Al Zahra'a, 1991). (Arabic)

Baker, Raymond William. *Islam Without Fear: Egypt and the New Islamists* (Cambridge, MA: Harvard University Press, 2004).

Baker, Raymond William. *One Islam, Many Worlds of Muslims: Spirituality, Identity, and Resistance across Islamic Lands* (New York: Oxford University Press, 2015).

Baker. Raymond William. *Sadat and After: Struggles for Egypt's Political Soul* (Cambridge, MA: Harvard University Press, 1990).

Banna, Hassan al. *Collected Tracts of the Imam Martyr Hasan al-Banna* (Cairo: Dar al-Shihab, n.a.). (Arabic)

Bayat. Asef. *Making Islam Democratic* (Stanford, CA: Stanford University Press, 2007).

Bayat, Asef. *Post-Islamism: The Changing Faces of Islamism* (New York: Oxford University Press, 2013).

Benard, Cheryl. *Civil, Democratic Islam: Partners, Resources, and Strategies* (Santa Monica, CA: Rand, 2003).

Bishri, Tareq al. *The Arabs in the Face of Aggression* (Cairo: Dar al Sharuq, 2002). (Arabic)

Bishri, Tareq al. *The General Features of Contemporary Islamic Political Thought* (Cairo: Dar al Sharuq, 1996). (Arabic)

Bishri, Tareq al. *Muslims and Copts in the National Community* (Cairo: al Hay'a al 'Amma lil Kitab, 1980). (Arabic)

Bishri, Tareq al. *The Political Movement in Egypt 1945–1952*, 2nd edition (Beirut: Dar al Sharuq, 1983). (Arabic)

Crooke, Alastaire. *Resistance: The Essence of the Islamist Revolution* (New York: Pluto Press, 2009).

256 BIBLIOGRAPHY

Cameron. A. J. *Abu Dharr al Ghifari: An Examination of His Image in the Hagiography of Islam* (New Delhi: Adam, 2006).

Esposito. John. *The Future of Islam* (Oxford: Oxford University Press, 2010).

Esposito. John. *The Straight Path* (Oxford: Oxford University Press, 2010).

Esposito, John L. and Dalia Mogahed. *Who Speaks for Islam: What a Billion Muslims Really Think* (New York: Gallup Press, 2007).

Fatah, Nabil Abdul. *Veiled Violence* (Cairo: Khattab Press, 1994) (Arabic).

Fuller, Graham. *A World Without Islam* (New York: Little, Brown, 2011).

Ghazalli, Muhammad al. *The Battle of the Mushaf* (Cairo: Nahdat Masr, 1996) (Arabic)

Ghazalli, Muhammad al. *Between Reason and the Heart* (Cairo: Dar al Iltisam, 1973) (Arabic).

Ghazalli, Muhammad al. *Bitter Truth* (Cairo: al Ahram Markaz al 'Alam al Arabi, 1993). (Arabic)

GhazallI, Muhammad al. *The Bombshell of the Truth* (Damascus: Dar al Dustur, 2002). (Arabic)

Ghazalli, Muhammad al. *Culture Among the Muslims* (Cairo: Dar al Sharuq, 2010) (Arabic).

Ghazalli, Muhammad al. *From Here We Know* (Cairo: Nahdat Masr, 1997). (Arabic)

Ghazalli, Muhammad al. *Islam and Political Tyranny*, 6th edition (Cairo: Nahdit Masr, 2005). (Arabic)

Ghazalli, Muhammad al. *The Prophet's Sunnah between the People of Hadith and People of Fiqh* (Cairo: Dar al Sharuq, 1991). (Arabic)

Ghazalli, Muhammad al. *Renew Your Life*, 9th edition (Cairo: Nahdit Masr, 2005). (Arabic)

Ghazalli, Muhammad al. *The Secret behind Arab and Muslim Backwardness* (Cairo: Dar al Sahwa, 1985). (Arabic)

Ghazalli, Muhammad al. *Towards a Substantive Interpretation of the Surahs of the Holy Qur'an* (Cairo: Dar al Sharuq, 1995). (Arabic)

Ghazalli, Muhammad al. *Women's Issues between Rigid and Alien Traditions* (Cairo: Dar al Sharuq, 1994). (Arabic)

Huntington, Samuel. *The Clash of Civilizations and the Remaking of World Order* (New York: Simon & Schuster, 1996).

Hudeibi, Hassan al. *Callers Not Judges* (Cairo: Dar al Tauzir wa al Nashr al Islammiyya, 1977). (Arabic)

Huwaidi, Fahmi. *The Banned Articles* (Cairo: Dar al Sharuq, 1998). (Arabic)

Huwaidi, Fahmi. *Iran from Within* (Cairo: Markaz al Ahram lil Targama wa Nashr, 1987). (Arabic)

Huwaid, Fahmi. *Islam and Democracy* (Cairo: Markaz al Ahram lil Targama wa Nashr, 1993).

Huwaidi, Fahmi. *The Qur'an and the Sultan* (Cairo: Dar al Sharuq, 1999).

Izetbegovic, Alija Ali. *Islam Between East and West* (Indianapolis, IN: American Trust Publications, 1993).

Izetbegovic, Alija Ali. *The Islamic Declaration: A Program for the Islamization of Muslims and the Muslim Peoples* (Sarajevo, 1990). https://en.wikipedia.org/wiki/Islamic_Declaration

Lawrence, Bruce. *Shattering of Myth: Islam Beyond Violence* (Princeton, NJ: Princeton University Press, 1998).

Lewis, Bernard. *Islam and the West* (Oxford: Oxford University Press, 1993).

BIBLIOGRAPHY   257

Magd, Kamal Abul. *A Contemporary Islamic Vision: Declaration of Principles* (Cairo: Dar al Sharuq, 1991) (Arabic).

Magd, Kamal Abul. *Dialogue Not Confrontation* (Cairo: Dar al Sharuq, 1988). (Arabic)

Mitchell, Richard, *The Society of the Muslim Brothers*, 2nd edition (Oxford: Oxford University Press, 1993).

Qaradaw, Yusuf al. *Elements of Comprehensiveness and Flexibility in Shari'a* (Cairo: Dar al Sahwa, 1985). (Arabic)

Qaradawi, Yusuf al. *Fiqh of Jihad: A Comparative Study of Rulings and Philosophy* (Cairo: Dar al Wahba, 2009). (Arabic)

Qaradawi, Yusuf al. *Fiqh of Priorities: A New Study in the Light of Quran and Sunnah* (Cairo: al Wahda, 1995).

Qaradawi, Yusuf al. *Ghazalli as I Knew Him* (Cairo: Dar al Sharuq, 2000). (Arabic)

Qaradawi, Yusuf al. *Islam and Secularism, Face to Face* (Cairo: Dar al Sahwa, 1987). (Arabic)

Qaradawi, Yusuf al. *Islam and Violence* (Cairo: Dar al Sharuq, 2004). (Arabic)

Qaradawi, Yusuf al. *Islamic Awakening: Between Legitimate Difference and Reprehensible Divisions* (Cairo: Dar el Sahwa, 1990). (Arabic)

Qaradawi, Yusuf al. *The Islamic Awakening: The Concerns of the Arab and Islamic Homeland* (Cairo: Dar al Sahwa, 1988). (Arabic)

Qaradawi, Yusuf al. *The Islamic Renewal* (Cairo: 1999). (Arabic)

Qaradawi, Yusuf al. *Non-Muslims in Islamic Society* (Beirut: Muasassat al Risala, 1983). (Arabic)

Qaradawi, Yusuf al. *The Role of Values and Ethics in the Islamic Economy* (Cairo: Maktabit Wahda, 1995). (Arabic)

Qutb, Sayyid. *In the Shade of the Quran* (Leicestershire, UK: Kube Publishing Ltd. for Islamic Foundation, 2007).

Qutb, Sayyid. *The Literary Dimension of the Quran*, 17th edition (Cairo: Dar al Sharuq, 2004). (Arabic)

Qutb, Sayyid. *Milestones* (Damascus: Dar al 'Ilm, n.a.). (Arabic)

Qutb, Sayyid. *Social Justice in Islam*, revised edition (New York: Islamic Publications International, 2000).

Rahnema, Ali. *An Islamic Utopian: A Political Biography of Ali Shariati* (London and New York: I. B. Tauris, 2000).

Rodinson, Maxime. *Islam and Capitalism* (New York: Penguin Books, 1977).

Roy, Olivier. *The End of Political Islam* (New York: I. B.Taurus, 1994).

Roy, Olivier. *Globalized Islam: The Search for a New Ummah* (New York: Columbia University Press, 2004).

Safran, Nadav. *Egypt in Search of Political Community: An Analysis of the Intellectual and Political Evolution of Egypt, 1804–1952* (Cambridge, MA: Harvard University Press, 1969).

Said, Edward. *Covering Islam: How the Media and the Experts Determine How We See the Rest of the World* (New York: First Vintage Books, 1997).

Said, Edward. *Orientalism* (New York: Knopf, 1979).

Schwartz, Stephen. *The Two Faces of Islam* (New York: Doubleday, 2001).

Shehata, Samer S. ed. *Islamist Politics in the Middle East* (London and New York: Routledge, 2012).

Tamimi, Azzam S. *Rachid Ghannouchi: A Democrat within Islamism* (Oxford: Oxford University Press, 2010).

258 BIBLIOGRAPHY

Mark, Taylor. *The Moment of Complexity: Emerging Network Culture* (Chicago: University of Chicago Press, 2001).

Trimingham, J. Spencer. *Sufi Orders in Islam* (Oxford: Clarendon Press, 1971).

Waines, David. *An Introduction to Islam* (Cambridge: Cambridge University Press, 1995).

Wickham, Carrie Rosefsky. *The Muslim Brotherhood: Evolution of an Islamist Movement* (Princeton, NJ: Princeton University Press, 2013).

Glossary of Non-English Terms

Entries are primarily from Arabic, although several key Hebrew and Turkish expressions are also included.

'alim (pl. 'ulama)	Islamic scholar
Amir	leader of a politicized and often militant Islamic group
'aqida	doctrine the Arabic word connotes that which is held onto, binds, knots, fixes firmly
Ashura	day of mourning in Shi'i Islam for the martyrdom of Hussein, the Prophet's grandson
ayah	sign from God; verse of the Qur'an
bida'	unacceptable innovation
da'wa	the call to Islam
dhikr	remembrance
faqih (pl. faqihs)	an Islamic scholar, specially trained and recognized by peers as qualified to contribute to *fiqh*; commonly but misleading translated as jurisprudence
fatwa (pl. fatwas)	religious opinion by an Islamic scholar
fikr	social theory and philosophy
fiqh	Islamic legal reasoning, based on interpretation of Qur'an and *Sunnah*; the work of trained specialists known as *faqihs*; subject to challenge and correction as a fully human endeavor (note: in Western scholarship, commonly translated as Islamic law. Centrist Islamic scholars would likely regard this translation as misleading and an understatement of its scope.)
fitra	nature
gizya	the tax on non-Muslims, provided for by a contract according to which they were exempted from military service and received protection and legal right
hadith (pl. hadiths)	traditions of the Prophet that illuminate his thoughts and actions, accompanied by their sources; term is interchangeable with *Sunnah*, although some scholars argue there are fine distinctions in usage

GLOSSARY OF NON-ENGLISH TERMS

hajj	pilgrimage to Mecca, held annually and prescribed for all Muslims once in their lifetime
hakemeyya or hakemeyyet Allah	God's sovereignty
halal	religiously permitted
haraba	war against civilization
haram	religiously forbidden
hayat	social life (Turkish)
hegab	headscarf that covers the hair but not the face
hudud	punishments provided for in *Shari'ah*
ijtihad	an effort to interpret the sacred texts
imam	faith (Turkish)
islah	reform
Islam haraki	movement Islam
Islamic world	also called Islamdom, the complex of societies and cultures in which Muslims and their faith have been prevalent and socially dominant
istikhlaf	the divine call to humanity to act as God's regent on Earth
jahilliyya	the pre-Islamic age of ignorance
jihad	struggle for the faith in both spiritual and physical senses
al jihad al Kabir	the great jihad or personal struggle to be a better person
al jihad al sughayir	the lesser struggle to defend the community
khatam al nabiyeen	the Seal of the Prophets, Qur'anic naming of the Prophet Muhammad
khawaga	foreigner in long-term residence
khums	payment of one-fifth of acquired wealth
khutbah	sermon
marja' (pl. maraji')	the highest rank of authority among Shi'a religious scholars
marja' al-taqlid	the "source of emulation" to whom the faithful turn for guidance on religious and other matters
marja'iyya	collective of *maraji*
maslaha 'amm	the common good

GLOSSARY OF NON-ENGLISH TERMS 261

Medrestu'z Zehra	university project of Sa'id Nursi
mu'allim al inqilab	revolutionary mentor
mufti	an Islamic scholar qualified to issue a religious opinion or fatwa
mugadid	an Islamic scholar who is thought to appear every century to renew Islam
al mujta'a al ahaly	communal society
mustakhlifun	those charged to act as God's regent on earth
al Muwahhideen	the Druze, distinctive and eclectic sect that believes in one God
al nas	humanity, the common people
neqab	face veil
nushuz	an attitude suggesting unfaithfulness
qadi	judge who decides cases in accord with *Shari'ah*
riba	usury
sahaba	companions of the Prophet Muhammad
al Sahwa al Islammiyya	the Islamic Awakening
shaikh	a trained religious teacher or guide; entitled to give the Friday sermon.
Shari'ah	the provisions from Qur'an and *Sunnah* to regulate human behavior; (note: in Western scholarship, commonly translated as Islamic law. Midstream Islamic scholars would likely regard this translation as misleading.)
sherif (pl. sherifs)	descendent of the Prophet Muhammad
shumeleyya	comprehensiveness
shura	consultation
Sunnah	the record of all deeds and words of the Prophet; the second source of Islam, after the Qur'an; term is interchangeable with *hadith*s, although some scholars argue there are fine distinctions in usage
surah (pl. surahs)	chapter of the Qur'an
tafsir	exegesis
tafsir bi-al-diraya	this alternative to the classical approach meant a reliance on reason and interpretation
tafsir bi-al-riwaya	Quar'anic commentary that relied primarily on inherited classical sources

262 GLOSSARY OF NON-ENGLISH TERMS

al Tagdid al Islami	the Islamic Renewal
takfir	declaring Muslims to be unbelievers
takhlif	the divine trust to humanity to live life in accordance with God's laws, calling for righteous deeds and action against evil.
talab al 'ilm	travel in search of knowledge
ta'lim	formal schooling
tanzim sirri	secret apparatus
tarbeyya	proper upbringing
tariqa (pl. turuq)	a school or order of Sufism
tarshid	guidance
tawhid	the Islamic belief in the oneness of God
tikkun olam	healing the world (Hebrew)
ummah	Islamic community
'umra	recommended but not prescribed pilgrimage to Mecca at times other than the *hajj*
usul al fiqh	the "roots" or fundamental methods to guide efforts of Islamic scholars to understand the sacred texts
usuli	opportunistic
waqf (pl. awqaf)	Islamic endowment
Wasittia	the centrist Islamic midstream
wilaya	a historic and therefore not binding concept of rule that precludes the rule of women and non-Muslims
wilayet al faqi	rule of the *faqih*; the Iranian system of government in which a leading Shi'i religious leader exercises absolute authority
zahid	ascetic
zakat	religious obligation owed to support those in need
zhikr	Sufi ritual of remembrance of God, marked by collective chanting and swaying body movements
zimmah	contract of protection of non-Muslims in an Islamic society
zimmi	"protected" non-Muslim people subject to a covenant according to which they were exempted from military service and received protection and legal rights in return for which they paid a special tax called the *gizya*

Index

For the benefit of digital users, indexed terms that span two pages (e.g., 52–53) may, on occasion, appear on only one of those pages.

'Abd al- Ra'uf, Sayyid, 116
Abdou, Muhammad, 73, 213–14, 216–17
Abdul Hamid II, Sultan, 97
Abu Dharr al Ghifari, 16–37
'adl, 2–3
Affan, Osman ibn, Caliph, 21, 152–53, 161
Akkad, Mustafa, 200, 201, 203
Ali, Imam, 17, 181, 183–85, 186
Ali, Muhammad, 200–30
amirs, 11–12. *See also* extremism
anti-Western Westernizers, 46, 94
Arabi, Ibn al, 30, 31–32
asceticism, 2–3, 4, 5–6, 20–21, 72, 118–19, 131–32, 144, 161, 192, 203, 217, 231–32

Baghdadi, Abu Bakr al, 58
Banna, Hassan al, 38–69
believing revolutionary, 176–99
Bezels of Wisdom, 30, 31–32
Black Shi'ism, 183, 184

Central Asia, 59
challenger civilization, 237–38
civilizational Islam, 234
Clark, Ramsey, 229
companions of the Prophet, 10, 24, 25, 202, 223–24
compassion, 7, 9, 16, 29, 36, 67, 77–78, 86, 111, 118–19, 122, 127–28, 129–30, 144, 150, 161–62, 168, 169, 170, 183–84, 186, 188, 190, 191, 192–93, 207–9, 231–32, 238, 239
consumerism, 57, 173–74, 175
creative destruction, 237

da'i, 33–34, 36–37, 202–5
Damascus, 54

Dar al Islam, 53–54, 55
Da'wa Party, 160
democratic contagion, 66–67
dhikr, 17
du'a, 33–35, 59, 192–93, 202–3

economic man, 170
end of history, 135
Ennahda party, 63

Fadlallah, Muhammad Hussein, Ayatollah, 114–51
Fanon, Frantz, 183, 187, 192, 198
faqih, 141
female infanticide, 189
Fisk, Robert, 150–51
fitra, 18
FLN, 179–80
Floyd, George, 225–26
Foreman, George, 205–6

Gallipoli, Battle of, 88
Gama'a al Islamiyya, al, 80
Ghandi, Mahatma, 35–36, 104
Ghannouchi, Rachid, 61
Ghazalli, Abu Hamed al, 49–50
Ghazalli, Muhammad, Shaikh, 21, 27, 33–34, 35, 44, 53–54, 55, 69, 70–86
God's regent on earth, 136. See also *istikhlaf*
Gorbachev, Mikhail, 210–11
Gorgeous George, 221–23
Gülen, Fethullah, 105

Hakemeyya, 57
Hallaj, Mansur, 5
Hamas, 41, 61, 85, 139, 188

264 INDEX

Hudaibi, Ma'mun al, 78
Huntington, Samuel, 8, 172, 237–38
Hussein, Imam, 114–52

Ibn Ali, Hussain, 162–63
Ibn Saud, 76
Imam Reza, 178–79. *See also* The Kind Imam
indispensable nation, 135, 237
Iran's "earthquake", 139–42, 145, 160, 185, 188–97, 198–99
Islam haraki, 30, 36, 165, 166–67, 191
Islam's Jesus, 3–4, 106, 177, 207–8, 231, 238. *See also* Muslim Jesus
Islamic Awakening, 3, 6–8, 9, 13, 14, 15, 22–28, 30, 35, 36–37, 38, 41, 43–45, 153–54, 160, 162–63, 166, 176–77, 182, 188–89, 191, 195, 197–99, 206, 207–8, 209, 212–13, 216, 217, 231, 238
Islamist Imaginary, 38
Istikhlaf, 16, 29–30, 136, 158, 172, 183

Jackson, Jesse, 225–26
jahilliyya, 53–54, 200–1
jihad by word, 87–113

Kamel, Mustafa, 88, 89
Kazim, Musa al, Imam, 152
Khalafalla, Muhammad, 78
khawaga, 39
Khoei, Sayyid Abul Qasim al, Ayatollah, 153
Khomeini, Ayatollah, 28, 36, 84–85, 140, 141, 165–66, 184–86, 196–98
Kind Imam, 178–79. *See also* Imam Reza
King, Jr, Martin Luther, 35–36, 103–4, 203

Lenin, 56–57

Malcolm X, 205, 224, 226
marja' al taqlid, 123, 129, 136, 139–40, 148, 153
Mashhad, 178–80, 181, 182–83
Materialism, 104, 155, 173–74
Mecca, 18, 19, 22–23, 76, 194, 203–4
Medina, 76, 169

The Message, 18, 200, 201, 230, 234
message of remembrance, 237, 239
midstream Islam, 5, 6–7, 8–9, 12, 13–14, 23, 53–54, 73–74, 80–81, 83, 85, 86, 94–95, 120, 163–64, 188–89, 194–95, 204, 205, 206, 209, 210, 216, 231, 235, 239
Milestones, 53, 55, 56–58
Mo 'allem-e enqilab, 176
Mokkatam Hills, 40
Monotheism, 1–2, 4, 18, 20–21, 25–26, 27, 28, 31, 33, 76, 109, 183, 193–94, 229–30, 235, 239
Mu'awiyya, 21–22, 54
muezzin, 200
Muhammad, Elijah, 204, 205, 224
mujahid, 17
Mursi, Muhammad, 47–48, 59–61, 62, 63, 64–67
Muslim Jesus, 3–4, 5, 6–7, 9, 14, 17, 29–30, 72, 87–89, 106, 107, 117–19, 127, 128–29, 144, 162, 207–8, 216, 217–18, 231–32, 233, 234. *See also* Islam's Jesus
Muttalib, 'Abbas ibn 'Abd al, 19
Mysticism, 5

Nagshbandi circle, 90–91
Najaf, 116–17, 125–26, 153–54, 165, 166
Nation of Islam, 204, 206, 224
New Islamic Trend, 73–75, 79, 80
Nursi, Sa'id, 87–112

one and many, 29–33
Osman Ibn Affan, Caliph, 21, 152–53, 161

partnership in faith, 137–38
positive action, 96, 104

Qa'id Ibrahim Mosque, 1
Qutb, Sayyid, 30–31, 38–69

Rabaa al 'Adawiyya Square, 67–68
Red Shi'ism, 183, 184, 191, 192, 198–99
righteous rebellion, 54
Risale i-Nur, 96, 97–98, 104, 106–7

Sadr, Ayatollah Baqir al, 152
Safran, Nadav, 134

INDEX 265

Sahaba, 24
Sahwa al Islamiyya, al, 73
salamu 'aleikum, 19
Sarakhsi, Muhammad Abu Bakr al, 16
Savak, 181
seal of the prophets, 238
secularism, 7, 27, 43, 44–45, 79, 100–2,
  104, 106, 107, 234
Shahada, 18, 19
Shariati, Ali, 176–99
Shi'ism, Black, 183, 184
Shi'ism, Red, 183, 184, 191, 192, 198–99
Shirk, 25
Sonje, 224
Sufism, 5, 50, 90–91
surah, 6

tafsir bi-al-diraya nur postacıları, 97–98
tafsir bi-al-riwaya, 97–98
Tahir Pasha, 91
Takfir, 53–54
tawhid, 20–21, 25, 27, 125–28, 136, 158,
  194, 198
theocracy, 57

Till, Emmett, 225–26
Till, Mamie, 225–26

'ulama, 54, 83, 191
Umayyad Dynasty, 54
Urfa, 87
usul al fiqh, 153–54

Vietnam, 214–16, 224, 227, 228, 229

Walt, Stephen, 149
Wasittia, 6–7, 8–9, 74–75, 77
Westernization, 42–43, 44–45
Women, 6, 18, 74, 84–85, 101, 114, 128–
  29, 132, 135–38, 188, 189–90, 203, 204
wretched of earth, 179, 198

Yazdi, Mohammad Tag Mesbah,
  Ayatollah, 185–86

zahid, 202
zakat, 16, 137, 154–55
Zionism, 127
Zuwaihri, Ayman, 58